NEXT-YEAR COUNTRY

SOCIAL CREDIT IN ALBERTA
Its Background and Development

A series of studies sponsored by the Canadian Social Science Research Council, directed and edited by S. D. Clark.

Next-Year Country

A STUDY OF RURAL SOCIAL
ORGANIZATION IN ALBERTA

By

JEAN BURNET

UNIVERSITY OF TORONTO PRESS

TORONTO   BUFFALO   LONDON

Reprinted in paperback 1978
University of Toronto Press
Toronto   Buffalo   London

Printed in Canada

ISBN 0-8020-6340-3

Foreword

THIS is the third of a series sponsored by the Canadian Social Science Research Council through a special grant from the Rockefeller Foundation relating to the background and development of the Social Credit movement in Alberta. It focuses attention upon the community basis of the movement. The Hanna area was chosen for study not with the idea that this area was typical of the Alberta rural community but rather with the idea that it revealed more clearly than other areas not so severely hit by the drought of the 1930's the kind of disturbances within the Alberta social structure which made possible the rise of the Social Credit movement.

What emerges in this study by Dr. Burnet is a picture of a community lacking a solid foundation on which to erect a stable social organization. Reduction of population, the resettlement of part of the area by people with an Eastern European cultural background, the strengthening of the ties of village and country, the development of rural co-operative schemes, the reorganization of the municipal and educational administration of the area, the change to lease-holdings and the increase in the size of holdings, the shift from wheat farming to stock raising and the promotion of large-scale irrigation projects were solutions which offered themselves in meeting the problem of developing a satisfactory form of community life. With the deepening of the depression and the worsening of drought conditions during the 1930's, however, none of these solutions seemed adequate. The whole social structure appeared to be on the verge of collapse. Although war-time prosperity brought relief, many of the fundamental problems of community organization remained unsolved. Indeed, with technological improvements in agriculture, and the drain of labour off the farms owing to the continued growth of urban industries and service occupations, some of these problems were greatly intensified in the post-war years of the late forties. At the time Miss Burnet completed her study in 1946 the new agricultural revolution was only just making its effects felt.

The significance of this study, as one of a number relating to Social Credit, is to be found in its analysis of the strains and stresses of the local community structure of Alberta. Dr. Burnet is not concerned with showing how the Social Credit movement grew up. That task is left to other studies in the series. Even if she had made the attempt, she could not have explained, in terms of the problems of the local community, why this movement developed at the time and in the way it did. The personality of Mr. William Aberhart, the leader of the movement, was in itself an important factor in determining its character. Important also were such factors as the American background of a large element of the southern Alberta population, the unfortunate experience with the two-party system of government in the early history of the province, the effort to secure political reform through the organization of a farmers' party, the relation of the Alberta economy to the wider Canadian and world economies, the peculiar ideological appeal of social credit as a monetary theory, the constitutional rigidities of the Canadian federal structure, the growing conservatism of the U.F.A. political leadership and the failure of the provincial Government to deal effectively with the problem of public and private debt, and the spreading distrust in Alberta as in other parts of the Western world of democratic institutions and of the leadership of "politicians" or "intellectuals." What Miss Burnet's study shows is not what factors produced the Social Credit movement but rather what factors operated in the life of the local community to provide favourable ground for its development.

In a very real sense Social Credit was a movement of the local as well as of the wider community. The mass meetings held by Mr. Aberhart and his fellow workers, the organization of local study groups, and the campaign of propaganda carried on through radio and by the distribution of Social Credit literature did more than build a strong political party capable of winning the provincial election of 1935. Such activities reached down into the life of the local community and gave to that life a new meaning. Persons resident in Alberta in the years that witnessed the growth of the movement attest to its importance as a local social reorganizing force. A population disillusioned by the collapse of the hopes brought West by early settlers, and made socially apathetic, was given an idea to believe in and a programme to work for. Nowhere were the effects of this more felt than in the organization of the local community.

As a solution to the problems of rural community organization, Social Credit, of course, was bound to fail. Miss Burnet's study provides some understanding as to why that was so. In the life of the

local community it is possible to see this movement in some perspective. Like many other solutions which offered themselves, Social
Credit did not really alter the character of rural society. In the end,
its significance as a social movement is to be found not in the accom-
plishments of its reform programme but in its arousing, at a dark
moment in the history of the people of Alberta, of a new hope in the
future. How dark that moment was for certain people in Alberta is
revealed in this study of the drought-stricken community of Hanna.

S. D. CLARK

The University of Toronto

Preface

THIS is a study of problems of social organization of the rural community. It is concerned with a drought-afflicted wheat-growing area of Alberta, of which the town of Hanna is the centre. In this area the problems of rural social organization have been acute. The area was settled only a short time ago; it is dependent upon wheat growing, and it was hard hit by drought and by depression. Hence the task of building a satisfactory community life has been difficult, and has not yet been accomplished.

The Hanna area is in the east-central part of the province. The Saskatchewan border is its eastern boundary, on the south it reaches to Acadia Valley and to the ranching lands along the Red Deer River, on the west to the more favoured farming districts beyond the Hand Hills, and on the north to the neighbourhood of the Canadian Pacific Railway line running through Castor and Coronation.

The name of Hanna, the one town of the area, can fittingly be applied to the whole. It is so applied in popular speech, although the residents of the town have at times protested against this.[1] Hanna is not the geographical centre, being located near the western edge, but it is the service centre. It has 1,800 people, whereas none of the hamlets and villages has as many as 400. Many goods and services can be obtained only in Hanna, and farmers who ordinarily trade at one of the villages frequently travel long distances to the town. Both the size of Hanna and the range of its facilities are related to the fact that it is a Canadian National Railways division point.

The whole area, as well as being the service zone of one town, was settled at the same time. It was opened in 1909 for homesteading, and filled up rapidly within the next three years. Since then the population has fluctuated greatly. Many of the original settlers moved on after a short stay to more promising fields. The good prices and good crops of the war years brought a new influx, followed by a new outflow during the drought and depression of the 1920's. Economic revival at

[1]*Hanna Herald*, July 30, 1931; May 10, 1934.

the end of the twenties again resulted in an increase of population and
the catastrophic thirties in another decline.

Census figures, available for every fifth year, show some of the
changes in population. Census Division No. 5, which coincides roughly
with the Hanna area, had only 75 residents in 1901, and 283 in 1906.
By 1911 the number had jumped to 13,170, and by 1916 to 24,500. The
peak was reached in 1921, when the population was 31,220. By 1926 it
had fallen to 24,669, and though it rose in 1931 to 26,651, in 1936 it
was 21,359 and in 1941 only 18,926.[2]

Most of the early settlers were of Northern European background—
British, Scandinavian, and German. In the course of time the proportion of British people has decreased, and several minority groups
have become marked off from the rest of the population. The largest
of these is the German-Russian group which is now prominent in the
rural districts near the town of Hanna.

Throughout the area wheat farming is the dominant economic
enterprise, although most of the land is classified as marginal or submarginal for the growing of wheat. The impact of drought and of
market fluctuations on the wheat economy has led to the inclusion of
all the rural parts of the Hanna area in the Special Areas. These are
the districts that during the late twenties and the thirties were put
under the jurisdiction of a board appointed by the provincial government because they were considered unsuitable for agricultural settlement.[3]

Although certain conditions are common to the whole area, Hanna
is not a single community. It can be subdivided into a town and several
villages, village-centred rural communities, and rural communities
without village centres. The inclusion of all of these makes possible
the investigation of problems of social organization which lie not in
the structure and functioning of one community, but in the relations
among several.

On the other hand the area is small enough to allow some examination of problems of local community organization. General studies
of the West have shown that it is possible to predict from soil and
rainfall maps the areas which have a fluctuating population and unusual social unrest. The physical environment operates, however,
through its effects on social organization. Within the limited Hanna
area may be seen the manner in which this occurs.

The fact that Hanna was settled only a generation ago has been
important in its adjustment. Ways of life which have evolved in one

----

[2]Dominion Bureau of Statistics, *Eighth Census of Canada, 1941*, and preceding
censuses of Canada and of the Prairie Provinces.
[3]Cf. Statutes of Alberta, 1938, c. 92; 1939, c. 34; 1940, c. 28.

environment are seldom suited to another. The fiats of nature[4] must be learned by long-term observation, and techniques adapted to them; common understandings must be reached among community members. Therefore the people of a new community are usually restless. Further, Hanna was settled at a time when severe problems were facing even those rural communities which had once been stable. The developments in technology and in industrial-capitalist organization that had taken place by the early years of the twentieth century both increased the farmer's resources and presented him with problems, problems which might be expected to be even greater in new areas than in old.

The wheat economy also poses special problems, particularly in the area of severe drought. Wheat growing in the dry belt can support only a sparse population, and it gives widely fluctuating yields. Thus it presents a situation to which adjustment is difficult.

Two types of adjustment must be made. The first is economic. The demands of the natural environment and of the economic system of which the region is a part must be met. If settlement is to be stable, they must be met on a long-term basis, by "a way of living that will carry through the years."[5] That social and cultural forces are involved in this is shown by the varying degrees of economic success attained by different ethnic groups in similar situations, and also by the marked interdependence of technology, social organization, and ideology in any established rural society.

In addition, a form of group life must be worked out that affords satisfactions comparable to those offered by other communities. The importance of this is assumed in many studies of rural life, in which rural depopulation is related to the lack of recreational facilities for young people and to the emphasis on city ways in the schools and not to the lack of economic opportunities in the country in comparison with the town. The organization of the family and of the community are vital aspects of welfare. It was in recognition of this fact that a committee appointed in the 1930's by the Alberta Minister of Agriculture to investigate and report upon the problems of the drought area stated: "The problem of successful settlement in the dry areas is as much a sociological problem as an economic one, and until such time as it is treated as such, no permanent solution will be provided."[6]

Field research for this study was carried on from June to September, 1946. Data were gathered chiefly by means of observation, interview-

[4]J. M. Gillette, *North Dakota Weather and the Rural Economy*, p. 80.

[5]E. C. Hughes, "A Proposal for [the] Study of the Dynamics of Rural Culture and Institutions," p. 1, quoting C. C. Colby.

[6]*A Report on the Rehabilitation of the Dry Areas of Alberta and Crop Insurance, 1935-36*, p. 59.

ing, and the reading of the files of the *Hanna Herald*. Various studies and government reports dealing with Western Canada or the western United States served to suggest and to check hypotheses. No attempt has been made to take into account the changes which may have occurred in Hanna since the field work was done. When references are made to the present, the time meant is the summer of 1946.

Professor S. D. Clark of the University of Toronto, editor of this series, and Professor E. C. Hughes of the University of Chicago gave helpful advice in the planning of the research and in the analysis and interpretation of materials. Two Albertans acted as assistants for short periods: Miss M. H. Spencer helped gather information about the town of Hanna and Mr. S. R. Mealing information about the village of Oyen. Mr. and Mrs. J. K. Sutherland, hospitable hosts and able informants, were two of many kindly and co-operative Hanna people. A committee of readers, acting on behalf of the Canadian Social Science Research Council, made many useful criticisms. Assistance for publication was provided by the Canadian Social Science Research Council and the Publication Fund of the University of Toronto Press. The editor and staff of the University of Toronto Press gave generous help in the preparation of the study for publication.

J. B.

The University of Toronto, 1950

Acknowledgments

GRATEFUL acknowledgment is made to the following authors and publishers for permission to quote from copyright material: D. Appleton-Century, *Especially Babe* (1942), by R. Ross Annett; Columbia University Press, *Rural Trends in Depression Years* (1937), by E. de S. Brunner and I. Lorge; Stanford University Press, *The Railroader* (1940), by W. Fred Cottrell; Rivington and Company, *In the Shadow of the Rockies* (1930), by C. M. MacInnes; The Viking Press, *Imperial Germany and the Industrial Revolution* (1915), by T. B. Veblen.

Contents

NEXT-YEAR COUNTRY

CHAPTER ONE

The Dry-Belt Economy

THE RURAL community of the Hanna area has failed to adjust to the physical environment and to the world economic situation. This is the most obvious and the most pressing fact about its organization. The Plains Indians and the few cattlemen who preceded the agricultural settlers made a long-run adjustment to natural conditions, although their supplanting can be interpreted as failure to adjust equally well to the world economy.[1] The wheat farmers have as yet adapted themselves to neither. Their income has fluctuated widely and has shown a downward trend, except for the recent war and postwar years. Responses to the changes in income so far have not solved the basic problems and have increased the difficulty of developing a satisfactory form of community life.

The Hanna economy is based on wheat. Over one-third of the land is unoccupied, over half of the occupied land is unimproved, and the yield of the improved land is low because of lack of rainfall, so that less wheat is produced than in several other parts of Alberta. Nevertheless, wheat is the most important product of the area. Census Division No. 5 includes not only the Hanna area but also ranching lands immediately north of the Red Deer River. In 1935, of 4,317 farms in the Census Division, 2,318 or 53.7 per cent were classified as wheat farms; in 1940, of 3,847 farms, 2,991 or 77.5 per cent were so classified.[2] Little livestock is raised, and of the area devoted to field crops 90 per cent is almost always used for wheat and oats, the former being grown to much the greater extent.[3] Experiments have been made with other

[1]Great Plains Committee, *The Future of the Great Plains*, pp. 1-17.
[2]Dominion Bureau of Statistics, *Eighth Census of Canada, 1941*, vol. VIII; Dominion Bureau of Statistics, *Census of the Prairie Provinces, 1936*, vol. I. The classification is in terms of the main source of income.
[3]See Appendix, Tables I - III.

grains, such as flax, but they have been even less suited to the area than wheat. If most of the land were used for pasture rather than cultivation, soil-drifting would decrease. However, forty acres or more of grazing land are required for each animal, and in drought, when wheat cannot grow, stock cannot be raised for lack of feed and water.

The region is capable of producing the highest quality of wheat. Dry-belt wheat is both hard and high in protein content.[4] There is some basis for the Hanna Board of Trade motto, "The Best in the West When We Get It," and the boast of local farmers that their wheat sells the whole North American crop.

The difficulty is that the Hanna farmer cannot count on a good crop, and not until recently has he been able to count on good prices. The natural environment is extremely variable. So has been the price of wheat. Hence the income of the Hanna farmer has fluctuated widely.

When conditions have been good, wheat has brought a fabulous return, even from light soils. In 1916 one farmer had a yield which brought him $2,900 from only thirty-four acres. Others remember even more lucrative crops. When conditions have been bad, nothing has grown profitably. Gardens have failed, and feed for stock has had to be shipped in from outside. Knowledge of these facts limits diversification. A grizzled and stooped New Brigden farmer remarked in September, 1946: "Not much in her this year. This country has beat us again. Man's a blame fool to keep trying. But what else is there to do? There's nothing better than those berries [wheat] when the price is right. You can raise hogs or sheep or cattle and work away with them all year round, but the berries have them all beat if you can just carry on until there's a crop and the price is right. A man keeps waiting."

The hope of riches if a bumper crop and good prices coincide also keeps some people from leaving the area.[5] A district agriculturist who in 1938 was trying to persuade people to accept government aid in

[4]On a map issued by the Board of Grain Commissioners, Ottawa, showing the protein content of wheat grown in 1932, a small tract of land just east of the town of Hanna is the only part of Alberta indicated as having wheat with "distinctly more than average" protein, and the rest of the Hanna area is shown as having wheat with "slightly more than average." W. A. Mackintosh, *Prairie Settlement: The Geographical Setting*, p. 148. See also W. E. Bowser and A. G. McCalla, *Cropping for Profit and Permanency*, Plate II, facing p. 9.

[5]In Ross Annett's novel, *Especially Babe*, a dirt-farmer replies (p. 12) to the urging of a government man that he move: "I know them kind of places you'd move me to. Places where you can raise enough vegetables an' such to just live on. One crop of wheat and I'll make more money than them folks do in a lifetime." Similar sentiments were voiced by a number of farmers in speaking of people who had moved north or returned east.

moving from the dried-out areas said that his greatest fear was that it would rain. If it did, he claimed, he would need another ten years to convince the people that they ought to leave. The dry belt is "next-year country" because its people still feel that every crop they plant may be "a million-dollar crop."

Hanna is part of the Northern Plains, and, as a marginal area, exhibits in extreme form the peculiarities of the Plains. These may be summarized as unpredictable variability near the margin for profitable cultivation.[6] The average annual rainfall is so low that a variation of a few inches makes the difference between a good crop and a failure. Other agricultural hazards are numerous, and as unpredictably variable as the rainfall.

Even the soils of the Hanna area, while generally fertile, differ greatly from place to place.[7] The land is prairie and rarely too hilly to be arable. Most is within the brown-soil belt; a small portion to the northwest is in the transitional or dark brown belt. The soils are predominantly loams of medium or heavy texture, rich and well adapted to grain production.[8] Farmers stress, however, that the best lands are likely to be immediately alongside of the worst, that one quarter-section may have productive soil and the adjacent quarter be barren.

Rainfall is the chief limiting factor in Hanna farming. That the rainfall is low is important for the fertility of the soil, since heavy rains would make for the leaching of important plant foods. Unfortunately it is often so low as to be inadequate for crops, though most of it comes in the growing season when it is of greatest use. It is also extremely variable. Between 1913 and 1945 the annual rainfall was as high as 25.1 inches and as low as 7.6 inches, in the years 1940 and 1919 respectively. The average from 1913 to 1945 was almost exactly

[6]Cf. C. F. Kraenzel, W. Thomson, and G. H. Craig, *The Northern Plains in a World of Change*, p. 16.

[7]For a detailed study of the soils, see F. A. Wyatt and J. D. Newton, *Soil Survey of Sounding Creek Sheet* and *Soil Survey of Sullivan Lake Sheet*. The Sounding Creek Sheet very nearly coincides with the Hanna area as defined for this study. It includes 120 townships, or 2,764,800 acres, in the form of a rectangle 90 miles east and west by 48 miles north and south. Its southern limit is 144 miles north of the international boundary, and its eastern limit is the Saskatchewan boundary.

[8]The blowout-phase loam is less fertile than the others. Though unusual, it is not peculiar to the region. The name is derived from shallow depressed spots or "blow-outs," irregular in shape, from 6 to 18 inches deep and from 5 to 15 feet in diameter. Often they are almost bare, or only lightly covered with grass. In some places they make up almost half the land surface, though usually they cover a considerably smaller area. Cf. Wyatt and Newton, *Soil Survey of Sounding Creek Sheet*, pp. 24-5.

13 inches, with the figures for the five years 1927, 1931, and 1934 to
1936 omitted and the figures for 1941 and 1944 incomplete. This may
be compared with the 20 inches considered to be the lower limit for
humid-area agriculture. The amount of rain in April, May, June, and
July varied from 1.6 inches in 1924 to 11.9 inches in 1942, with an
average for the twenty-four years 1913 to 1926, 1935, and 1937 to
1945 of 6.7 inches.[9] The variability in rainfall is spatial as well as
temporal. The Hand Hills area gets more rain than the flat lands.
In Hanna as in Sublette, Kansas, "a rainfall reading is good only for
that particular can."[10]

Dust storms are a result of the low rainfall and light soil, and of
high winds and inadequate farming practices. They have become a
more and more important hazard as the soils, especially in the brown-
soil zone, have been stripped of their grass cover and planted in
grain.[11] A dust storm is vividly portrayed by a Hanna farmer:

The morning is usually fine and clear, with maybe just a gentle breeze
blowing. We farmers are all out in the fields ploughing, seeding, summer
fallowing—doing any one of a score of jobs and duties that fall to the
farmer's lot ere the soil will produce. The breeze comes on just a little
stronger, and a few small particles of soil start to drift gently along the top
of the cultivated land. These tiny soil particles soon loosen up other little
particles. Very soon, with the increasing wind, the whole surface of the
field is gently sifting along, always moving, always gathering fresh momen-
tum by rapidly increasing volume. There is nothing spectacular yet. But
wait—away off to the northwest a heavy black cloud is forming between
sky and earth. Black, yes, black as night. It sweeps towards us rapidly at
forty, fifty, sixty miles an hour. We turn, each individual one of us, looking
for the nearest shelter. Teams are unhooked as quickly as possible, and
if no stable room is near turned with their heads away from the storm.
Those of us with tractors either make for shelter or stay with the machines
as long as possible. . . . The air gets colder. The huge black wall is now
only a mile away. A minute, and with a blast like the roar of a thousand
lions it is upon us. We are alone in a sightless mass of hurtling soil, stinging
sand and thumping clods. We lose all sense of direction. Unless one happens
to be within hand's reach of a fence progress in any calculated direction is
almost impossible. We can only stand buffeted by the blows of a thousand
hammers, or drift helpless, choking, blinded. This is the black blizzard.

[9]A Report on the Rehabilitation of the Dry Areas of Alberta and Crop Insurance, 1935-36, p. 33, gives available data for the years 1913 to 1934. The Department of Agriculture for the province of Alberta supplied information for the years
1935 to 1945.
    [10]E. H. Bell, Culture of a Contemporary Rural Community—Sublette, Kansas,
p. 79.
    [11]E. S. Hopkins, A. E. Palmer, and W. S. Chepil, Soil Drifting Control in the
Prairie Provinces. The planting was done in response to wheat market booms,
which made cultivation of even the lightest textured lands highly profitable.

For hours the tortured soil is torn and ravished until the storm ceases. Then we look out on the fields which we have tilled. They are as smooth as if polished by a giant plane. Here and there a few wheat plants, stricken, stand on roots still remaining in the hard subsoil. With to-morrow's sun they will probably fade and die. Millions in rich top soil is gone forever. That is the black blizzard, the most appalling thing in nature.[12]

Dust storms permanently decrease the fertility of the soil, accentuating the deterioration which occurs through continuous wheat growing and through water erosion. They contribute greatly to the decreasing productivity of large tracts even in good years. They are a factor in the downward revision of the yield considered to be a good or a bumper crop. A succinct description of their destructive force is a farmer's reply to a compliment on the winning of several wheat competitions in the twenties: "The land that that wheat grew on blew away from me."

Numerous other hazards play a role in crop production. Hail can destroy a promising crop within an hour. Few Hanna farmers have escaped being "hailed out" completely at least once. High winds are frequently disastrous. Frost, not so great a hazard at Hanna as in many other parts of the West, causes considerable damage in the wettest years, when the crop is slowest in maturing.[13] Grasshoppers and other insects come in plagues. Residents of the area tell of watching hordes of insects approach, and of passing a promising field of grain in early afternoon and a few hours later seeing the field stripped bare by grasshoppers.[14]

The importance and the variability of the different hazards are suggested by census data. In Census Division No. 5, Alberta, crop failure in 1930 occurred on 428,442 acres. In 1935 it occurred on 207,714 acres, and in 1940 on only 27,175 acres. Drought was the cause of failure for 87,159 acres in 1930, for 97,623 acres in 1935, and for 1,196 acres in 1940. Hail or rain was accountable for failure on 306,507 acres in 1930, on 49,904 acres in 1935, and on 22,448 acres in 1940. Wind was listed as a cause of failure only in 1930, when it affected 29,487 acres. Insects damaged less than five hundred acres in 1930 and 1940, but 48,455 acres in 1935.[15]

A graphic linking of the factors involved in wheat farming was made by a farmer located a few miles west of Hanna in commenting

[12]J. K. Sutherland, "The Black Blizzards and What We Must Do about Them" (unpublished radio broadcast).

[13]Wyatt and Newton, *Soil Survey of Sounding Creek Sheet*, p. 7.

[14]Cf. O. E. Rölvaag, *Giants in the Earth: A Saga of the Prairie*, pp. 341 ff.

[15]Dominion Bureau of Statistics, *Eighth Census of Canada, 1941*, vol. VIII, and preceding censuses of Canada and of the Prairie Provinces.

on his crops from 1909 to 1945. His remarks have to do with one particular farm, but statistical records are largely corroborative.[16] The first year he spent in the area was inclined to be dry, and the second was very dry. In 1911 and 1912 there was abundant rainfall and the crops were good. The year 1913 was dry, but residual moisture helped; 1914 was also dry. The next two years brought abundant rainfall and heavy crops, but there was considerable frost damage in 1917. A long drought began in 1917, a year of little moisture and light crop. The last year of the First World War was very dry, and there was a crop disaster because of drought and frost. The next three years were inclined to be dry; 1922, though on the dry side, brought a fair crop, and 1923 the first abundant rainfall and bumper crop in many years. In 1924 it was dry and the crop was a failure. In 1925 it was inclined to be dry and there was damage from insects, so that the crop was light. The 1926 rainfall was medium and the crop fair. A wet year followed with a bumper yield, but in 1928 a wet year did not result in a good crop because of tremendous damage from frost. Then came three years of light crops, with dry weather and in 1931 very great damage by grasshoppers also. In 1932 there was a fair amount of moisture and a reasonable yield, but the price of wheat fell very low. The crop was practically a failure in 1933 and 1934 because of drought and grasshoppers; it was somewhat better in 1935, but suffered damage from frost. The next two years were very dry and the crop failed. In the three years from 1938 to 1940, there was a fair amount of moisture and a fair crop, with a light rainfall and a light crop in 1941. The year 1942 was wet and there was a bumper crop, but the next three years were dry again and the crops very light. The spring of 1946 was exceedingly dry, and dust storms were frequent; rains from early June until mid-July aroused hopes for a bumper crop, but a three-week dry spell followed by rains which interfered with the harvest meant that the yield, though a little better than average, was still small.

The net income per acre depends not only upon the yield of wheat but upon the costs of production and upon prices. While some of the costs of producing wheat vary with the yield, others are inflexible. During the drought and depression years, wheat prices often sunk below production costs.[17] They fell to nineteen cents a bushel for high

[16]See Appendix, Table IV.
[17]Regarding costs of wheat production in the West, see D. A. MacGibbon, *The Canadian Grain Trade*, pp. 462-70; E. S. Hopkins, J. M. Armstrong, and H. D. Mitchell, *Cost of Producing Farm Crops in the Prairie Provinces*, pp. 22-32; G. E. Britnell, *The Wheat Economy*, pp. 76-9; R. W. Gardner, "Wheat Production Costs," *Canadian Chartered Accountant*, XXXIV, 1939, pp. 165-9.

quality wheat, though the average price for a season was never so low.[18] Fluctuations were so rapid and so great that a farmer who had heard radio reports of prices immediately before driving into town often received four or five cents a bushel less than he expected.

The Dominion Department of Agriculture's system of land classification in the West from the standpoint of wheat growing takes account of both the natural environment and the economic environment. Four classes are relevant to the Hanna area. Class I includes parcels of land which produce fewer than 375 bushels of wheat for sale from each quarter-section. Such land is submarginal for wheat production and might better be used for grazing. Class II consists of parcels of land which yield between 375 and 517 bushels of wheat for sale from each quarter-section. This land is marginal. It might, in the long run, give the farmer sufficient return to induce him to continue production, but, because of the high variability of yields at Hanna, the use of marginal parcels for specialized wheat production involves considerable risk. Hence Class II land might better be used for combined wheat-growing and grazing units. Class III includes parcels from which the estimated amount of wheat for sale ranges from 518 to 795 bushels per quarter-section. Such land is fair for wheat growing. Class IV is made up of parcels from which 796 to 999 bushels per quarter-section is obtained, and which are good for wheat production.[19] In other parts of the West higher ratings are necessary. Within the Hanna area well over three-quarters of the land is in Class I, and most of the remainder in Class II. Only a very few parcels are classified as good land. That is, the vast tract of land centring in Hanna is, from the point of view of wheat growing, almost wholly submarginal and marginal.[20]

Attempts have been made to stabilize both yield and income and to check the downward trend. Yield has been improved little as yet through the work of the federal and provincial departments of agriculture in developing new varieties of wheat and new techniques of wheat growing. The efforts of the grain companies, boards of trade, chambers of commerce, service clubs, and farmers' organizations in

[18]Regarding wheat prices, see W. A. Mackintosh, *Economic Problems of the Prairie Provinces*, and A. Stewart and W. D. Porter, *Land Use Classification in the Special Areas of Alberta and in Rosenheim and Acadia Valley*, p. 73. In the autumn of 1931 at Fort William, Ont., where wheat brought almost twenty cents a bushel more than in Hanna because of freight and elevator charges, wheat was selling at nine and sawdust at ten dollars a ton. Toronto *Globe*, Dec. 6, 1932.

[19]Stewart and Porter, *Land Use Classification in the Special Areas of Alberta and in Rosenheim and Acadia Valley*, pp. 33-4.

[20]Cf. Canada, Department of Agriculture, *P.F.R.A.: A Record of Achievement*, p. 49.

research and education have also failed. Although conservatism is one factor in the failure of educational campaigns, poverty, which prevents the taking of a long view, is no less important.[21]

Improvements in the marketing of wheat have benefited the Hanna area less than more productive parts of the West. They have been made slowly. The Grain Growers' co-operative movement did not fulfil all the hopes held for it. The movement for the re-establishment of the Wheat Board which operated from 1917 until 1920 failed. The Wheat Pools which were formed in the 1920's and enjoyed a few years of success were hard hit by the depression of the 1930's. The Wheat Board set up during the Second World War and still in existence has, however, brought a measure of price stability, and if it continues to function may solve part of the problem of Hanna and the western wheat-growing region generally.[22]

Hail insurance helps stabilize income by countering the effects of one major agricultural hazard, but some Hanna farmers have felt unable to afford the insurance and others may have been helped by it to continue to work land that should have been abandoned.

Although changes in agriculture in the Hanna area have taken place over the years, they have for the most part not directly affected yields or net income per acre. They have been in the size of holdings and the form of tenure rather than in the ways of controlling natural and economic forces.

The size of farm holdings has increased.[23] The original size, 320 acres, was dictated by government policy. It had become evident elsewhere by 1909 that the 160-acre homestead was uneconomical in the subhumid prairie regions, and the free quarter-section was supplemented by an equally large pre-emption, for which the nominal sum of three dollars an acre was paid. Some settlers increased their holdings further by the use of South African veterans' scrips, which entitled their holders to half-sections. In the course of the years farms have been greatly enlarged. In the 1920's and early 1930's, thousands

[21]The situation is frequently one such as W. O. Mitchell depicts in the Saskatchewan area. Enterprising farmers who wish to try new methods, such as strip farming and irrigation, are prevented from changing their practices by lack of funds. Other farmers, perhaps less destitute, thus have no model to show them the economic advantages of change. W. O. Mitchell, *Who Has Seen the Wind*, especially pp. 20-1, 242-4.

[22]Cf. H. Moorehouse, *Deep Furrows*; L. A. Wood, *A History of Farmers' Movements in Canada*; W. A. Mackintosh, *Agricultural Co-operation in Western Canada*; C. R. Fay, *Agricultural Co-operation in the Canadian West*; W. P. Davisson, *Pooling Wheat in Canada*; H. Boyd, *New Breaking: An Outline of Co-operation among the Farmers of Western Canada*.

[23]See Appendix, Table V.

of acres which had been abandoned as people moved away were taken over by those who remained, for grazing or grain growing. To some extent this was necessary to keep in check pests, weeds, and soil-drifting. The sale of farms by the discouraged at low prices permitted the formal acquisition of land. The Special Areas Board also helped people increase their holdings. The Board was set up to administer those parts of Alberta which "include a considerable amount of land which by reason of insufficient rainfall, inferior quality of soil, and other causes, cannot by the use of ordinary methods of agriculture be made to yield over a period of years produce in sufficient amount to provide the persons farming such land with the means of livelihood," and in which "a large proportion of such lands has been abandoned by settlers and investors due to their inability to secure an adequate livelihood or compensation therefrom."[24] By the late 1930's all of the Hanna area was included in the Special Areas. The Board controlled most of the land—that which was never alienated from the Crown and the large proportion which had reverted to the Crown—and leased it at low rates. In 1946 two or three cents an acre was charged for grazing land, and a sixth or an eighth of the crop, with the first five bushels an acre exempt, for arable land. Improvements in machinery also permit larger holdings. A half-section is now regarded as barely enough even for a single man. Farms of over a thousand acres are common; farms of six or seven thousand acres are not rare, nor are they considered to conflict with the policy of the Special Areas Board of discouraging wheat and cattle "barons."

The increase in the size of holdings is related to the extensive use of machinery. From the beginning the wheat farmers have employed machinery, but whereas formerly horses were used for power, now tractors and self-propelling combines are used. "You don't have to feed a machine all winter, or watch it starve when feed gives out," the farmers remark.[25]

[24]Statutes of Alberta, 1938, c. 92, quoted in Stewart and Porter, *Land Use Classification in the Special Areas of Alberta and in Rosenheim and Acadia Valley*, p. 69.

[25]A newspaper account of depression hardship made reference to the economy of using a tractor: "A typical example of the doggedness of our people is found in the following incident accidentally brought to our attention. A farmer living a few miles north of Hanna cropped about two thousand bushels of wheat last year from little better than two hundred acres. Living expenses, crop payment, and seed for this year left no wherewithal to purchase feed for spring work. His horses wintered poorly and without feed could not be worked. Unable to arrange credit for feed, a second-hand tractor was purchased on deferred payments and credit arranged for gas. Misfortunes never come singly, he had the ill luck to be thrown off a saddle horse, breaking three ribs. No hospital for this man! He strapped a piece of canvas tightly around his body and today is driving that small tractor in

Mechanization has gone so far that horse-drawn vehicles are thought dangerous. Expensive automobiles and tractors are used for many farm tasks, even, on occasion, for fetching the cows. A farmer's son, one of the few from the area to go to university, explained his interest in engineering in terms of the mechanization of farms: "A guy on a farm can see some use in engineering. You grow up with machinery and you get interested in machines. At school the subjects that are most interesting are the ones that explain machines."

The alternative to mechanized farming is a combination of grain growing and stock raising, but this is usually adopted only if machinery cannot be obtained. A nineteen-year-old boy and his father discussed the matter with an interviewer:

"There's two ways to farm in this country," said Bill. "One way is to raise stock and the other way to farm is with a big machine outfit—lots of machinery. Both ways take up a lot of land. Tractor farming for wheat is all right because you can make money even in the light crops, provided you have enough land. You've got to have a big farm or else it doesn't pay to use all that machinery."

"Bill's the farmer in the family," his father explained, "but even he doesn't like sheep much."

"Oh, I don't really mind them. But I'd rather run a tractor. Machinery for me!"

"Well, now, you see we're all out for machinery in our family. But I took to sheep because I didn't have the machinery to begin with. It takes a big outlay at first to have a large machine outfit for wheat farming. Machinery doesn't multiply itself the way my sheep do. There was a smaller outlay for the sheep at first, so I took to sheep."

Changes in the form of tenure have taken place, too.[26] At first both the ideal and the actuality were for the farm to be owned by one man and operated by him and his family, with occasional hired help. This form of tenure is widespread, and its stability and efficiency have rarely been questioned. It is, or has been until recently, the ideal in many parts of North America, the rural counterpart of the "Own Your Own Home" and "Own Your Own Business" ideals of towns and cities.[27] Since land was free or cheap, the ideal was realized in the

---

a four-hundred acre program of spring work. The moral is, 'You can't keep a good man down.'" *Hanna Herald*, April 24, 1930.

[26]See Appendix, Table VI.

[27]Cf. R. T. McMillan and O. D. Duncan, *Social Factors of Farm Ownership in Oklahoma*, p. 3: "The belief that agriculture and the nation are best served when a goodly proportion of those who till the land own the acres they work is deeply rooted in American life." See also L. A. Salter, Jr., *Land Tenure in Process*, p. 1: "General opinion in this country has long held that an ideal agricultural economy must be based on the widest possible measure of full and free ownership of farm lands by those who operate farms."

first years of the Hanna area. Few people were tenants, fewer still were farm managers.

Most farmers could not, however, stay unencumbered for long. Cash-crop farming, unlike subsistence farming, makes heavy demands upon credit, and dry-belt wheat farming makes especially heavy demands because of variable incomes. Loan companies at first urged people to borrow, and they did so readily. Even in 1914, when the first contraction in the Hanna economy took place, mortgages were common.[28] The First World War ended the period of abundant credit,[29] and when it was over Hanna had entered upon a period of drought broken only for a few years before the disastrous thirties. Borrowing, even from government agencies, became almost impossible. In late 1929 and early 1930, the *Hanna Herald* attacked the Canadian Farm Loans Board for "blacklisting" the drought area. The paper quoted from a letter received by a farmer who had asked for help: "Since the application form was sent to you, the Board have decided that for the present at least, and until conditions improve, they will not consider applications from certain districts in this Province where land values have deteriorated because of adverse seasons."[30] Eventually the paper was able to laud a change in policy.

Soon the debt burden was crushing.[31] To pay taxes or to pay the interest on old debts was almost impossible. Interest was called "the crop that never fails." Foreclosure became a terrifying spectre to farmers, many of whom lost their machines, their crops, and even their land. There sprang up a host of stories of people working all night to harvest a crop and get it into town before it could be seized, taking advantage of errors in foreclosure papers, and outwitting or intimidating process-servers. One story is reminiscent of the tales of Paul Bunyan:

A farmer who was deeply in debt, a man of immense stature, was being harassed for an unpaid machine account. This farmer was down to two very small horses and a walking plough. Finally the machine company sent a collector who had been a heavy-weight wrestler to intimidate the farmer

[28]The newspaper in that year carried the item: "November 1st, usually known as 'Mortgage day,' is constantly on the minds of all farmers. Instead of November 1st being a day of pleasure, it is usually a day of sorrow and worry, as it is on that day that the agents of the various machinery companies pay their official visit to their debtors. This was quite evident in this district when they made their last visit here. Charity begins at home." *Hanna Herald*, Nov. 12, 1914.

[29]For a detailed study of farm credit, see W. T. Easterbrook, *Farm Credit in Canada*.

[30]*Hanna Herald*, Nov. 14, 1929.

[31]Cf. Royal Commission on Dominion-Provincial Relations, *The Case for Alberta*.

into paying up. The collector drove up to where the farmer was ploughing summer fallow. The farmer was well aware of the pugilistic reputation of this particular collector. As the collector drove his car near the scene of the ploughing he was somewhat appalled by the muscular appearance of the lean, lanky, hungry farmer. Instead of asking for money, he asked where another farmer lived in the vicinity. Our ploughman was a firm believer in the usefulness of first impressions. He took a firm stand in the dusty furrow, and with the plough handle grasped in one hand, raised plough, horses and all. With this dangling mass he pointed over towards the highway that the collector had just left, murmuring huskily that he reckoned Farmer Brown lived over that way, and the quickest way to get there was to turn completely around and start making tracks. These directions were, rumour says, implicitly obeyed.[32]

Debt led to the overthrow of old tenure patterns as, parcel by parcel, land reverted to the Crown. The new form of tenure is part ownership, part leasehold, still with family labour, and with much smaller encumbrances.[33] Not only has credit been greatly restricted, but experience has led to a fear of new debts and heroic efforts to reduce old ones.[34] Even food is skimped that mortgages may be paid. Many of the debts not paid have been cancelled or reduced.

The Special Areas Board has encouraged leasehold tenure. Its policy aims at preventing over-population. The Board by 1946 controlled 65 to 70 per cent of the land in the area as a whole, and in some districts 90 or 95 per cent. This land it sells only in unusual cases, and does not lease except to people who already have holdings in the area. So little is charged for leases that it is sometimes to a farmer's advantage to let all but the quarter-section of land on which his buildings are revert to the Crown and to lease what he needs. Payment for leases, if rigorously extracted, approximately equals what taxes would be and it frequently is not demanded. In allowing land to revert, therefore, the farmer simply saves a few years' taxes. Leasing also permits the exchanging of poor lands for better.

The new form of tenure has not solved the fundamental problems of the area. Although it paves the way for government conservation measures, as yet these have not been introduced widely. Irrigation has been discussed for thirty years as a remedy for basic dry-belt problems.

[32]J. K. Sutherland, "The Rain That Didn't Come" (unpublished radio broadcast).
[33]See Appendix, Table VII.
[34]An example of the distrust of credit arrangements was given by a Victory Loan canvasser in a rural district. He had collected $17,000 and was being praised by local organizers in the presence of a Calgary man. The latter asked how much he had secured at once, and how much had been promised for later dates. The canvasser replied that all had been paid, whereupon the city resident claimed that he ought to have obtained pledges for as much again. In telling of the incident, the local man said, "If I had tried to sell any bonds on time, I wouldn't have sold any at all, either way!"

Surveys have indicated that thousands of acres are irrigable and the East Central Irrigation Association has tried to get government action in the matter, but irrigation projects have not been carried out. Moreover, people are not unanimous about their desirability. Some are convinced that they would be far too costly. Irrigation, then, although it may be important in the future, has not yet provided a means of adjustment.

The Hanna area has not worked out a solution to the problems presented by its geographical and economic situation. It is marginal or submarginal for wheat growing, but under existing conditions of price and technology even less adapted to other types of agriculture. The failure of Hanna residents to solve their economic problems doubtless has social and cultural roots. Farming practices, the division of labour, standards of living and modes of tenure and inheritance brought into the area from more humid regions have proved ill adapted to the dry belt and have delayed economic adjustment. In turn the failure in the realm of economics has had adverse social and cultural consequences, at both the household and the community level.

CHAPTER TWO

The Rural Household

FOR THE Hanna family or household group the economic situation presents serious problems. The large size of the farms, the high degree of specialization and of mechanization, leasehold tenure, unpredictable fluctuations in yield and income, all affect adversely the standard of living and the social organization of the household. They thrust upon the household many social and economic tasks and at the same time impair its ability to perform them. Hence it cannot offer to its members a satisfactory way of life.

To provide for their members a consistently high standard of living is the aim of most families or households. It is a more important aim for the farm family than it is for the city family, because the farm family is to a greater extent both the consumption-unit and the work-unit. The standard of living is related to food, clothing, housing and house furnishings, farm facilities, and working conditions. It affects health, comfort, and contentment. Certain aspects of these are physical. The human organism needs a sufficient quality and quantity of food, sanitary arrangements, clothing, and shelter to survive and to function efficiently. Other aspects, at least as important, are psychological, social, and cultural, such as the standards for comparison which people draw from their own past experience and from their ideas about conditions in other places. Unless their standard of living is adequate, people cannot be well and happy.

That the standard of living in the Hanna rural community has been unsatisfactory is suggested in a 1943 newspaper editorial:

The war has accelerated the movement of boys from the farm to the city that has been going on for years. In discussing the subject, the Sedgewick Community press suggests that the attitude of the parents of farm boys is largely responsible for the young people's dissatisfaction with farm life.

16

"It is not denied that farmers have hard struggles and many discouragements, but constant dwelling upon them does not help to better conditions. . . . Many farmers, if they knew of the struggles and discouragements of thousands in the cities, would get a truer perspective of their own situation. . . . It is the atmosphere of the farm home, and the fact that its disadvantages are dwelt upon so much that drives so many farm boys away from farms." If the community press should carry its reasoning further it would get at the real root of the problem. The job is to make the parents more contented. They see homes in towns and cities equipped with electricity, water systems and, in many places, gas heating, while the great majority of farm homes have to put up with primitive conditions—oil lamps and water carried from the pump are relics of the past as far as the urban centres are concerned. The introduction of electricity to farm homes would make a tremendous difference. The average home equipped with electricity uses the current for at least half a dozen different jobs. If a farm could have electricity for lighting, running a refrigerator, operating an electric iron, a radio, and even for cooking, what a boon it would be to the farm housewife. If the farmer could use the current for power it would be a great help to him. If the nation is to keep the boys on the farms of this country plans will have to be made to make farm life more attractive. To do this the farm home will have to be equipped for modern day life.[1]

The diet of the dry-belt farmer in prosperous times compares favourably with that of many other rural residents of North America. It includes an abundance of the products of the farm itself, fresh in summer and preserved in winter. Meat, fowl, vegetables, milk and cream, butter and eggs are readily available, and are supplemented by purchases from the village and town stores. On trips to town or through the mailman or co-operative neighbours the farmers get bread and cakes, cereals, meats, fresh imported fruits, canned goods, salt, sugar, and flour. Food is rarely skimped. Housewives are proud of their lavish tables, and of their ability to accommodate large numbers of unexpected supper guests. The pride in feeding threshing-crews well has survived the heyday of the crews.

Back of the custom of abundant meals lie several factors. Primary is the heavy physical labour by all members of the family which is demanded by the farm economy. Supplementary are the cultural pattern brought from earlier rural areas, especially the American West and Midwest, and the impossibility of selling farm products during part of the history of the area.

Not only is food abundant in good times but it is also well cooked. Cooking skill is highly regarded, and the farmer's wife, in spite of her many other tasks and her lack of facilities, tries hard to win praise for her meals. "Good plain food, well cooked," is her goal. If she is suc-

[1] *Hanna Herald,* Feb. 18, 1943.

cessful, her neighbours are aware of the fact and discuss her ability to set a good table as an important virtue.[2]

Even in prosperous times the diet of the Hanna farmers is not perfect, however. It is not free of the faults general throughout Canada and especially rural Canada. The chief faults, in terms of the highest present-day nutritional standards, are an over-abundance of starchy foods, a shortage of citrus fruits, and a scarcity of fresh meats, fruits, and vegetables in the winter season.

The primary causes of the deficiencies are ignorance and faulty eating customs. Much modern food knowledge has been recently acquired and imperfectly disseminated. Ignorance of nutritional facts was widespread prior to war-time educational campaigns. Even where the knowledge has been acquired, customs concerning food and cooking have been slow to change. A housewife's observation, "It's all in what you're used to: it's what you're used to that's tasty," is a shrewd one.

The deficiencies tend to be great in rural areas because of slower acceptance of new ways and of difficulties in securing and in storing needed foods. Cities have abundant and varied supplies at almost all times, although sometimes costs are prohibitive to those with small incomes. In small towns and villages and on farms many foods are not accessible. Moreover, whereas homes in the city frequently have excellent refrigeration facilities, in smaller centres and on farms refrigeration is largely lacking.

In Hanna it has been difficult to secure foods considered desirable by nutrition authorities. Few fruits are available. Saskatoons, which are becoming rare, are almost the only native fruit, and adapted fruit-trees have to be able to endure the droughts, the early frosts, and the high winds. Some farmers keep no cows for milk nor hens for eggs. They do not want to destroy their relative freedom from chores, or to associate themselves with subsistence rather than cash-crop farming. Hence articles of diet usually obtained on the home farm have to be bought. The resulting financial strain is probably greater than that on a town or city household, if rural people need more food than urban because of their heavy labour and outdoor life.[3]

---

[2]As early as 1922 "high living" in the matter of food was condemned by a rural resident as a factor in the deepening depression. In a letter to the *Hanna Herald*, Jan. 26, 1922, he said: "Hundreds of families could cut their living expenses in half and still have plenty of good wholesome food to eat. We do not eat the most healthy foods but the food that pleases the taste best, such foods often being most unhealthy as well as most expensive." The letter provoked an indignant reply, *ibid.*, Feb. 9, 1922.

[3]Cf. P. Sorokin and C. C. Zimmerman, *Principles of Rural-Urban Sociology*, p. 76.

Moreover, unless he lives near by, a farmer usually does not go every day to the village or town. If he sells cream he may go three or four times a week in good weather, but when it rains or snows, when there is much farm work to be done, or when the automobile or truck breaks down, it may be impossible to get in for weeks at a time. Many houses in the Hanna area have neither cellars nor refrigerators for storage: a well is often the makeshift icebox. Preserved foods must be substituted for fresh ones, with a dietary loss.

Much of the water in the Hanna area is made unpalatable by the presence of alkali and other substances. These are not only unpleasant but nauseating to many people.[4] To avoid them it is necessary to buy distilled water or water from wells free of the offensive substances. In some isolated parts of the area all the water must be bought. Places along the Wardlow railway line, for example, have few wells. The farmers have barrels of water brought in by the railroad once a week.

In frontier times the diet of farm people in the Hanna area was grossly inadequate. Farmers were isolated from village stores and many foods were unavailable both at the stores and from nature. The many bachelor households were additionally handicapped by lack of time and of culinary knowledge and skill. The *Hanna Herald* in 1913 attributed the mental illness of a homesteader in part to lack of proper food, and added: "Many a lonely homesteader puts in his hard day's toil and retires at night on a meal quickly made by his own hands and scant because after working in the field he has not the inclination to go to the trouble of preparing a better one."[5]

In the drought and depression of the 1920's and 1930's food conditions were even worse. People could not afford to buy as much as before. The failure of village stores removed sources of supply. The stricken farms themselves could provide little food. Gardens failed completely. There were no vegetables or fruits to can even if canning had been within people's means. Feed for livestock could not be grown, and the amount shipped in from outside was hopelessly inadequate. Relief supplies from government agencies, the Red Cross, and the churches, and fruit and vegetables secured at low cost by the co-operatives were almost the only available foods. Some supplies were distributed to all residents, whether on relief or not, but in many districts 90 per cent or even 100 per cent of the population were on government relief. The relief supplies, however, were both insufficient and badly distributed. They were given out from town and village

----

[4]A district nurse expressed the opinion that the water might be casally related to acne and appendicitis, which are very prevalent in the area.

[5]*Hanna Herald*, June 5, 1913.

centres, either by residents or by special officers not fully acquainted with the rural situation. Sometimes the farmers' organizations tried to remedy matters by getting supplies whose distribution would be in their own hands.

Semi-starvation was for many the result of drought and depression. Premier William Aberhart in 1935 talked of people in Alberta having nothing to eat for days. He said: "There are children in Alberta who have not tasted butter or milk in the last three years although they live on farms. Their fathers have to sell all the milk the cows produce to live. . . . Children are crying for food out in Alberta tonight. The boys and girls are hungry. . . ." He added that in the dry belt the people were living on gopher stew.[6] Mr. Aberhart's statements produced great indignation,[7] but at most he exaggerated conditions which needed no exaggeration to be shocking. A diet of potatoes and milk has become legendary in the Hanna area. A trucker who delivered relief supplies in the 1930's told of a woman who wept when he filled a tub with vegetables for her and her children, and said they had had no vegetables for three years.[8] Probably the effects of malnutrition in the thirties will be evident for many years.

Dry-belt clothing during bad times lacked warmth and comfort as well as attractiveness. There was no money to buy garments, and cast-offs sent from the East could not meet the need. "There are women in Alberta who have worn nothing but gunny sacks for the past three years, dresses made from the bags in which the binder twine was wrapped," said Aberhart.[9] As in his statements about food he probably exaggerated, but the stout cloth of flour sacks and sugar sacks was put to many ingenious uses. Amusement was derived from instances in which the lettering was not thoroughly bleached and could be read on the articles of dress.[10] When such materials ran out, both adults and children had to try to keep warm in scanty, torn clothing.

Housing, grounds, and farm buildings afford an easily observed indication of levels of living. In this regard there is marked deterioration in quality as one goes eastward from Calgary to Hanna. Before the severe drought area is reached, the homes and farm buildings

[6]*Ibid.*, Sept. 19, 1935.
[7]*Ibid.*, Sept. 19, 26, 1935.
[8]Annett depicts a family including two small children which lived on oatmeal and potatoes after the relief flour was gone. The older of the children had seen oranges and apples in the stores but neither had tasted them. A can of peaches was regarded as a great treat. Both children were pale from malnutrition. There is little reason to consider the picture overdrawn in these details. R. R. Annett, *Especially Babe, passim.*
[9]*Hanna Herald*, Sept. 19, 1935.
[10]Cf. K. Strange, *With the West in Her Eyes*, p. 228.

along the highway have a fine appearance. They are almost all frame buildings, large enough for a family of five or six. Some are one and a half storeys high, some two or two and a half. They are in good repair, neat and well painted. Often they have a generator for electric power and a windmill. Flower gardens are near the houses, and trees border the roads leading to the highway. Ten or fifteen miles west of Hanna the dominant type of building changes to an unpainted grey shack. Home, chicken coops, barn, garage, and granary are of this form. The house is small, shabby, and without running water or electricity. Attempts at gardening have had little success. Trees are planted near the house, but the climate prevents them, as well as flowers and grass, from thriving. Even farmers with a considerable income live in poor housing. Comfortable and attractive stucco houses, with electricity and running water, are few.

The small, unpainted buildings had their origin as bachelors' shacks quickly put up on homesteads.[11] If the frontiersman had any help, it was usually from a neighbour with more experience in building; carpenters were seldom employed. Sometimes the coming of wife and family could be met by additions to the shack, but rarely by a new and better house. The demands on space as the youngsters grew up coincided with drought and depression years. Then building and even repairs could not be financed, and in addition land values in the area fell and no higher price per acre was paid for a farm with good buildings than for one with poor. By the time prosperity returned, the children had left home and the small old house was adequate for the few family members who remained. Leasehold tenure also discourages spending time and money on buildings, because of fear that the lease may not be renewed. On almost all farms with above-average buildings, some improvements are recent and there is a son who is confident of inheriting his father's holdings.

Evidence of the condition of farm buildings is found in the Stewart and Porter report of *Land Use Classification in the Special Areas of Alberta and in Rosenheim and Acadia Valley.*[12] The area studied includes a considerable amount of land to the south and west of the Hanna area. The surveys used were made in the late 1930's. Of 7,581 buildings, 4,421 were occupied. These were ranked, in comparison with those in other parts of the province, as good, fair, and poor. The number of good buildings was 41, of fair buildings 569, and of poor buildings 3,811. Of the 3,160 unoccupied buildings, 943 were usable and 2,217 useless. In the early 1940's further abandonment and deterio-

---

[11]Frame buildings were sometimes preceded by sod shanties.
[12]P. 51. See also Appendix, Tables VIII and IX.

ration occurred, and many buildings were moved or destroyed for lumber.

Uncleanliness and discomfort frequently result from lack of running water and the rudeness and smallness of the buildings. The lack of facilities and the amount of work to be done force the housewife to give first attention to keeping clean the utensils used in milking and in separating. Other things are washed in somewhat cursory fashion. Also, hanging work-clothes in the kitchen and cooking food for livestock there cause unpleasant odours.

The houses, like frame buildings in other areas, are fire hazards. Frequently in winter a stove or lamp has set fire to a house or barn. Wells are inadequate to meet such emergencies. The result of a fire is almost invariably the total destruction of the building and its contents, and sometimes the loss of life.

Communication facilities are items in the standard of living and also influence the satisfaction given by other items. Communication has two aspects—communication within the community, and communication with the world outside. The telephone, the local newspaper, and local roads have to do chiefly with the first. The book, the periodical, the city daily or weekly newspaper, the radio, the railway, and the mail-order catalogue have to do chiefly with the second. The two are closely related, however. The automobile and the highway are of importance for both.

Isolation is a frequent problem on the frontier. It might be expected to be less acute in the Hanna area than on some other frontiers because of the advances in transportation and communication which had taken place by the time of the opening up of Alberta, the absence of forest in the Hanna region, and the extreme rapidity of settlement. On the contrary, isolation was a severe hardship. The first settlers found it difficult to travel to and from Brooks, Stettler, and Castor, at various times the nearest railway towns, by horse or by oxen for supplies. They sometimes got lost in winter storms or blizzards. They suffered grievously from loneliness, which seems peculiarly acute in prairie lands where the absence of neighbours can be verified at a glance.[13]

[13]C. M. MacInnes said of a region settled earlier than Hanna: "Surely few things can be more overpowering for a stranger than the immensity of the prairie, when for miles in all directions there is nothing to be seen but an unending succession of lonely hills or a flat expanse of plain. The settler's loneliness is increased by the fact that he can see, beyond the shadow of a doubt, that he is absolutely alone, a certainty which the backwoodsman, surrounded by the forest, never has. The little shack that has been built with such labour, sinks into insignificance in that vast ocean of emptiness, and its builder realises his puniness as he has never realised it before. It was bad enough in the summer, when there was work to do

The women were more isolated than the men, who in the course of their work met their neighbours. The women spent their lives within tiny shacks, engaged in ceaseless heavy toil. They could not get skilled medical aid in childbirth. Frequently, when the men were busy with harvest or a round-up, they were completely alone for days, with "nothing to keep them company but the dreary moanings of the prairie wind in the dry grasses and about the buildings, or in the still cold nights, the lugubrious yelp of coyotes to add the last touch to their loneliness and desolation."[14] Isolation bore especially heavily on well-educated Englishwomen who could find little female companionship of any sort and none of the sort to which they were accustomed. "Prairie madness" was considered to be a result of loneliness.[15] The women's dread of loneliness and its consequences increased the hardships of the men by preventing redress of the sex ratio, which on an agricultural frontier is usually soon adjusted.

The hardships of frontier isolation were severe enough to lead to great efforts at contact. Economic survival demanded co-operation for threshing and other farm work, and the threshing-crew became an important means of bringing people together. Newspapers were started. Railway lines were extended. Mail-order services grew popular. The telephone was widely used, and the battery radio came to be regarded as almost a necessity. Cars became numerous, and one of their important uses was to take people to movies in the nearest village or town. These facilities spread as a result of social contacts, but, more important, they served to increase contacts. In the free-spending frontier atmosphere, especially in the years when wheat brought large cash incomes, the amount of money spent on means of transportation and communication was astounding to outsiders.

Drought changed matters. Depopulation increased the problem of communication. The density of population was soon less than in 1912 and 1913. Poverty denied the people access to almost every means of communication. Newspaper circulation dropped, and many country weeklies failed. Great numbers of telephones were disconnected. Cars either wore out and were made into Bennett buggies and Anderson carts[16] or were not used because gasoline had to be hoarded for use

and when the prairie was astir with life, but in the winter it often became almost unendurable." C. M. MacInnes, *In the Shadow of the Rockies*, pp. 325-6. Cf. E. B. Mitchell, *In Western Canada before the War*, pp. 148-51; W. P. Webb, *The Great Plains*, chap. xi, especially pp. 148-51. It may be that MacInnes's view is that of an easterner, but during the early days many Hanna settlers were newly come from eastern areas.

[14]MacInnes, *In the Shadow of the Rockies*, p. 326.

[15]Cf. M. Harrison, *Go West—Go Wise!* pp. 19-20, 146-8.

[16]These were horse-drawn vehicles, named after depression-time premiers of Canada and of the province of Saskatchewan, respectively.

in tractors and because there was no money to buy a licence. Radios were kept in use longest, and almost all families had them, but eventually they too wore out or were sold.

Although in the 1940's ingenuity and better times effected some improvement, isolation of farm households within the local community persists. The number of persons per square mile has remained low. In Census Division No. 5, including the town of Hanna which increased in population from 1,490 in 1931 to 1,622 in 1941, the population density was 3.47 persons per square mile in 1931, 2.78 persons in 1936, and 2.46 persons in 1941. It is probably even lower in 1946, since men in the services in 1941 were counted as residing at their permanent address.[17] A man is sometimes sixteen miles by road from his neighbour. Isolation is increased by the bad state of the roads. Even Highway No. 9, running through the area from east to west, is gravelled for only a small part of its length. Side roads are almost impassable in rainy or snowy weather. Newspapers have not been started again, and the *Hanna Herald* and the *Cereal Recorder* are the only ones in the area.

Increasing mechanization has added to the isolation of households. Wheat farming is an individualistic occupation. When everybody's crop ripens and has to be harvested at once, if it is to escape hail or frost, co-operative effort is hard to secure. At first the farmers had to work together, but new machines, notably the combine, have removed the necessity.[18] The farm work can be done by the family with perhaps a part-time hired man. Hence the family is economically less dependent on its neighbours.

The telephone and the automobile have not regained the role they once had in the community. When there were strong neighbourhood ties, these facilities had great importance in social life, but now that the ties are weak, they provide little aid to local communication.

Telephones are, of course, numerous once more. They would be costly because of the distance between farmsteads if it were not for mutual telephone systems and barbed-wire telephones. Mutual systems are co-operative: subscribers help install the lines and keep them in repair. Barbed-wire telephones use fences for transmission. Usually one person on each circuit has a government telephone to connect the community with the outside. Most homes are served by either a mutual or a barbed-wire telephone. The instruments are, however, not much used for "neighbouring." Tales of "joshing" friends over the

[17]Calculated from the Dominion Bureau of Statistics, *Eighth Census of Canada, 1941*, vol. II, and preceding censuses of Canada and the Prairie Provinces.

[18]Cf. E. H. Bell, *Culture of a Contemporary Rural Community—Sublette, Kansas*, pp. 73-4.

telephone and of listening in on the party line almost all refer to the past.[19]

The case of automobiles is parallel. Cars and trucks are thought to be necessities, and farmers own one or both, in a recent model. People drive forty or fifty and even seventy or eighty miles to a moving-picture show or a dance. They boast of their disregard of distance as do the plainsmen of the United States dust bowl.[20] They have the means for visiting neighbours, but the same means serve for visiting friends fifty or a hundred miles away, or in large cities and towns.

Communication within the local community has broken down. There has been a decrease in common understanding and common participation, and a weakening of social co-ordination and control. But communication with the broader community has increased. The depression heightened the farmers' realization of their dependence upon the outside world. They are aware of the impact upon their lives of political and economic events throughout the world, and follow them closely. Chief among the facilities used to get information in the rural Hanna area are the radio, the movie, the mail-order catalogue, and other literature.

The radio plays a vital role. The farmers listen devoutly and intelligently to news broadcasts, including the all-important weather bulletins. The broadcasts are often timed to coincide with the farmers' meals and bedtime.[21]

The movie supplements the radio, although the movie is attended chiefly for entertainment and the radio is considered at least as much a source of information as of entertainment. The movie is one of the chief attractions of the town, especially on a Saturday night. The size of towns is often explained in terms of their having or lacking a moving-picture show. Hanna has a well-constructed movie house, the proprietor of which shows pictures also in near-by villages. The pictures and the newsreels are of good quality and recent issue.

The catalogues of the big mail-order houses are found in almost all farm homes, even those of non-English-speaking farmers, and influence greatly the standards of the people. They and other printed

[19]Cf. Strange, *With the West in Her Eyes*, pp. 160-3.
[20]Bell, *Culture of a Contemporary Rural Community—Sublette, Kansas*, pp. 64-5.
[21]The farmers are not the fanatic followers of radio serials and comedy programmes that some city people are: even the housewife must too often leave the living-room to tend her garden or her fowl to listen to programmes without interruption. Programmes of old-time music and farm broadcasts rank next to news broadcasts in popularity.

matter are received through weekly or semi-weekly rural free delivery systems. The amount of literature obtained thus is often great, and is supplemented by periodicals and newspapers bought during visits to town. One farmer of little formal schooling listed the papers and magazines he and his wife received: *Calgary Herald, Hanna Herald, Western Producer, People's Weekly, Family Herald and Weekly Star, Farmers' Union Herald, Western Farm Leader, Liberty, Maclean's, Chatelaine, Readers' Digest, McCall's, Woman's Home Companion, Ladies' Home Journal, Country Guide, Country Gentleman,* and *Co-op News.*[22] Other farmers subscribe to or buy regularly almost as many newspapers and periodicals. In summer the literature is not thoroughly read, but it is given a good deal of attention when work is slack. Of less ephemeral literature not so much is available. Farmers buy books occasionally at town drug stores—which have a limited supply—or on trips to Calgary. They also make use of the extension services of the University of Alberta. The complaint is made, however, that few of the books sent out are of interest to the majority of the farm people.

The *Hanna Herald,* the weekly published in the town of Hanna, gives more attention to problems beyond the immediate locality than most country newspapers. Its news is largely local, but its editorial comments combine a keen regard for the local situation with a broader outlook.

The automobile and the railroad enable the western farmer to see the outside world as well as hear of it. His partial freedom from work in winter gives him a chance to travel. "Taking a trip" to visit relatives in the East or in the United States is one of the important goals of the people. It is frequently attained, except during depression. Frontier restlessness and wanderlust may be a factor in the greater mobility of the western than of the eastern farmer.

However, the sectionalism of Canada limits the Hanna wheat farmer's integration with the outside world. The sectionalism is expressed in many ways: in antagonism between the parts of the Dominion, in talk of secession, in ignorance of and lack of sympathy for other regions, even in variations in speech. The western farmer reveals intense sectional feeling, as might be expected from his disadvantageous position. When he looks beyond the local community, he does so in the manner of a member of a minority group. He feels that his problems are unique. He shows no sense of fellow-feeling

[22]This farmer, a leader in farmers' organizations, is known as a "great reader" and an exceptionally well-informed man. He is an inveterate writer of letters to newspapers, has given series of radio broadcasts, and has written at least one magazine article. The list was verified during a three-week stay on the man's farm.

with Ontario or Maritime farmers and, though he talks of secession from Canada and affiliation with the western United States, he resents any suggestion that the American farmers' difficulties are comparable to his. He says of eastern farmers that, "They don't know what it's all about," of American farmers that, "They haven't anything to worry about." In this respect he is still isolated.

Contact with the outside world makes Hanna farmers even less content with their local community. Although such contact affords satisfaction in itself and because it makes available goods and services, it brings dissatisfaction through acquainting the people with other ways of living. Not only do they see the advantages of city life without being made fully aware of the disadvantages, but also they learn of the low prestige of rural as against urban traits in modern society. The minority-group frustrations already experienced by the Westerners are increased, and become particularly galling because the situation is different from that they knew thirty years ago when western agriculture was expanding.

In working conditions, the wheat farmer has some advantages over city workers and other rural workers. He, unlike the factory hand, is not subject to the discipline of supervision, and unlike the less specialized farmer is relatively free of the pressure of farm chores.[23] He has few such daily tasks as feeding stock in winter, and even in summer he can often take time off.

The wheat farmer on the other hand suffers some serious hardships. At various times he is under great pressure to get work done, and must work long hours for weeks at a time. That is the case at harvest time, and also early in the season if rains interfere with planting. If a machine breaks down, the farmer must give up sleep in order to get it repaired. Formerly the needs of his horses set a limit to his day. The tractor has removed the limit, and indeed the high initial and maintenance costs of the tractor often make extra work necessary. The risk or uncertainty involved in wheat farming is a severe hardship. Like other farmers the wheat grower is subject to unpredictable natural hazards. Like urban workers he is profoundly influenced by the unpredictable business cycle and other market conditions.

The effect of these hazards was poignantly expressed in a series of broadcasts made in 1939 and 1940 by a Hanna farmer. With monotonous frequency he told of people who were in great need of the money expected from the sale of their produce and whose hopes were blasted, after months of waiting, by either natural or economic forces. Each

23Cf. E. A. McCourt, *Music at the Close*, p. 28.

time the thought in the people's mind was expressed in the phrase, "What's the use?"[24]

Two devices have been developed to relieve the strain. One is a stress upon next year's prospects. Poe's couplet,

> Hope springs eternal in the human breast:
> Man never is, but always to be, blest,

is apt as an expression of the dry-belt farmer's outlook. As soon as disaster strikes one year's crop his attention is focused on the future. He takes pride in this characteristic, and in the designation of the area as "next-year country."

The second device is dry-belt humour, which can be classified as "gallows humour." A farmer gives examples:

Our drought frame of mind has developed a sense of humour all its own. For instance, just as soon as the seed is in the ground we hear of the almost innumerable farmers in the hospital with cricks in their neck, or else a broken back from looking up for rain. There are the stories of children from five to seven years old who have rushed into the house in fear and trembling on seeing their first shower of rain. There are the stories of frogs who had forgotten how to swim, and there is the story of the visiting lady in the small prairie town hotel who was given the water the fish was boiled in to wash with. There are stories of men harvesting their grain crops with a hoe. Then as the drought becomes more intense, the imagination is drawn to still greater laughter. For instance, there are the stories of the gophers who have to get down on their knees to reach the scanty grass, of the cows with green tinted spectacles. When the winds come and the black blizzards blow, we have stories of the farms that we can't keep at home, or the farm that went down to Dakota leaving only the postholes.

Then again there are the test stories as to the degree of wind velocity it is safe to work in. Some farmers swear by the chain method; that is, a chain is hung on the end of a pole, and if the wind and dust hold the chain out in a horizontal position the farmer decides it is too tough and enters the house. Another test is that a gopher is thrown out into the whirling vortex of sand and dust and if the gopher starts to burrow in the storm as if he was in mother earth, then the farmer decides it is a day to ponder on Einstein and the fourth dimension.[25]

A strong and well-integrated social unit might provide satisfactions to counterbalance the inadequacies in the wheat farmers' standard of living. The household of the Hanna area is not such a unit. Several characteristics impair its stability and make it especially vulnerable to the drastic changes in income typical of the dry belt.[26]

[24]J. K. Sutherland, "The Roast Beef of Old England and the Pork Chop of Canada"; "The Last Load of Wheat"; "The Rains That Didn't Come"; "Two Better Halves"; "The Freezing Chill of Frost, the Hurtling Masses of Ice" (unpublished radio broadcasts).

[25]Sutherland, "The Rains That Didn't Come."

[26]Cf. R. C. Angell, *The Family Encounters the Depression.*

A considerable number of households in the Hanna area are not "normal" households. They do not consist of a married couple with or without children, but of one or more bachelors. Many of the home-steaders who stayed on through the drought years did not marry. The region was unattractive to women, especially in the poverty-stricken twenties and thirties. The sex ratio in the rural parts of Census Division No. 5 in 1941 was 134 males to 100 females, a ratio maintained since the early twenties. For the Census Division as a whole, there were 155 single men per 100 single women, and 106 married men per 100 married women.[27] Since the sex ratio is slightly more balanced in the urban areas, the imbalance between the numbers of single men and single women in the rural areas was even greater. The bachelor households now frequently consist of elderly men whose property will revert to the Crown for lack of heirs. The property is in some cases only a half-section from which the men have made a bare living, but in others it is a farm distinctly above average.

The family, sometimes with the addition of a hired man, is the household unit among the rest of the community. While childless families are infrequent, the families are not large in comparison with such rural ones as those of the French Canadians. One man said that in the township in which he lived, the most densely populated in many miles, there were forty-six people, composing twenty or twenty-one households. Half of these were bachelor households. Of the rest, a family of four children and their parents was the largest. Families of five and six children are exceptional. German families of eight or ten, once common but now rare, are spoken of with amusement. With the use of machinery a small family is sufficient for the work of the farm. With wide fluctuations in income it is a hardship to have to provide for a large family. However, from the point of view of social self-sufficiency, the small family is at a disadvantage.

Lack of community of interest puts the family at a further dis-advantage. In the ideal type of rural family the members spend much time together and thus develop many bonds of interest.[28] In the wheat-farming family of the drought area, the amount of common partici-pation is small. Unlike the head of the urban family, the farmer does not have his work day limited by law. In the busy seasons of sowing and harvest he leaves the house early in the morning and returns late at night. Even darkness does not stop his work if risk is involved in delay; men at times drive their tractors until 2 A.M. and start work

[27]Dominion Bureau of Statistics, *Eighth Census of Canada, 1941*, vol. II, and preceding censuses.

[28]Cf. Sorokin and Zimmerman, *Principles of Rural-Urban Sociology*, pp. 347-8.

again two hours later. During the day few duties on a mechanized farm require co-operation, if more than one man is at work, and few bring the men to the house and garden and chicken coop where the housewife and her daughters are busy. The farmer may get home for his midday meal more often than the city worker, but if he is working far from the house he sometimes eats in the fields. When trips are necessary for repairs to machinery or for purchases usually only one person can be allowed to go. In the winter the men are away less, but the children may be absent. The low density of population makes it necessary for pupils to "bach" or board near the school, going home for week-ends only if the weather is fine.

For recreation, farm families separate along age and sex lines. The married couples do not participate as units, as city couples tend to, and the young people keep apart from the older ones. Division is apparent at parties, school meetings, and agricultural meetings, and even in town restaurants. Picnics, formerly frequent in the Hanna area but now rare, are family affairs, but the families gather chiefly at meal-time and then usually with such outsiders as the hired man and bachelor neighbours.

Although economic interdependence is strong in the dry-belt family, probably stronger than in the urban family, its integrating effects are diminished by a strongly patriarchal authority system. All family members from an early age make vital contributions to the farm economy. A similar situation produced on earlier North American rural frontiers a democratic and equalitarian form of family,[29] and, in the dust-bowl wheat community of Sublette, Kansas, a family pattern giving the young an unusually high status.[30] Two factors prevent such developments in the Hanna area. Because of their European background, many settlers are used to a strict patriarchal system, and try to maintain it. Because of the cash-crop economy, the father receives almost the whole of the family cash income, and out of it pays the household expenses and distributes pocket money. The only part of the cash income received by another member of the family is the egg-and-cream money, which may be claimed by the farmer's wife. The persistence of the patriarchal type of family in a situation where the division of labour favours a more equalitarian type is a source of friction.

The patriarchal system involves sons doing adults' work without wages or a voice in the management of the farm. They must ask their

[29]Cf. J. R. Burnet, "Ethnic Groups in Upper Canada" (unpublished Master's thesis, University of Toronto, 1943), chap. IV.

[30]Cf. Bell, *Culture of a Contemporary Rural Community—Sublette, Kansas,* pp. 76-86.

fathers for the use of the car, for pocket money, for direction in the work they are doing. As long as they are unmarried and on the farm, they are thought of as "young fellows," even when over fifty years old, if their fathers are alive and in control.[31] Dissatisfaction over lack of responsibility, initiative, and money leads some young men to quarrel with their fathers, and to "row out" and leave home.[32] In the summer of 1946, several youths acted in this manner. Others after their war service stayed in town as loafers, living on their gratuities and on gifts from indulgent mothers, rather than return to the farm.

The fact that the Hanna-area family is pecuniary in its outlook also detracts from its strength, especially during depression. Both the recency of settlement and the cash economy make the Hanna family, and probably the Alberta farm family generally, more concerned with money than the rural family is often thought to be. The economic may be "by no means dominant"[33] among the motives leading to settlement in a new area, but it can never be ignored, and in the early years of settlement economic concerns occupy the centre of attention. Interest in economic affairs in the Hanna area was fed by the type of farming. Wheat farming required the use of expensive machinery and the sale of the crop. A strongly materialistic philosophy developed, and was enhanced by the fluctuations in cash on hand from year to year. The Hanna farmers came to derive their standards almost if not fully as much from the market-place as city dwellers.[34] The amount of "money talk" in dry-belt newspapers and novels is great. In good times, free spending is a point of pride. Money is squandered light-heartedly on amusements and luxury goods. Gambling for high stakes is a matter

[31]The usage is reminiscent of the use of the term "boy" in County Clare (C. M. Arensberg and S. T. Kimball, *Family and Community in Ireland*, p. 56).

[32]The preoccupation of some agricultural experiment stations in the midwest and western United States with father-son arrangements is related to the problem. Several bulletins have advocated father-son agreements as potential contributors to "the stability, permanence and wholesomeness of farm and community life" (J. B. Cunningham and H. C. M. Case, *Father-Son Farm Business Agreements*, p. 5). The conditions against which they are directed are seen in the introductory sentences in one such bulletin, P. S. Eckert, *Father-Son Farming Arrangements*, pp. 2-3:
"When a farm boy finishes his schooling, usually he is ambitious to test his talents against the problems of the vocation which he selects. He wants to feel that he is needed and that his activities fit into the scheme of things. If he decides to devote his energies to cooperating with his father on the home farm, he should feel or at least have the opportunity to experience the thrill of responsibility and the satisfaction of seeing his own work well done.
"Personal satisfactions are important, sometimes more important than the monetary consideration involved. Nevertheless, the purely personal factors are often neglected by the parents of grown sons."

[33]W. A. Mackintosh, *Prairie Settlement: The Geographical Setting*, p. xiii.

[34]Cf. Sorokin and Zimmerman, *Principles of Rural-Urban Sociology*, p. 79.

for boasting. Retrenchment in hard times is made more difficult by the extravagant ways of life developed during prosperous years and by the importance attached to money and the things money buys.[35]

The lack of any accepted principle of inheritance is another factor weakening the Hanna family. Inheritance is an important problem in all rural communities. The choice of an heir to the family farm and equipment, the motivation of non-inheriting sons to contribute their labour to the farm, and the orientation and education of all children except the heir toward the outer world involve strains which may disrupt family units. The strains can be eliminated only where a low birth-rate prevails and where the labour of a large family is not necessary for the efficiency of the agricultural system, or where a definite rule of inheritance obtains which is economically suited to the rural situation, or where free or cheap lands make it easy to establish more than one son on the land, or where, in individual cases in a community, division of the family property is possible. In Hanna the problem of inheritance is new, but it is becoming pressing. The homesteaders are almost all in their sixties. Many farms will have to change hands in the next few years. Yet no solution to the problem has emerged.

The fact that Hanna men as a rule do not cling to the ideal of keeping the farm in the family hinders the growth of inheritance customs. In many rural communities land is not a commodity to be bought and sold, but the object of an emotional attachment strong enough to outweigh considerable hardship. One dry-belt farmer showed such attachment when he explained his staying on the farm in the thirties when his neighbours were leaving by saying, "I'm enough of a peasant to have reverence for my land." Emotional ties stem largely from the prospect of passing on the land to a son. Hanna farmers do not look forward to this. Some, having come to the West full of optimism, were thoroughly disillusioned when drought and depression dispelled their hopes of riches or even security. They became determined to give their children a chance somewhere else.[36] Others surrendered the ideal of passing their farms on to sons when private ownership of a whole farm became disadvantageous and difficult to maintain.[37]

[35]The Hanna farmers recognize this when they discuss their frugal German-Russian neighbours, and prophesy that their sons who cannot recall the days of poverty and simple fare will be less staunch in the face of "the next depression."

[36]The statement heard by Bell in an area similar to Hanna, in Kansas, "If I had a boy who wanted to be a farmer I'd kick him all over town," states their point of view. Bell, *Culture of a Contemporary Rural Community—Sublette, Kansas*, p. 53.

[37]Cf. *ibid.*, pp. 54-5; E. O. Moe and C. C. Taylor, *Culture of a Contemporary Rural Community—Irwin, Iowa*, p. 55.

The removal of hope of securing the family land makes it harder to get the co-operation in farm work of the young people and to equip them to earn a livelihood. It destroys an advantage which is claimed for the rural family over the urban family in training the young. On the farm the boy or girl is said to be able from earliest youth to observe and practise the occupation in which he or she is later to engage. In the Hanna area, however, the child must do work until he is grown up which he has no assurance of being able to continue. Preparation for a career away from the farm is made difficult by lack of funds and by inadequate schools which equip students only for unskilled city jobs. Thus the young people are faced with a serious problem of occupational adjustment.

The weaknesses in the household are only one aspect of the instability of the Hanna rural community, and their consequences are hard to isolate. There are, none the less, symptoms of community disorganization which seem largely due to the problems of the household. Running away from home is common among teen-age boys. There are many cases of sex irregularities within the family group. Incestuous relations between father and daughter or stepfather and daughter are frequently and circumstantially discussed. Adulterous relations are talked of enough to seem frequent in occurrence. Divorce and separation also are not rare. Statistics on these phenomena are not available for the Hanna area, and if they were would be based on too small a sample to be significant. However, the ratio of divorced persons to the total population fifteen years of age and over was, in 1941, .209 per hundred for Census Division No. 5, .168 for Canada as a whole, and only .108 for the rural population of Canada; and the ratio of separated persons to the total population fifteen years of age and over in 1941 for Census Division No. 5, although it was lower than the rate for the country as a whole, was slightly higher than that for the rural population. Thus at first glance the vaunted stability of the rural family is not in evidence in the Hanna area.

The natural and economic environments of the Hanna area have in them factors making for a thinly scattered population. To this, a system of community organization based upon strong and self-sufficient household units would appear to offer promise of adjustment. It is obvious, however, that in the dry belt there are also forces weakening the household. These include the low standard of living, the lack of primary group contacts, and the uncertainty of obtaining a livelihood or of keeping the land which carries with it what hope there is of obtaining a livelihood. Compensation for the deprivations suffered in the household group would be required in other areas of social organization if the community were to be stable.

CHAPTER THREE

Ethnic Division

ONE ETHNIC group frequently succeeds in working out an agricultural way of life where another group has failed. In the Hanna area this has not occurred.[1] In part of the area the bearers of the Anglo-Saxon culture are being supplanted, but the people supplanting them are proving little more successful in adjusting to the dry-belt environment. The adjustment they are making is at most a short-run one. It is in their failure to achieve successful dry-belt settlement rather than in the conflict of their culture with the dominant one that the newcomers present a problem.

In its frontier days, Hanna had no ethnic problem. The homesteaders were mostly from eastern Canada, especially Ontario and Nova Scotia, the midwestern and western states, Great Britain, and Scandinavia. Although among those from the United States were Germans and German-Russians,[2] these people had become familiar with American ways of life and some of them, indeed, coming from Montana or the Dakotas, had had experience in living on the Northern Plains. There were a few Syrians, a somewhat greater number of Chinese *restaurateurs* and laundrymen, and one or two Chinese farmers.

All the settlers mingled freely, except the Chinese. No group, not even the large Anglo-Saxon one, was isolated enough to maintain its own set of community institutions. Economic and social pressures promoted full co-operation. Neighbouring, in the rich sense in which that word is used in many rural societies, was practised without regard to ethnic lines. Farm women tell how members of different ethnic groups

[1]E. C. Hughes, "A Proposal for Study of the Dynamics of Rural Culture and Institutions," p. 2.
[2]Cf. J. D. Hicks, *The Populist Revolt,* pp. 14-15.

exchanged recipes with them, and helped feed threshing-crews and guests at bees, weddings, and dances. Men speak of work and of informal social relationships with members of different groups. It was not long before cultural differences disappeared.

Indicative of the fusing process is the fact that in the Hanna area settlers from the United States rid themselves of their old political loyalties more rapidly than in other parts of Alberta. An observer in the Oyen district, some seventy miles southeast of Hanna, wrote:

There is one feature which I am at some loss to explain and that is the lack of American nationalism among the American immigrants. In other parts of the Province where there are large numbers or even small numbers of Americans, they have continued to celebrate the Fourth of July and cry "Allah" at the sound of the President's voice, nor does this tendency weaken with the second generation. In the Oyen territory I have never heard a single one of the standard remarks, that prices are lower in the U.S.A., that Canada ought "to realize her North American destiny" and cease to be a "British dependency," etc. I can offer three suggestions to explain this apparent acceptance of Canadian citizenship. First, the Americans are the largest group by far, so that they have not been in the position of members of a minority continually explaining themselves to their neighbours, after the fashion of minorities. They have thus not insisted upon their separate identity. Second, the political issues in the province have been so controversial and the campaigns marked by such intensity of feeling that a strong local interest has been supplied which has acted to make the Americans forget themselves in the hurly-burly. My third attempt to explain the lack of American nationalism is this: that the Americans were the original settlers of the district and that their part in "opening it up" has centred their affections upon it. In the more northern part of the province Americans have generally come either a little later or in a smaller proportion to the rest of the settlers.

With the onset of drought and depression, the ethnic composition of the Hanna population changed. Many immigrants came from Europe just after the First World War, and more in the late twenties. The census records considerable increases in the numbers of people of Danish, Czechoslovakian, German, Polish, Roumanian, and Ukrainian birth between 1921 and 1931.[3] In the thirties the Special Areas Board discouraged new settlers, but nevertheless one ethnic group established itself. It consisted of about ten families of Germans who had come to the Saskatchewan dry belt in 1922. Some of these bought lands in Alberta before the Special Areas were set up, and afterwards subdivided their land to enable others to come and settle near them.

The later immigrants, unlike the pioneers, have not been assimilated easily. The Saskatchewan Germans form an ethnic colony, as do

[3]See Appendix, Table XI.

certain Ukrainians. Such segregation is usual when aliens enter already crystallized social structures rather than frontier societies.[4]

The most numerous and best organized ethnic group is the German-Russian, located in the immediate neighbourhood of the town of Hanna. It is the most distinct minority in the region, the only one looked upon by the dominant group as a threat. It presents the greatest ethnic problem of the Hanna area.[5]

The first German-Russians came in with the rest of the home-steaders, by way of the Dakotas and Washington. They were accepted as members of the community. Some of their customs—for example, their ways of cooking—were thought barbarous, but others were imitated. People were friendly to the German-Russians and there was no hint of their being difficult to assimilate. In the twenties many more German-Russians entered the area, coming directly from Europe.[6] As discouraged Anglo-Saxon settlers moved out, the new arrivals bought many farms, especially in the good Hand Hills district southwest of the town of Hanna. In the thirties immigration stopped, but the German-Russians had a high rate of natural increase. Now they are estimated to make up three-quarters of the rural population near Hanna.

The German-Russians apparently adjusted well to east-central Alberta. The drought and the great depression set in soon after the arrival of many, and during the thirties their ministers had to ask for gifts of clothing for them. Their hardships did not last long, however. By the forties their homes were among the most pleasant and prosperous-looking in the district. The cars they drove were new and expensive. Their neighbours thought them highly successful, although less so than the Mennonites and Hutterites elsewhere in the province.

The success reveals a culture adaptable to migration and to the Hanna environment. The German-Russians had sustained one migration before coming to North America. They had gone from southern Germany to Bessarabia and the Volga colonies in the eighteenth and nineteenth centuries, especially while Catherine the Great offered German immigrants special privileges. Their ways of life had changed so little in the course of migration that a minister who had worked in southern Germany could identify by the accent and customs of the people the locality from which their ancestors had migrated to Russia two centuries before.

[4]For a study of such groups in rural America, see E. de S. Brunner, *Immigrant Farmers and Their Children.*
[5]The German-speaking minority is the largest in Alberta. Cf. E. B. Gerwin, "A Survey of the German-speaking Population of Alberta."
[6]Cf. Appendix, Table XII.

The German-Russian culture has those elements of strength which are associated with the culture of folk societies. Religious prescriptions and church organization are important and the family ties are strong. Isolation supports these traits.

Peculiarly important in the Hanna environment is a strong emphasis on the virtues of industry and frugality. To such an emphasis the English-speaking settlers subscribe, but in their culture the ascetic ideals come in conflict with the practice of "pecuniary emulation." The German-Russians, like the Mennonites and Hutterites whose background is almost identical,[7] do practise an ascetic way of life. This enables them to surpass their neighbours in adapting to the rigours of the Northern Plains and to the special hardships of drought and depression. The English-speaking farmers attest to this. In discussing their progress, they invariably mention that the German-Russians are "good, hard-working farmers" and "know how to live frugally." The importance of the sectarian spirit is shown in the fact that the only groups with which the German-Russians are compared unfavourably are the actual sects, the Mennonites and Hutterites.

The German-Russian settlers of the Hanna area were in the old land mostly Lutherans. A few were Baptists, a few Adventists. They quickly established congregations in the new country, and the importance of the church among them is striking. The white-walled, silver-spired church buildings dominate the German rural neighbourhoods. In the town of Hanna a Lutheran and a United Church serve the German-Russians. Almost the only difference between the two churches is that in the United Church the members are unusually self-reliant, able to conduct services well without the minister, whereas in the Lutheran the minister considers that the people depend far too much on him and do nothing without him. Before church union the United Church was Congregational and most of its members were originally Lutheran. Explanations given of the turning to Congregationalism throw light on the difference between the United and Lutheran Churches and also indicate the devoutness of the German-Russians. One explanation is that Congregational ministers "of their own kind" could come from the United States to serve the Alberta settlers. The other, which the United Church minister stressed heavily, is that in the Lutheran Church restrictions on lay participation make meetings impossible in the absence of the minister, and that the people became Congregationalist in order to have regular mid-week prayer services.

[7]Cf. C. A. Dawson, *Group Settlement: Ethnic Communities in Western Canada.*

In sharp contrast to the English-speaking farmers, the German-Russians support their churches well. They attend mid-week and Sunday services assiduously, and contribute generously. The Lutheran minister, interviewed in 1946, mentioned his congregation's staunchness, saying that the members hoped to get a new church soon. They had repaired the porch in 1945, and one man had promised to put a cross on top and a sign in front, though he hadn't "got round to it yet." A manse had just been bought at a cost of over $3,000, of which Hanna was to supply $800, Scapa $800, and the central organization of the denomination the rest. Hanna had already filled its quota, with several pledges of $100. This church had a Ladies' Aid which looked after the upkeep of the church interior, helped needy families—though not, the minister admitted, on the scale of the Salvation Army—and during the war did knitting for the Red Cross and sent boxes to boys overseas. There was also a choir composed of the unmarried members of the congregation, and a Luther League for young people. Confirmation classes were held for teen-age youngsters, lasting almost all day for several weeks. These classes presented an attractive picture:

I arrived at the church at 4:00 P.M. and when I opened the door the confirmation class was still in session. On one side were eight boys who looked neat, mended and scrubbed but not meek. On the other were six girls, two sets of twins among them, in crepe dresses with their coats over them. They looked like middle class Canadians and in no way could be singled out as Germans. They were thoroughly normal children, did not know their lessons perfectly, groaned at the amount of home work assigned and wriggled in their seats. None looked sulky or bored. The lesson concluded with the class gathering around the organ and singing. The boys and girls were separated here too.[8]

The United Church during the summer of 1946 opened a new church building in Hanna, erected after a proposal to merge with the English-speaking United Church had brought no response. The sincerity of the people was evident in the dedicatory service:

The dedication was to take place today, with morning and afternoon services. The first was to be at eleven, but as I approached at about 10:45 A.M. I saw a crowd outside. On the steps of the small white church stood the minister, the superintendent of Home Missions for the Alberta Conference of the United Church, and a group of men in their fifties or early sixties. Around them were gathered about a hundred people, singing German hymns. More were assembling as cars parked nearby or people hurried along the streets. It was a reverent group, although on the edge of the crowd a few joking asides were made in English, one being about the beer parlour. The modal age of the group would be in the late fifties or

[8]Field notes.

the sixties, although there were a number of babes in arms and young children and a few teen-agers present.

The dedication service was brief, with the superintendent officiating and the minister translating, and soon after eleven o'clock the congregation poured into the church. The interior was plain and white. There were ten pews on each side of the centre aisle, capable of holding six people. The women sat on the left, the men on the right, with one or two exceptions accountable to crowding. The body of the church was soon packed. About fifty people—also divided as to sex—sat on benches in the porch, ten or fifteen on benches in the aisles, and a variable number, up to a dozen or more, stood in the porch. All were dressed in none too wealthy or tasteful rural Sunday best. The women looked housewifely. Many of the old men achieved beauty and dignity. A few girls in late adolescence were the only people making attempts at shoddy smartness. The young people were also the only ones speaking English.

The service was like the usual United Church service, except that the congregation sat for hymns and stood for prayers and that the collection was taken after the service. A generous collection it seemed to be, too, with many bills. The scripture lessons were read by the superintendent, the minister, and four or five elders. A choir was led by the minister in a number of simple, melodious hymns. The visiting official gave his readings, sermon, and prayer in English. The minister translated, embuing the sermon with much greater dramatic power than it had originally possessed. Only two English phrases remained in the translation: bank accounts and baseball.

It was almost one o'clock when the service ended, and as I left I counted about thirty-five cars and trucks waiting outside. The congregation was slow to disperse. Most of the people stood outside in a dense group, talking.

In the afternoon a similarly crowded service was held.

The total effect was of humble and sincere piety among the people, and of dignity and power in the minister.[9]

The churches hold fewer meetings than English-speaking urban sects, but provide most of the formal activities of the German-Russians. The church leaders are the most respected members of the community. They are the elderly, pious, and comfortably well off rather than the learned.

Two religious ceremonies other than the services have social importance. These are weddings and funerals. The former frequently are a culmination of friendships begun at confirmation class or church. When carried out in full detail they are formidable events.[10] At

[9]*Ibid.*

[10]A wedding which was described began with the assembling of the guests at the bride's home for a mid-day meal, before all drove to Hanna for the fairly brief ceremony. The party then returned and the bride and groom knelt at the threshold of the house before taking places of honour at the table inside. Everyone wished them happiness, drank much wine, and placed donations in the bride's slipper which circulated several times. In the evening another meal was served of banquet proportions. The long hours of drinking and joking were interrupted by

funerals, "wakes" are still held. Burial is accompanied by noisy attestations of grief and includes a custom, deplored by a minister as cruel, of having the grave filled in by the mourners before the burial party leaves the cemetery.

Strong family organization like strong religious organization is characteristic of the German-Russians. The family is larger than among Anglo-Saxons or Scandinavians, and seems a more closely knit unit. Its somewhat different division of labour permits women to work in the fields with the men. Among its ideals are keeping the farm in the family and settling all children on farms. The strength of these ideals was suggested by the remarks of a Hanna resident who contrasted a prominent German-Russian family of the Hand Hills community with an Anglo-Saxon town family. The German family consisted of parents and ten children. In it the aim of the father and mother, who had retired to town, was to have all their children about them. They had settled four of their seven sons on near-by farms, and the rest were working in town. The girls had married farmers. All visited the parents, bringing their families with them, on Saturdays, and were visited by the parents on Sundays. The English family "had brought up three boys and put them through University." All three now lived far away, and were seen by the parents only once a year. The families were both successful, each in terms of the standards of its own group. The first had remained a close-knit family group, whereas the second showed a high degree of individualism.

The German-Russians, unlike the Anglo-Saxons, have well-developed customs concerning inheritance. A farmer when in his fifties or sixties transfers the farm to his son and retires to the town. A German minister's explanation is that his people in old age seek the sociability of a town because in Germany and Russia they lived in farming villages. But giving up the farm sometimes inflicts hardship on the old people. The men on occasion must live on the old age pension or eke out an inadequate income with casual labour, and when this is the case their status in the community is lowered. On the other hand, such customs of inheritance have meant that almost all the second-generation German-Russians are settled on farms, and that the home farm has seldom passed out of a family's hands. The land is transferred on more favourable terms than if sold to outsiders, and young men are given a strong incentive to remain in farming.[11]

a third meal at midnight and halted by the departure of the bride and groom on a trip several hours afterward.

[11] In a study of a Wisconsin farm community, its stability was found to be related to similar transfer practices. Cf. K. H. Parsons and E. O. Waples, *Keeping the Farm in the Family.*

Separation of the German-Russians from the rest of the community has helped their culture to endure. At the same time, endurance of the culture has maintained the separation. Since the twenties the German-Russians have been socially isolated. The fact that there were among the early pioneers a few German-Russians meant that those who came in after 1920 could learn the ways of farming from them and did not have to seek guidance from the Anglo-Saxon settlers. A foreign tongue and a strong and self-sufficient social system, built upon church and family, also have kept contacts with outsiders at a minimum.

The English farmers explain the segregation of the German-Russians by saying that the later immigrants were "a poorer type" than the pioneers. This is doubtful. Many who came in 1927 and 1928 were friends and relatives of early settlers.[12] The newspaper accounts of their arrival stressed that they were desirable neighbours.[13] The only complaint published was that ill health among them indicated laxness on the part of the medical authorities.[14] Probably, therefore, the English farmers mean simply that the German-Russian pioneers, many of whom had lived for a time in the United States, behaved more like themselves than did the late-comers.

The German-Russians have transplanted a folk society to east-central Alberta. In doing so they have made an excellent adjustment, for the time being, to the dry belt, but have contributed to the feelings of insecurity of the English-speaking farmers. Already shaken by the departure of their neighbours and by economic and social hardships, the English are disturbed at being in the minority. They talk of being "surrounded by foreigners," and of being "all alone now." They hint at a German conspiracy to take over the land. They complain that on

[12]The visit home of four pioneers in 1926 and 1927 was recorded in the *Hanna Herald*, Dec. 2, 1926. Many immigrants came out as a result of this visit.

"Four prosperous farmers of the Hanna district, who left Roumania more than ten years ago and came to settle in this country, left on the eastbound C.N.R. train, Tuesday morning, en route to their old home land. They were . . . well-known farmers of the Hanna district, who intend taking several months for a real holiday, and intend to enjoy themselves for the next three or four months with friends and relatives in the old land. They will sail from Halifax on December 6th.

"These men have all made good in this country; have prospered as a result of their faith in the land; have good comfortable homes and are naturally 'well fixed' or they would not be touring the globe as they are at present. Every one of these gentlemen came to this country with a very small amount of capital, but they have all farmed consistently and speak very highly of the country of their adoption. None of them would dispose of his holdings here, unless the purchaser could put up an attractive fortune in spot cash.

"The success of these four men is but an example of what many old country settlers, from Europe, have accomplished since coming to this country."

[13]*Ibid.*, June 2, 9, 1927.

[14]*Ibid.*, April 19, 1928.

their rare visits to German-Russian homes German is spoken and no attempt is made at translation into English.[15] They react to what seems a serious threat with heightened hostilities and more frequent assertions of superiority. In general they show the characteristics of residents of any area which is being invaded by members of another ethnic group.

The problem of at least a part of the Hanna area would none the less be near solution if the adjustment of the German-Russians were a long-term one. The Germans would simply replace the English, and the German way of life would become the prevalent one. A change in the ethnic composition of the population would be accompanied by a change in the method of farming, a pattern of development familiar in North American history.

But the adjustment of the German-Russians is only a short-run one. Forces are at work to upset it. One of these forces is inherent in the culture and has been a prime factor in the people's two great migrations. A large family system in which all the children are directed toward farming requires an abundance of land. Only one son can inherit the home farm; the others must go abroad. Hence there is an increasing pressure on the land. In east-central Alberta the large farm units made necessary by drought add to the pressure. This factor foreshadows the disruption of the German-Russian way of life.

Forces leading to contacts with the outside world and to assimilation also threaten the culture. Among these forces, the economic are pre-eminent. The German-Russians, like their neighbours, carry on large-scale cash-crop wheat farming, using modern machinery. This does not permit self-sufficiency. Farm equipment, food, and clothing must be bought; grain and other surpluses must be sold. Thus the heads of households must meet not only other farmers but also business men. The German-Russians recognize this necessity. At first reluctant to join co-operatives, now they form a large proportion of the members of the creamery, and at least 75 per cent of the members of the Hanna U.F.A. local. Through such contacts they learn the English language and English ways.

The schools also bring the German-Russians into touch with English-speaking people. Although some of the older immigrants, even the community leaders, are illiterate, the German-Russians are not opposed to education. They must be able to read in order to preserve their forms of worship; they must be able to write and to count in order to do business. School authorities say that, contrary to popular opinion,

[15]One woman told of visiting a German neighbour when a German-speaking fellow guest wanted very much to recommend a remedy for her arthritis. The hostess, the only bilingual person present, refused to translate what was said.

German-Russian youngsters are not removed from school earlier than other children to work on farms. Few German-Russians go beyond high school, but in the Hanna area few farm children of any origin do. The children do good work, though handicapped by the fact that German is spoken at home. They join in the activities centring in the schoolhouse, and when movies are shown take along non-English-speaking parents and grandparents. The factor of schools in one instance kept a German-Russian farmer from moving to the Peace River country. The man's wife reminded him that he had had no education because of his father's pioneering and insisted that his children should not be similarly handicapped. In the summer of 1946 two German-Russian families visited British Columbia with a view to moving there, chiefly to get better school facilities. The language spoken by the school-teachers and used in the text-books has prestige even where all the children are from German-speaking families, and is quickly adopted. The parental tongue falls into disuse. Absence of almost any German books but the Bible, and certainly of German children's books,[16] speeds the adoption of English. The Hanna ministers say that the members of the third generation whom they teach in confirmation classes do not know German.

A tendency to break away from the traditional churches comes with the loss of the German language. The first-generation immigrants, who speak and understand little English, are slow to accept a new language in their religious services. An article in the *Hanna Herald* in 1940 told of two rural Lutheran churches near Hanna which decided to discontinue the use of German during the war. The decision was made to allay suspicions of subversive activity or undesirable propaganda among the congregations in their services and meetings. To clarify the situation and to dispel rumours, the article pointed out:

1. The majority of members of these congregations, who never were citizens of Germany, are citizens of this country and as such recognize their duty toward both their government and their country.

2. According to Romans 13: 1-7, the question of loyalty to the country in which a Christian lives, and obedience to the government, becomes not only a matter of loyalty and obedience as a citizen, but of Christian principle and Christian doctrine. This teaching has been upheld by the Lutheran Church since its very beginning.

3. As a church we are interested in the preaching of the Gospel of Jesus Christ, and language is considered only as a means to accomplish this task. Some of our people are not sufficiently well acquainted with the English language in order to get the full benefit of God's Word when brought to them in this language. For this and for no other reasons have

[16]German weekly newspapers—notably *Der Courier* and *Der Nordwesten*—are received in many homes.

we employed the German for our preaching in the past. However, where our people have sufficient knowledge of the English to obtain the full benefit of a service in that language, there we consistently employ this; as is proved by the fact that approximately eighty per cent of the work of our Church in Canada and the United States is carried on in the English language.

In order to show that they are not engaged or interested in activity inimical to the country in which they reside, but rather in preserving peace and unity, the members of these congregations are ready to forego the privilege of hearing the Word of God in the language they understand best.[17]

German was resumed after the war for the sake of the older people. It makes the church less attractive to members of the third generation, however, and they either become lax or attend English services at the United Church or the Calvary Tabernacle (Christian Missionary Alliance).

Recently the Germans have actively tried to adopt English ways. Contact with the dominant group, the views of community leaders, and the influence of the war have made them want to assimilate. Contact with the English acquaints the German-Russians with another way of life which has certain advantages. Borrowing is done, consciously and unconsciously, with far-reaching and unforeseen results for the social and cultural system of the German-Russians.

Contact also teaches the German-Russians that their way of life is thought to be inferior. The English-speaking farmers condescend to the Germans, although they proclaim them "good people" and thus include them among the respectable, from which group certain English are excluded. Their frugality is commended, but a low living standard deplored. German cooking is said to be "tasty," but is not relished by the English nor considered healthful.[18] Industry is acclaimed, but the taking of children from school for work and the "exploiting" of women are condemned. The economic advance of the Germans is praised, but it is hinted that sharp dealing may be responsible for their success.[19]

[17]*Hanna Herald,* June 20, 1940.

[18]In discussing the war, one woman said: "When they couldn't do anything else to keep them out, many of the Germans were examined and rejected on health grounds. It's the way they eat. A lot of them had stomach trouble and ulcers and I don't know what all. They don't eat the way we do. Some of them are good cooks, but they fry everything in fat, even their vegetables. They cut up their cabbage and carrots fine and put them in a pot with a little water and put in lard and seasoning, and the water boils off and they cook in the fat. We had neighbours out here and they were Germans and we'd have them over for dinner occasionally and the man wouldn't eat my meat because it wasn't cooked in a lot of fat."

[19]Grounds may exist for the charge. Ethical rules are usually considered to apply in full force within one's own group rather than in inter-group relations.

Awareness of their low prestige makes the German-Russians eager to become like their English neighbours. The eagerness is encouraged by the German leaders, the most prominent of whom are the ministers. They have had wider contacts than the rank and file, and they favour assimilation. The highly respected United Church minister several times during an interview stated that his was an old and dwindling congregation and that "It is right that it should be so." Presumably it was he who had suggested merging with the "English" United Church of the town. A Lutheran minister apologized for holding services in German, saying that he preferred to preach in English but could not do so altogether because of the old people. Another's demeanour was described by an interviewer: "Throughout I felt he did not want 'Lutheran' to be identified with 'German' only. He told of a previous minister who, when sent bills by the gas company bearing 'German Lutheran Church' as the address, took them back in great disgust saying that he would not pay until it was listed as the 'American Lutheran Church.' He laughed about the incident but he was entirely on the side of the minister."

The effect of the war has been great. The German-Russians did not identify themselves with the German cause. They are apathetic even in local, provincial, and federal politics, like most pious European peasant immigrants,[20] and their sojourn in Russia cut their ties with Germany. A German agent came out to the area in the 1930's, and was not caught until almost the outbreak of the war. In spite of drought and depression and of the low status of the German-Russians he got little response. The chief signs of his activity were a few rash statements by youths of German origin. Newspaper accounts give no reason to think these serious:

A———, farmer of the Craigmyle district was in police court on Monday charged before Magistrate B——— with making statements likely to cause disaffection to His Majesty, contrary to the Defence of Canada regulations pursuant to the War Measures Act and was sentenced to serve 60 days in Lethbridge jail.

C——— of Delia who appeared in court as a witness stated that on the night of June 8th the accused made the statement that, "In two or three months we will be under Hitler's government."

Also, immigrants used to a family farm system are often slow in adopting the standards governing economic relationships in industrial society, which are usually implicit rather than explicit.

[20]Granted the separation of the German farmers from the other groups in the community, it is still remarkable that in a region where provincial and federal politics are hotly and bitterly debated, the views of the German-Russians are not well known. It is probable that many of them are Social Crediters.

D———, R.C.M.P., Hanna, gave evidence on the night of June 8th, having received a complaint he proceeded to the National hotel where he saw C———, and from information received located the accused and placing him with C———, asked C——— to repeat A———'s statement which C——— did. Accused was then put under arrest and after arrest denied even being in the National hotel that night. "The accused was sober and did not deny making the statement," Corporal D——— said.

[In summing up the case the prosecutor said that there had been many rumours concerning fifth column activity but this was the first case to be brought to court.][21]

E———, resident of the Hanna district, appeared in police court on Tuesday morning charged under the War Measures Act for adverse activities against His Majesty the King. Arrested by Constable F———, E——— was accused of making statements liable to dissuade recruits from enlisting. He was found guilty by Magistrate G——— and sentenced to two months at hard labour at Lethbridge accompanied by a fine of $100.00 or an additional two months if the fine was not paid. He was also found guilty under the Liquor Act and was fined $20.00 and costs or a jail term if the fine was not paid. In both cases the fine was paid.[22]

H——— of Scapa, charged under the War Measures Act of subversive action likely to cause disaffection to His Majesty's government appeared in police court on Tuesday and was sentenced to four months imprisonment by Magistrate G———. Arrest was made by Corporal D--———, R.C.M.P.[23]

At least one of the men on his release voluntarily joined the army. A German minister is said to have attempted subversive activity in Hanna, and to have been arrested after his departure. Some resistance was shown to the draft, but there is no evidence that it was greater than among other rural groups. The resistance might be explained by the group tradition of opposition to military service and by a fear of retaliation if Germany won the war. Fear also led to a reluctance to buy war bonds. A professional man in Hanna who took part in the sale of bonds reported that until the Allies appeared to be winning the Germans would buy none. He said that he could not understand this—a statement which in itself indicates that the Germans did not openly oppose the war effort—and that he asked someone about it. The person explained that the Germans had been told that any evidence of help to the Allies would be held against them when the Nazis ruled Canada, and that one of the worst pieces of evidence was the holding of war bonds. The German-Russians did participate in Red Cross activity and the sending of boxes to soldiers overseas. An outstanding patriot was a German farmer, three of whose children volunteered, one daughter and two sons. When the remaining son was drafted the farmer thought it unfair, but did not waver in his loyalty.

[21] *Hanna Herald,* June 13, 1940.
[22] *Ibid.,* June 20, 1940.   [23] *Ibid.,* June 27, 1940.

He was even suspected by German neighbours of "turning them in" when they attempted to dodge the draft.

In spite of their lack of sympathy for Germany, the German-Russians were identified with the enemy by the rest of the people and made the objects of hostility. The principal indications of the hostility were references to the use of the German language, accusations of draft-dodging, and the placing of stress on the slight evidences of subversive activity.

The use of the German language was a fertile source of complaint. The most friendly disposed often acknowledged that hearing German spoken on all sides was "hard to take" when things were going badly. The Chief Constable told of attempts to have the language suppressed: "There was a few people in town who wanted to make me stop them from talking German on the streets. And I says to them, 'How do you know they're talkin' German? Do you know German?' They says no, but they're sure that's what they were talkin'. And I said so was I, but there wasn't no way to prove it, and there wasn't no law against talkin' German anyhow, so they'd better watch out, because if they tried to make any trouble I'd pinch *them* for rioting."

The most frequent and bitter charge was that the Germans tried to avoid military service. Almost everyone told of "draft-dodging." A farmer's wife listed the devices she believed to have been used: "She began by a rambling talk of the Germans doing anything to keep their boys out of the army: sending the boys to University 'if they thought they could make the marks—and when they couldn't, there was a great to-do,' 'retiring' to town at forty or fifty years of age and coming out daily to help the son farm, etc. 'When they couldn't do anything else to keep them out,' she said, 'many of the Germans were examined and rejected on health grounds.' "[24] Typical anecdotes were related by the two Hanna lawyers. One told that a German family with one section of land and four sons had applied for exemption for all of them. The R.C.M.P. asked the lawyer about the family, and was told that each son had one quarter-section listed in his name and that all four were really not needed. The R.C.M.P. went out, asked a few questions, saw that each quarter-section had only about twenty acres cultivated on it, and in a little while the three youngest sons were called with no exemption allowed. To this day they do not know who gave the policeman his information. The other lawyer related that a German who came to see him about the draft suspected that a neighbour had betrayed him. The man's father had given the farm to him and gone to the coast for a couple of years; then he had returned, thinking it safe.

[24]Field notes.

A year after the war's end, the instances of pro-German activity and sympathy were frequently mentioned, although they were not exaggerated or discussed with fervour. The attitude of a professional man was typical:

I asked if there had been much feeling between the Germans and the town during the war. He said that it had been very unfortunate for the Germans that a real spy had been found amongst them. The people around here had actually left first Germany, then Russia, because of their desire to escape military service and they had left the States because they didn't like it down there. But the spy had gone around with a very good moving picture camera; he had got permission from the Government to use it in the schoolhouses. He had got the young men, or at least some of them, completely enthusiastic about Hitler's side. When the war was won by the Germans these young men would be the ones who would take over the town and have the money and be the rulers instead of just the opposite as it was then. The older Germans did not turn. They knew about war and they wanted no part of it. This spy was one of the higher ranking ones. When the King and Queen came through, the police here got a note from Ottawa to watch the spy so they picked him up on a thirty-day vagrancy charge. Afterwards they let him out, apologized profusely for their mistake, "and like a fool the spy stayed around." When war was declared they immediately picked him up. His mail had been censored all the time so they had a clear case on him.

I said, "That sounds more plausible than a rumour I heard that one of the clergymen was teaching them Nazi doctrines." He said hesitantly that the rumour was true. The minister had been in on the same line. He had gone to the States of his own accord when war started to try to prevent his sons being called up, but just as soon as they got down there his sons were called so he might as well have stayed in Canada.

He said that this all put the Germans in bad odour with the town, but there had been no outward trouble.[25]

Antagonism to the German-Russians was seldom expressed openly, and both English and Germans were reluctant to admit any friction. In a conversation between a Lutheran minister and an English interviewer, the subject of the war was introduced:

Without any coaxing on my part he swung into a statement that the German people here during the war felt that on the whole there had been no ill-treatment of them, except that with some individuals having sons killed by members of that same nationality they found it difficult to differentiate. It was phrased almost exactly like that, tactful and roundabout. "What they [the Germans in Hanna] did find hard was that when they were in restaurants some people would say very insulting things in a loud voice so that they could not help but be overheard," he concluded. He said the last with a little more emotion. As he had seemed to be trying to be fair and non-partisan before, I think he must have felt he had ample proof.

An English woman minimized difficulties to an equal extent:

[25]*Ibid.*

"How did the German-Russians get along here during the war years?"

"Oh, fine. They got along very well."

"No trouble at all?"

"Oh, no." The woman hesitated, then said casually, her voice dropping, "None to speak of."

"None to speak of?"

"Oh, at first some of them talked a bit freely, but they soon found they couldn't get away with it, and stopped." Obviously this was all she wanted to say on the subject, or even a bit more.

Of course, the reluctance to talk may have been a form of repression, indicative of strong emotions rather than indifference.

That the war-time bitterness has increased the German-Russians' wish to assimilate is evident. They have begun calling themselves Russian rather than German and parading their patriotism. A Swiss-German farmer said that in Alberta the German record for joining up was superior to the English. He told how two business men had talked a great deal about German-Russian draft-dodging until he showed them an item from the *Calgary Herald* giving enlistment statistics. He quoted many cases to prove that around Hanna the German-Russians had not tried to evade the draft any more than the English.

The money economy is another force breaking down the German-Russian way of life. It is an inevitable part of wheat farming, and the Germans have readily adopted it. The effect is a weakening of ascetic ideals, a decline in frugality, and an increasingly materialistic outlook, which makes the people more and more like the English-speaking farmers.

Finally, the cessation of immigration prevents the reinforcement of the German-Russian way of life. Since 1931 few people have come out from Europe.[26] As the generations familiar with Russia and the old culture die, the customs they observed are weakened.

Some second- and more third-generation German-Russians have merged with the English-speaking group. A Hanna man remarked that Germans born and brought up in this country were not at all bad: "You can't tell them from white people." With prosperity, their standard of living has come to approximate that of their neighbours, and both German-Russians and Anglo-Saxons point out that a generation is now rising which "hasn't known how to be frugal." Town women complain that the German-Russian girls are beginning to have "too much Canadian in them" to be docile domestic servants. The birth-rate is falling. There is an increase in the use of English. Few people as yet have left the farm for town and city, but more and more talk about doing so, and when this move does occur it leads to rapid

[26]See Appendix, Table XIII.

assimilation. Two cases of middle-aged people are instructive. An interviewer reported a German railroader to be belligerently insistent on good Canadian citizenship:

I asked two railroaders if they would mind giving me their names and one did with a joke about it being the Scotch spelling. The other said, "Mine's an odd sort of name," before he spelled it. He continued, not in a conversational tone but as if compelled, that he prided himself on being a good citizen, "not that I mean to apologize for what I am," but he felt it should be pointed out that he was a good citizen. He seemed strictly on the defensive throughout this. He came from the eastern part of Prussia which had been alternately Russian, Polish and German, "and I don't like any of them." His parents had been good citizens too, he said.[27]

A farmer's daughter, who because of drought was forced to come to Hanna to work when she was fifteen and who now was married to a railroader, was, in contrast to the man, most casual about her ethnic background, as if it was of no significance. When asked if she had been born near Hanna, she replied cheerfully: "Oh, no, I'm a Russian. I come from the centre of Russia, but it was a part which the Germans had once had something to do with so German was spoken there. That's why I know it instead of Russian." She had come to this country at the age of six. She had been brought up a Lutheran, but had joined the Church of Christ in Hanna and was one of the most enthusiastic workers in it. In the case of both these people leaving the farm was an important factor in assimilation.

Intermarriage, a telling index of assimilation, is as yet slight in the Hanna area. A minister said that few of the German-Russians married outside the group, and some young men from the district went as far as the German settlements near Medicine Hat to get a German bride. A woman who had a wide acquaintance among the German farmers could recall only two instances of intermarriage. In the first a German girl from the Hanna vicinity had while working in Calgary met and married an Irish-Scottish airman from Ontario. In the second a German girl had married a Scandinavian. Both marriages had taken place lately. The register of marriages in the Hanna district testifies to the rarity of intermarriage, but is of doubtful value because many marriages take place and are registered outside the judicial district. Newspaper accounts of weddings in the *Hanna Herald* are more complete, and they suggest the same thing. Like the adoption of an occupation other than farming, the tendency for intermarriage to

[27]Many German-Russians in the Hanna area have anglicized their names. In some cases this may signify assimilation or a desire for assimilation, in others it simply means regard for convenience in dealing with Anglo-Saxons.

increase in recent years is insisted upon by informants. With inter-marriage is linked the disruption of wedding customs, the weakening of the German-Russian churches, and other changes likely to impair the social and cultural organization of the group.

The rapidly achieved adjustment of the German-Russians, though still apparently strong, is weakening. It was no more than a short-run solution to the problems of the Hanna area. Its collapse can be fore-seen at present more in the speculations voiced everywhere about the third generation than in statistical or other factual indices. The German-Russian culture will probably not long survive the passing of the generations who knew life in the old country, and this will occur shortly. For a time the land may appear to be passing from the bearers of Anglo-Saxon culture to the German-Russians, but assimila-tion will soon make the new-comers indistinguishable from the people they supplanted.

CHAPTER FOUR

The Rural Village

THE PASSING of the village has seldom been as spectacular as in the Hanna area, where it occurred with great rapidity only a few years after the villages were founded. The importance of villages in rural social organization has long been stressed. In 1911 Galpin wrote:

> Take the village as the community centre; start out from here on any road into the open country; you come to a home, and the deep wear of the wheels out of the yard toward the village indicates that this home goes naturally to this village for trade, doctor, postoffice, church, lodge, entertainment, high school; the next road the same, and next and next, until by and by you come to a home where the ruts run the other way and grass grows a little perhaps in the turn toward this village, and you find that this home goes to an adjoining town for its major associations; between these two homes is the bounding line of the community.[1]

In the area thus marked off, the population has common social and economic experiences. Frequently the village gives leadership to the farming region surrounding it; Sorokin and Zimmerman call the villagers the "natural leaders" of the country people.[2] To the extent that this is true, the decline of the agricultural village is part of the problem of the decline of the rural community.

A few years after the first homesteaders took up land in the Hanna region, a number of hamlets and villages sprang up. They were all service centres. One or two were also the site of coal mines. The names of some, in the optimistic tradition of the West, indicate their rural outlook and their bright hopes—Sunnynook, Richdale, Cereal, Chinook, Excel, and Littlegem. All were on railway lines, or in localities which were expected soon to be served with railway lines. They were spaced

[1]C. J. Galpin, "The Social Agencies in a Rural Community," *First Wisconsin Country Life Conference*, p. 13.

[2]P. Sorokin and C. C. Zimmerman, *Principles of Rural-Urban Sociology*, p. 239.

so evenly, seven or eight miles apart, that they could be used in calcu-
lating distances. None experienced a railway boom, as Empress, a
little south of the Hanna area, did: Hanna was selected early to be the
division point and centre for the area. None the less their progress was
rapid. They soon had elevators, general stores, banks, lumber yards,
churches, schools, community halls, and restaurants. Some had two
banks; in 1914 Oyen had four lumber yards. Cafés and laundries run
by Chinese, hotels, and lively weekly newspapers were additional
enterprises in the larger villages. A substitute for newspapers was
space in the *Hanna Herald,* which devoted many columns to items
from the surrounding countryside. One village, twenty-five miles south
and slightly east of Hanna, was described in 1919, when the population
of the area was at its peak, as follows:

Sunnynook is surrounded by a beautiful rich country; fine farms; fine buildings; splendid location for a town, good roads, good thrifty farmers; good
soil; and water of the best quality. About eight years ago, one could count
the settlers on one hand, but today thousands of acres are broken and sown
with wheat.
    Already two banks are on the ground, also store, shop, lumber company,
post office, with many others coming.[3]

The villages were community centres after the ideal type of the
agricultural village in North America. They provided the necessary
economic and welfare services. They afforded a convenient gathering
place, and such occasions for getting together as shows, concerts,
dances, lectures, and sermons. Thus they increased the opportunities
of the farming people for meeting one another and forming relationships out of which grew strong rural organizations. They also provided
leadership to the rural community. Local news items of the period
between 1910 and 1930 suggest that ministers and teachers located
in the villages played an important part in the life of the surrounding
countryside.

The villages were small and served wide areas.[4] In these respects
they were like other villages of the Plains, which had been settled
more sparsely and in an era of better transportation than the humid
regions.

As frontier villages they were, of course, characterized by rowdiness
and lawlessness, which the presence of a hard-worked and poorly paid
member of the R.C.M.P. did little to check. A village near Hanna is

[3]*Hanna Herald,* May 22, 1919.
[4]D. R. Jenkins, in discussing agricultural villages in the United States, considered the typical "service station village" to have 1,200 people and to serve an
area of 80 to 100 square miles. D. R. Jenkins, *Growth and Decline of Agricultural
Villages.*

said to have been the model for the town of Hooch in the ribald writings of Bob Edwards, newspaperman of the old West.[5] Whether or not this is correct, the village is described by local people as having been "wide open" in its early years. Bootlegging, drunkenness, and gambling for huge stakes in establishments run by card sharps were the most publicized forms of disorder.[6]

A division of interest between their residents and the farmers limited the effectiveness of the villages as centres for the rural areas. Most of the business men, even though they owned farms, were regarded by the farmers as parasites and exploiters. Some were speculators, who hoped to make a fortune in the area and then move on. Some represented large companies the policy of which did not conform to the needs of the local farmers. Others received their supplies on credit from city wholesalers. The farmers did not regard them as "having the interests of the country people at heart," nor did the business men recognize any common interests with the farmers. The hopes of unlimited growth held even by tiny villages tended to accentuate the urban outlook of their populations. Something of this outlook was reflected in their boast of being "better towns than Hanna," though none was even half so large.

In the twenties the decline of these centres began. By the thirties many were ghost villages. Unincorporated places, like the one which had boasted of its prospects in 1919, dwindled away.[7] The counterpart of Hooch, in 1921 an incorporated village with over a hundred people, was disorganized ten years later. The only buildings on its site in 1946 were a church, a school—closed the previous year—a store and gas station, an elevator, half a dozen houses, and some barns. The larger places also shrank. Youngstown, in the twenties a thriving centre of over four hundred and fifty people, lost almost a fifth of its population between 1926 and 1931, and half of the remainder between 1931 and 1936. The agricultural school there was used only a short time and

[5]Cf. R. E. Gard, *Johnny Chinook.*

[6]Of the gamblers, who had followed the frontier from the Middle West of the United States, it was said that "if they had worked as hard in some honest game as they did at being crooked, they would have been millionaires."

[7]R. R. Annett's description of Benson would apply to any of them. In 1939 the fictitious dry-belt village was "nothing but a huddle of weathered shacks, most of them deserted." It had one street, and one elevator. The latter was the last of six, and it was closed. It had one store: "Ed Hindson's was the only store left. Ed had fallen heir to many jobs as people moved out. He was storekeeper, postmaster, sold gas and oil, if any; handled express and freight for the one train per week that the railroad ran over the branch. In fact, Ed did all the business that was done in Benson. And he had plenty of spare time. Ed was too old to move when the drought came. He said he was going to stay on in Benson until he just naturally dried up and blew away like the Russian thistle." *Especially Babe,* p. 8.

left to stand empty for many years. Its banks closed down. Its ministers were withdrawn. Finally it was reduced from town to village status in 1931.[8]

The decline seems to have occurred earliest in the eastern parts of the area. People speak of the drought "creeping westward."[9] Half a dozen of Hanna's business and professional men started out in Oyen, Cereal, or Youngstown, and in the twenties or thirties moved west, sometimes spending a few years in another village before reaching Hanna. Many buildings, through the efforts of a town drayman who seized the opportunity offered by the drought to develop a profitable house-moving business, took a similar route: the Richdale bank is now an apartment house in Hanna.

The decline was partly a result of changes in community organization, bound up largely with developments in technology occurring almost everywhere in Western European society. Automobiles and trucks made obsolete the old patterns in which villages served as centres of areas a "team haul" in radius. Improved transportation enabled farmers to travel distances formerly prohibitive. The farmers came to look to the larger centres, where greater variety in goods and services was available, for many things previously secured in the villages. The effect in east-central Alberta can be seen in the population changes of five of the ten villages of Census Division No. 5, which are just outside the drought area to the west in conspicuously more prosperous farming land.[10] The largest of the five villages is located in a district where excellent crops are secured with fair regularity.[11] Nevertheless a resident to whom a remark was made about the flourishing appearance of the village launched at once into an account of its decline. It had had doctors, but could not keep them. It had no dentist, and no movies. The government located its buildings in larger towns; banks did likewise. He went on to say that this was all to the good: "It benefits everybody, or will when the roads are improved." His own reason for remaining in the village was the climate, which he felt was unequalled.

In the drought area, the crop failures and the low prices for wheat have accentuated the decline of the village. In most rural areas this type of centre is not likely to disappear. There is merely evolving a

[8]See Appendix, Table XIV.

[9]Cf. Major D. Stuart, *Our Creeping Desert, Its Causes and Its Cure.* This is a widely read "scare" pamphlet.

[10]See Appendix, Table XV.

[11]Forty dollars an acre was paid for a parcel of land near it in 1946, a price over twenty times what was quoted for lands to the east.

new spatial pattern of villages, and a new division of labour in which
the bigger towns and the cities supply specialized and expensive goods
and services, and villages furnish those which are standardized and
frequently needed.[12] In the dry belt the complete wiping out of once-
busy hamlets and the failure of new centres to grow up makes the
future of the village less certain. The town of Hanna is growing, and
serving an increasingly large area. To the north and the south of it
no village shows any vigour. To the east, Youngstown, still with
about two hundred people, has pinned its hopes of survival on
irrigation. Chinook, with a hundred and fifty people, gives an impression of continuing decay:

Chinook is little more than a ghost town. Although it was Saturday
night the main street was deserted. There were a couple of farm women
shopping in the U.F.A. co-op, and across the street four men stood in the
co-op's oil and gas warehouse. In the café—a Chinese one—half a dozen
men were kidding one of their number who had just got trimmed for
a dollar at cribbage. They left shortly for Cereal. The garage was open,
with everyone in it busy. The hotel seemed quite deserted without a light
anywhere. It must be open—the school principal lives there. All the houses
are unpainted. Most of them are rickety with sagging roofs. The curling
rink lies flat on the ground, not so high as the surrounding weeds. Only the
schoolyard shows any sign of care.[13]

The secretary of Chinook is possibly the only municipal secretary
in the province who is an active farmer living outside the village.
This indicates a lack of people able and willing to fill the few offices
of the village government. Cereal has the great advantage over
Chinook of having a beer parlour, and one whose reputation draws
people from beyond its normal service area, yet it too is desolate in
appearance:

The hotel is, I think, the best building in Cereal except the new hospital.
The dining-room there is the only place serving meals since the café is
short of help. It—the dining-room—is quite luxurious if one's taste is
sufficiently bad. It is decorated with hordes of china bulldogs and cats,
ranging from two feet to an inch or so in height. One side is chiefly windows,
which are hidden by a mass of potted ferns and begonias. The pots are
home made of nail kegs or buckets covered with flour paste and the most
utterly weird collection of buttons, military badges, tin or metal coins, meat
tokens, bits of painted china and such-like rubbish. In a few cases the whole
lot of gewgaws is painted over with gold paint. The room is clean, which
surprises me because the hotel is run in a fashion which is casual to say
the least. I had to wait three-quarters of an hour because nobody could
find the cook.

[12]Cf. N. L. Whetten, "The Social and Economic Structure of the Trade
Centers in the Canadian Prairie Provinces, with Special Reference to Its Changes,
1910-30."

[13]Field notes.

Except for those on the main street, Cereal's buildings are in bad need of paint, and almost of support. Only one house is in good repair. It is also the only one with a well-kept yard. Yet houses are scarce: it has been difficult for new-comers, such as the school teacher, to get them.[14]

Beyond Cereal only one village has vitality. This is the incorporated village of Oyen. Although it is not typical of the dry-belt village, its relations with its hinterland do indicate the kind of role such a centre can play in rural community organization and thereby the social loss sustained from the weakening generally of village centres in the Hanna area.

Oyen is about seventy miles southeast of Hanna on the Goose Lake railway line. It is twenty miles from the Saskatchewan border and a few miles northeast of the productive Acadia Valley, residents of which, although outside the worst drought region, are within Oyen's service zone. It is in the heart of the dry area: its name, like the names of the villages between it and Hanna, has become a synonym for severe hardship from drought. In the land classification scheme developed by the Dominion Department of Agriculture there is more Class II (marginal) land near Oyen than immediately southeast of Hanna, but Class I (submarginal) land still dominates.[15] There is also a slightly denser rural population near it than anywhere else southeast of Hanna.

Oyen was founded a year or two before the First World War and for years followed the same course as other villages in the area. It had a population of almost 400 at the time of the 1921 census, fluctuated around that point until the 1930's, and then declined sharply. The postmaster said that by 1937 "it was just about done for" with almost no business except the handling of relief. In the late thirties, however, it began to revive. From a population of 298 in 1936 it rose to 326 in 1941 and to nearly 400 in 1946.[16] The increase was caused by the return of servicemen and by an influx of farmers, both active and retired. It has been accompanied by prosperity. Several new businesses, including a pool hall and a coffee shop, have been set up and the buildings of several others have been improved almost beyond recognition. Although few homes have been built between 1940 and 1946, many have had considerable money spent on them for additions, foundations, and paint, and most are in good condition.

[14]*Ibid.*
[15]Cf. A. Stewart and W. D. Porter, *Land Use Classification in the Special Areas of Alberta and in Rosenheim and Acadia Valley.*
[16]Dominion Bureau of Statistics, *Eighth Census of Canada, 1941,* vol. II, and preceding censuses of Canada and the Prairie Provinces.

Oyen is about twice as large as any village east of Hanna on the same railway line and in a wide stretch north and south. Youngstown, half-way between Hanna and Oyen, once surpassed it but now is completely outstripped. One reason for this is the distance of the two villages from Hanna. Youngstown was strong in the days before automobiles. Now the people near it find the thirty-five miles to Hanna is not too far to go even for frequently used goods and services. Seventy miles, however, is an inconveniently long distance. This is especially true since the highway is gravelled only as far east as Youngstown, except for a four- or five-mile stretch, and the condition of the roads makes travel hazardous, if not impossible, in wet weather.

It is because Oyen is far from Hanna that two important institutions are located in the village. It has the only bank east of Hanna, although other villages, and Oyen too, have Province of Alberta Treasury branches, which fulfil many of the functions of banks without having the same prestige. As the region declined and as motor transportation became more customary, the banks near Hanna closed first. Oyen's was the one to endure partly because the village already was the centre for a considerable area. The villages immediately to its left and right never had banks.

Oyen also has the Special Areas office for the Sounding Creek-Neutral Hills Area. Headquarters besides those in Hanna were needed for administering the eastern districts. The office was set up in Oyen in the late thirties because of its vigour, and since then has increased the importance of the village. Farmers frequently have to do business with the Special Areas Board because of the amount of land it controls and the seed grain it distributes. While in the village, they are likely to do their shopping, drink beer, and attend a show.

The fact that Oyen is far from Hanna and has the bank and the Special Areas office has outweighed several advantages that Cereal has over it. Cereal, fifteen miles to the northwest, has boasted a number of singularly able men. Oyen has had few to match them, though its territory is larger. Cereal also is slightly older, and has in its hinterland a pocket of good land such as is not found anywhere in Oyen's territory. None the less Oyen is two or three times the size of Cereal and infinitely more prosperous. It is likely that Cereal's new hospital, set up through vigorous and persistent co-operative effort in the face of the refusal of government aid, is the village's last bid for prominence. Difficulties regarding personnel and finance may make it a brief one.

The services offered by Oyen in 1946 were well summarized in a letter to the *Calgary Albertan* by the secretary-treasurer of the Board of Trade. It listed the enterprises that the village had to its credit: two large general stores, a dress shop, two hardware stores, a furniture store, five implement dealers, three large garages and filling stations, a utility and power company, three grain companies, a flour mill, a branch of the Bank of Toronto, a drug store, a barber shop, a laundry, a butcher shop, a Masonic Hall, a first-class motion picture theatre, two restaurants and a coffee shop—the larger restaurant being "one of the best eating houses east of Calgary"—a lumber yard, four churches, a new hospital fully equipped, a large dormitory unit in conjunction with the high school, a first-class licensed hotel with twenty-four rooms, the headquarters of Acadia School Division No. 8, the Special Areas office, medical, dental, veterinary, and beauty-parlour services, golf links, a large curling rink, and an athletic and ball park. In addition a memorial hall was being planned, and the village had "one of the nicest avenues of trees east of Calgary."[17]

Although some of Oyen's businesses claim for it a wide service zone, in the lives of some farmers in the zone the village plays a simple role. They go to it chiefly for the bank, the Special Areas office, the hospital, the implement agencies, the high-school dormitory, the lumber yard, and the veterinary service, and do their ordinary shopping at smaller centres such as Excel, Lanfine, Benton, Sibbald, or New Brigden. In the autumn they are frequently in Oyen. That is the time for the receipt of the greater part of the year's cash income. During the rest of the year a crisis in their affairs is necessary to bring them to the village. They are within Oyen's outer, but not its inner, orbit. Their patronage is essential to the prosperity of the village and increases its ability to serve the rest of its hinterland, but they are not intimately associated with its economic and social life.

More closely tied to the village are the farmers who do most of their shopping there, and have at least a minimum of social intercourse with the villagers. They belong to Oyen's inner orbit. Some go there only two or three times a week, and less at busy times like harvest. Others go four or five nights a week in winter, to skate, play hockey, curl, play poker or bridge, knit, drink beer—in short, to act like villagers. A few even do odd jobs there when work on the farm is slack. The young people actually live in town, though they return to the farm to sleep, eat, and work.

The boundaries between the outer and inner orbits are hard to define except in terms of participation in village life. Distance from Oyen is involved, but some people six miles away belong to the outer orbit whereas some twenty-six miles away belong to the inner

[17]*Calgary Albertan*, May 8, 1946.

orbit. It is little more difficult to go twenty-five miles than fifteen by car or truck. The determining factor may be proximity to a minor shopping centre which can fulfil day-to-day needs. It may be the location of relatives and friends. Farmers may pass an otherwise adequate shopping centre because their relatives or friends live in or go to Oyen; conversely, they may turn their backs on Oyen because their friends are in Excel. For these reasons, a map of Oyen's inner and outer zones would not look like a pair of concentric circles, but would show one zone scattered piecemeal throughout the other until the hinterland of another village centre is reached. The extension of services does not distinguish the two orbits. Rural electrification is still no more than an aspiration. The only service limited to the vicinity of Oyen is the telephone, which in general does not extend more than ten miles beyond the village. Density of population does not set off the one zone from the other. A few farmers have moved to be near the village school, but the quality of the soil prohibits much concentration of population. The tendency has been not to move to a farm near the village, but to move into the village and go out to the farm at seed-time and harvest. Nevertheless the difference between the inner and outer orbits is a significant one.

The lack of any sharp dividing line between the villagers and the farmers of the inner orbit is the chief feature of their relations. There is little co-operation on a formal level, such as there might be in the management of a power plant supplying rural electricity or of a Fair Association. There is rather a lack of divisive activity and a tacit sharing of facilities which, if either village or country were more aggressive and prosperous, might be the possession of only one group or a cause of bickering between the two.

One feature of the lack of division is the number of farmers who live in town. These are not all retired men who have moved out of their sons' way. They are for the most part active farmers who during the working season are on their farms. Of twenty, not more than five are retired, and two or three of these, in the words of a villager, "haven't retired very hard." Almost all until moving to Oyen in the last five or six years were within its inner orbit in terms of social participation. In spatial terms, ten came from within a ten-mile radius, five more from within a twenty-mile radius, two from thirty miles away, and three from thirty-five miles away. The only people who did not belong to the inner orbit before moving are three of the retired men, two of whom lived twenty and one thirty-five miles from Oyen. The others had come into Oyen a great deal, had been well known there, and had had friends among the villagers. Settled in the village, they do not form a separate group.

Many business men own or have an interest in a farm but this is not so effective in softening the line between villagers and farmers as the fact that farmers live in the village. The business men with farms include not only old-timers who homesteaded in the district but also many later arrivals. The business men do not work the farms themselves nor do they belong to farmers' organizations. They undoubtedly understand the farmers' problems, but not noticeably more so than other members of the community.

The somewhat passive sharing of facilities by village and country is shown in regard to the new hospital, opened in June, 1946. The president of its board is a retired farmer who lives in Oyen but still goes out to his farm a good deal, the secretary is a prominent villager, and the other members are farmers from various parts of the fifteen townships the hospital serves. It has a contract system, and according to the secretary "absolutely all" the rural people and most villagers are contract patients. The villagers who can afford to go to Calgary for any serious illness are contract patients for the sake of supporting the local hospital. On the other hand, unlike the Cereal hospital, Oyen's is not the result of intense united effort in the community but of the provincial government's health policy. The $59,000 required to build and equip it was far beyond the locality's means.

The school also is a passive rather than active unifying agent. The village and the farming region are both within the larger school unit, Acadia School Division No. 8. Interest in its administration is low. However, the separation of village and country is no longer dramatized as it once was by different school boards. The Oyen board has ceased to function. Asked if it still met, a teacher replied, "The members meet each other on the street, but that's all." There also is the unifying effect of the mingling of farm and village youngsters, especially since the establishment of a high-school dormitory.

The Mutual Telephone Company was organized as a farmers' co-operative, and its president and the board members are farmers, but it is located in the village and almost every village house is served by it. Similarly the U.F.A. co-operative, though it does not represent active joint effort, is located in Oyen and patronized by villagers.

Formal co-operation occurred in the special case of the War Loan and Victory Loan campaigns. The loan committee was important in community life chiefly because its success strengthened local pride. According to one account, the loan subscriptions totalled over

$1,500,000. The first quota of $23,000 was set in the expectation of poor returns, but over $90,000 in excess of the quota was gathered. After that the quotas were steadily raised and consistently exceeded until the ninth loan. Then the quota of $250,000 was not quite reached. Although the chief organizers of the drives were Oyen men, there were rural collectors, of whom a villager on the committee said "they were the best men a man could ask for." Activities on behalf of servicemen also brought villagers and farmers together. The war-time activities, however, were only a temporary joint enterprise.

Although Oyen has been incorporated for a long time, this has not set it off from the rural community, because of the dearth of aggressive action in the village council. The council consists of three men who each year choose a mayor from among themselves, and a salaried village secretary. The electors are the property owners of the village, including farmers who own village land, and number about two hundred. The secretaryship is either a part-time position for a prominent and public-spirited business man, of the sort who sits on the council, or a full-time job for a person who has been on relief or who is a retired farmer.[18] There used to be a village constable, but the last one was said to be officious and also was so crippled that he had difficulty in getting about. Since his death the only law officer has been the Royal Canadian Mounted Police officer who is stationed in the village, and who also serves the countryside around.

Leadership in the village government is very nearly a vested interest. The men who have held public office are few in number. They may be characterized in terms of occupation, of achievement, and of age. They are, first of all, business men. Not only is business considered to provide the most useful form of training for municipal government, but professional men and civil servants, however able, well educated, and forceful in personality, frequently have neither time nor opportunity for participation in village politics.

The council members are also men whose ability as financial managers seems established. The people of Oyen at times advocate lavish expenditure when discussing provincial and federal politics: they are seldom so reckless when the local tax rates are directly concerned. Sometimes indeed caution is taken for financial ability.

In age the councillors are in their fifties or early sixties. Younger men do not feel a sense of responsibility about village affairs, nor are

[18]The salary paid to the secretary varies widely. In recent years it has been $325 when the job was held by a merchant, $560 when it was held by a crippled septuagenarian who had been on relief, and $690 when it was held by a retired farmer who received $300 more for services to the Wartime Prices and Trade Board.

they looked upon as suitable candidates by their fellow villagers. The councillors have not always been men of middle age or more, however, since the same people have been filling the positions for about twenty-five years. They have grown older with the community.

While a reputation for common sense is an asset for a candidate for a village post, a pleasing personality or the ability to meet people is not necessary. It is enough that a person does not arouse dislike. In Oyen the mayor has few occasions to represent the village to outsiders, and in any case he is not elected directly.

The councillors' interest in village affairs is by no means perfunctory. It is not demonstrative: people who talk too much or too wildly about village affairs are distrusted. Far from regarding their task with fanatic zeal, the leaders in Oyen's municipal affairs look upon it as a duty. They feel that everyone ought to do something for the community, and that on prominent merchants fall the responsibilities of public office. Rarely does a successful business man remain aloof from the village government. A merchant who is definitely not a "joiner" and spends his spare time in his garden was serving his first term as councillor in 1946. "There are a lot of organizations in town," he said to an interviewer, "but I'm not much for that sort of thing. The council, though—well, I ran for that because I figured they needed councillors."

Public confidence in the regular councillors is not entirely based on belief in the worth of the men themselves. Many people vote for them out of habit. The policies of the council are cautious, and reflect the villagers' opinion that Oyen is too small to embark upon ambitious schemes. Lacking any specific grievance, the voters elect the same candidates time and time again. Then, too, there seems to be no one else both capable and willing who could count on public support. Some possible candidates are fitful in their interest in public affairs, or have no clear idea of the village's wishes and needs, or are generally disliked, or are new to the village. These characteristics bar them from office. Also, for anyone to be effective in Oyen's village government the friendship, or at least the goodwill, of the leaders now established seems essential. That means that the aspirant must have something in common with them. There is no specific way in which they can stop him from offering himself as a candidate, but the men of whom they disapprove are regularly defeated.

Village elections do not arouse much interest. Village government is thought too unimportant to be of concern. It has no effect on one's ordinary life. Conversation in the cafés and in the hotel lobby turns at times to provincial or dominion politics, but never to village affairs.

There are no platforms and no campaigns in village elections: acclamations are common. Elections are fought, to the extent that they can be said to be fought, on the personal merits of the candidates, who make no speeches and put up no posters. Usually the "safe" man is elected.[19]

Cautious in all matters, the council takes little initiative in the development of public utilities. There is no water system and no sewage disposal system. Perhaps half a dozen houses have tap water from a reservoir. Rather more have cesspools or some such arrangement. The light plant is a private enterprise and highly inadequate. Power is direct current instead of the more usual alternating current. The plant is not large enough for its load, and the houses farthest from it have only feeble lighting and erratic power. Roads and sidewalks are almost the sole services provided by the village council. They are no better than those of other villages: there are two blocks on Main Street with cement sidewalks, a few boardwalks, and little else. A village fire engine has not been used for a long time, although the village secretary can explain in detail how it operates. The office of fire chief has lapsed. The attitude of the council in these matters is shared by the village at large. It is that if Oyen continues to grow improvements will be in order, but meanwhile economy is desirable. Clearly depression-bred wariness and apathy combine to make the council so inactive that differences between the incorporated village and the surrounding farms are not dramatized.

The rural areas, on their part, have no local self-government. They are included in the Sounding Creek-Neutral Hills Special Municipal Area. The farmers are in a position only to elect members to the council of the Special Area, which is purely advisory, and to criticize and complain. This prevents them from developing and exercising initiative, but it also prevents the struggles between village council and rural municipality which used to embitter relations on occasion.

The country and village are between them able to support organizations of various kinds adequate to their needs, organizations which neither could maintain alone. The farmers are thus able to participate in a large number of activities which without an accessible village they would lack. The villagers form the core of the organizations, especially when the farmers are busy at seeding or harvesting, but the farmers attend as they can and as they wish. Both derive advantages and contribute essential support.

[19]The emphasis on safety is a heritage of the depression. The provincial government did not salvage the village councils as it did the municipal governments. Allowing rural municipalities to carry on with only as much financial help as they absolutely needed would probably have produced the same conservatism in them.

This is the case with the four churches located in Oyen, only one of which is primarily rural. The churches are the United Church, the Roman Catholic Church, the Church of England, and the Pentecostal Church. The first has the largest congregation and the greatest influence in the community. It includes the majority of the business men, among them those who fill the village offices. Its ordained minister, although he has rural stations, can spend more of his time in Oyen than the other clergymen.

The Roman Catholic Church is close behind the United in the matter of membership, and has an advantage over it in not having its priests changed so frequently as the ministers of the United Church. The present priest has been there for three years. It has a serious disadvantage in the matter of lay leadership. Only three of the business men are Roman Catholic, and of these two are reserved men who keep apart from the rest of the community. Many of the congregation are elderly, and for that reason inactive. Some of the Ukrainians of the district, who have not lost their group identity and form the only ethnic minority in the village, compose another passive element.[20] Although there is no obvious prejudice toward them, and other Ukrainians in Oyen are indistinguishable from the rest of the population, these take no part in the ordinary social life of the community. The Roman Catholic Church suffers as well from a lack of discipline in the congregation. The unusual laxness of the Oyen Roman Catholics is attributable to the size of the territory which the priest has to cover, the personality of the priest, and a split in the congregation. The Oyen priest has to cover a huge rectangular parish about eighty miles east and west and almost fifty miles north and south, a much greater territory than that of the United Church minister. He is an energetic person, with a conception of the place of the church in the lives of the people not less but more ambitious than that held by his congregation. This is a disadvantage rather than an asset. His activities on behalf of the young people have alienated the conservative without bringing compensatory gains, and his co-operation with and cordiality to his fellow clergymen have further offended the pious. The division in the congregation is between orthodox Roman Catholics and several Greek

[20]The members of the group, few in number, include two or three farmers living in town, some C.N.R. section hands, the shoemaker, and the only full-time carpenter of the village. They are middle-aged or older, were born in the old country, and are not fluent in English. Their occupations do not enforce many contacts with their English-speaking neighbours. The farm families form something of a sub-group. Their men have more intercourse with the rest of the villagers than others of the group, whereas the women, partly because of language difficulties, keep apart. The other men are all bachelors.

Catholics. Although there is no enmity between the two the Greek Catholics are rather loosely attached to the main body. They do not attend regularly, and remain away for long periods if the priest in any way displeases them.

The Church of England has no resident minister, so that its congregation is not at all organized. The clergyman, who has a field as large as that of the Roman Catholic priest, visits Oyen only at intervals. He is too overworked to spend much time in visiting and has almost no contact with his congregation. He told of talking to an old lady south of Oyen who had not been called upon by a minister for a year, and said that such infrequent pastoral visits were the general rule. Anglicans tend either to give up going to church or to attend the United Church services. The United Church minister, on hearing that a family was Anglican, said, "Oh, I'm glad to hear that. I mean, if he's not Pentecostal, or just disinterested, or Catholic, he may come to us when the Anglican minister isn't around. We have quite a few more or less apostate Anglicans." He then named four families as examples.

The Pentecostal Church has not the vigour it once had. It has never been large, but at one time was expanding sufficiently to justify shifting its main meetings from the open country to the village. This was about 1939, when times were still hard and its minister was unusually able. His mastery of evangelical techniques was seen in a sermon he preached in 1946 as a guest speaker:

He opened the Bible at Revelation. From 8.15 to 9.04 he read or quoted Scripture from memory, rejoiced in his own salvation and declaimed against the "many false beliefs of our time." He spoke with incredible rapidity in a low but powerful voice, his Scottish burr rendering what he said nearly unintelligible. He skipped from Samson and Delilah to Elijah, from the atomic bomb to Christ's second coming, from Russia to his own salvation with breath-taking agility. He described how on the day when "Christ's bride is taken up" some persons would be taken from the field, some off trains, others off ships and still others from their beds. In pantomime he pitched hay, shovelled coal, gave frantic orders from a ship's bridge, and sat up in bed startled to find himself alone.[21]

After this man left the church lost members, partly because succeeding ministers have not equalled him in preaching powers and partly because the young jobless men who were most attracted to the Pentecostal Church have disappeared. At present, in 1946, the church is on the outskirts of the community. Its minister has no dealings with other clergymen. Its congregation is more than half rural. It condemns the community; the community ignores it.

[21]Field notes.

More numerous than any congregation are those who do not go to church. They include a Jew, a Jehovah's Witness, and a Mormon, who are the sole representatives of their respective faiths. Similarly in the countryside around there are many people who do not attend services, including men who drive their wives to church but do not go themselves. This is not astonishing: rather it is astonishing, in view of the complete lack of interest in church services in other dry-belt rural communities, that the Oyen churches include farm people at all. The United Church board has on it a retired farmer and another farmer living just beyond the village. The Anglican minister told of farmers driving their wives to his services. The Roman Catholic Church also has farmer members. It is only by comparison with churches of the same denomination in other communities that the Oyen Catholic Church seems lacking in rural support.

The organizations for men in Oyen are few and weak, but in all of them farmers take part at will. The Board of Trade was reorganized in October, 1945, after lapsing in 1936. Its brief minutes indicate unsuccessful activity and declining attendance. The Board was said to have been revived by one man to act as a spur to the council, and to have had little success because he himself has shown more zeal than insight and because the rest of the village have had no interest in stimulating the council to act. A member of the Board of Trade executive described some of its activities:

The Board of Trade doesn't actually do anything. It suggests things to the council instead. Now take lately. It's made some suggestions, and all of them were bad. One was for a village well. There is a village well, over by the fire hall. Nobody much uses it, though. There isn't enough need for a village well to justify putting one in. The cost of drilling one would be more than it was worth.

Then the Board of Trade recommended a community pasture for cattle and that cattle be kept out of the village limits. That was the action of just a few. They just wanted to get something for themselves. They weren't interested in the community—just for themselves. You could just see them get up—practically came out of the barn to that meeting. There isn't any land available for a pasture near enough to the village. There weren't enough that wanted it anyway. It was just a few who brought it up. Most of the people just didn't bother to vote against it. I was there, but it wasn't any use opposing it then. These fellows had all turned out just for that. They just used the Board of Trade to grind their axes. Well, the council's not going to impose on the whole village just for the benefit of a few men. There are men who figure they can get something from going to the Board of Trade. Some of them have no idea of managing at all, but they're always hollering. Well, on the Board of Trade they can just sit there and holler at the council. They get the public notice, you see, only they don't have to do any work.

The Masons are very strong. Almost all Protestant men belong to the order including the farmers. A branch of the Canadian Legion has been organized, but as yet has shown little strength. It is vaguely thought to be sponsoring an effort to build a community hall. Sports are represented by a Community Sports Club, the golf club, and the curling club. A tennis club is defunct. The curling club, usually the most thriving recreational association in a western town, had in 1946 just been revived after four years in which the rink had been used to store wheat. The golf club varies from as few as eight to as many as twenty-five members.

The Oyen Community Sports Club and its relation to the other clubs was described by its president. Asked what the club did, he replied diffidently and vaguely:

Well, we try to back all sports. When we first formed we had some idea we were going to raise a little money for a Community Hall. We were going to charge for ball games, and hockey games, and such. That was just to give us a start. The most part of the money would have to be donations, of course. The idea didn't work, chiefly because there were hardly any ball players. The hockey players were high school boys mostly, especially last winter with the dormitory, but the rink is just open air—no good for charging admission. Of course the boys that played got the fun out of it. We didn't get them a coach or anything: someone else coached them. But our club backed them. They were from the school, really, but we backed them. Take like for instance—well, we backed them. You see, the idea of the club was to take in all the sports in town. We were supposed to co-ordinate them, you might say. Now the golfers, they wouldn't come in. We wanted them but they said no. They were already established, you see. And the curling too.

No farmers play golf, but almost all curl. Curling is in the winter a major village-country link, drawing the country men from distances as great as fifteen and twenty miles. Hockey teams and baseball teams are less effective. They are singularly inactive, and would in any case draw boys and young men only.

Among the men poker, pool-hall, beer-parlour, and loafing cliques are important informal groupings. From these most of the farmers are cut off at busy seasons because their homes are out of the village and because their work days are so long, but some belong. One of the beer-parlour cliques, for example, includes several farm men and women.

In contrast to the men's organizations, the women's are centred in the churches. The men have no equivalent of the United Church Ladies' Aid, the leading women's club of the town. It keeps its members in a state of almost feverish activity. Although they seldom do anything more significant than drink tea, they do it as a formally organized group. The Catholic Women's League is less active, for the same reasons, probably, as is the Roman Catholic Church. The third women's organization is the Red Cross, which overshadowed the Ladies' Aid during the war. There are also bridge clubs. They are usually shortlived, since few women play bridge and a departed member is hard to replace.

Since the hardships of rural life bear most severely upon the women, it is an important fact that the participation in formal associations of the wives of farmers living in the village itself and in the inner orbit of its hinterland is greater than that of the men. The wives of the farmers living in the village figure disproportionately among the office-holders and active members of the women's associations. The women living outside the village are also more a part of it than their husbands. They not only belong to the associations, but also attend regularly the various meetings. They even participate in the bridge clubs. One woman living eight miles out was president of the Ladies' Aid for a time. Moreover, the farm women do not act as a group in the innumerable petty feuds within the organizations.

Between the ladies' and the men's organizations there is one sharp contrast. The men do not struggle for office and sulk if they are not successful. Leadership is regarded by them as an obligation which it is well to avoid. The women appear more eager for positions, particularly such positions as the presidency of the Ladies' Aid, entailing little work and much prestige. The one position which necessitates work in most organizations is that of secretary. In Oyen the job of secretary usually settles upon one able woman, while the presidency flits from person to person without much plan.

The contrast indicated is frequent in modern North American society. The jostling for positions involving prestige seems related to the limited opportunity afforded women for the expression of ambition outside the household. A recent survey, conducted in Manitoba, has shown that in a village in which the women, rather than the men, had opportunities for achievement and recognition outside the community, the women were more harmonious and less clamorous for prestige than the men.[22]

Joint activities among adults are limited rather strictly to theatre-going, visiting, and bridge-playing. The village-country line is not more definite here than elsewhere.

A rigid system of social stratification in Oyen might create barriers to the full participation of the farmers in its social life. No such system

[22]P. J. Giffen, "Adult Education in Relation to Rural Social Structure, a Comparative Study of Three Manitoba Rural Communities," chap. II, especially p. 98.

exists. The village has only the beginnings of a class structure. Its socially superior group consists of a dozen or more people, including leading business men, the station agent, the school inspector and the school division secretary, and their wives.

All the village business men do not "belong." Among the more prominent, three are almost completely isolated socially. Two of these are Roman Catholics, but it is by temperament .rather than by religion that they are kept apart. They are highly respected, and are members of the village council, but attitudes towards them call to mind the adage that "respect ne'er breeds true love." They and their wives play bridge together, and are each other's guests at Thanksgiving, Christmas, New Year's, and other holiday seasons, but they mingle little with the rest of the villagers. The third isolated business man is also reserved in temperament, and in addition has been in the village less than a year. His wife takes as little part in society as he. As for the others, not only are their businesses lower in prestige in the village and in the ranking system of the broader society, but they also have special disabilities which play a role in their exclusion. In some cases these are disabilities which are ignored in people otherwise fully acceptable: a fondness for wild parties falls into this category. The new-comers, the crippled, the young, the drunkards, the "queer" or those fond of the company of labourers—all tend to be kept out of the upper circle.

Several factors blur the clarity of the social structure. One is the wide acquaintance of a leading family. The members of the family, which includes two daughters, are all active in many spheres of village life, and their home is a natural centre for people from various age and socio-economic groupings. Included among their visitors are farmers. The family at one time had a farm, and kept some of its friends from that time. It exercises no care to keep its socially heterogeneous acquaintances separate. It would therefore have to be ignored by anyone who wished to be exclusive.

The edges of the upper stratum are further softened by the fact that, while the core is composed of middle-aged people, there are a number of younger couples who are accepted by it but mix rather more with villagers of their own age. In the case of these couples, one member may be older than the other. If so, the degree of participation with the older and younger sets is a matter of personal preference.

The upper stratum is also less sharply differentiated than it might be because of a division between the "respectable" and the drinking groups in the community. There is no sharp line of cleavage nor bitter hostility. Oyen is not split into armed camps. Nevertheless a consider-

able number of people look with disapproval upon those who indulge
in drinking. The attitude of the men is generally not uncompromising
disapproval of liquor in all its forms, but a vague distaste for the beer
parlour. They go into it occasionally, but the noise, the dirt, and the
behaviour of their fellow customers do not attract them. Since the
people who dislike liquor or the atmosphere which accompanies it in
the Oyen beer parlour include not only some of the "best people"
but other members of the community as well, the social divisions thus
created cut across divisions forming along class lines.

There are farmers in both the non-drinking and the drinking
groups. Oyen, like many western centres, boasts that it sells more
beer than any other place of comparable size in the province. The
amount sold is partly due to the farmers who come in on Saturdays
and on week-day afternoons. They crowd the beer parlour and they
drink a great deal. Generally the retired farmers in town do not follow
this practice, although one or two inconspicuously drink a considerable
amount. Oyen has to get its hard liquor from Hanna, so that beer is
the staple drink.[23]

Division among the upper-class women in the ladies' organizations
is another factor weakening class lines. There is rivalry among the
women for office and for influence. Further, one or two capable women
not in the top group assume a fair share of leadership. Some of the
upper circle accept these women completely. A few treat them as
upstarts, thereby incurring the disapproval of everyone else.

The top-ranking men are subject to the assimilating influence of
the curling rink, the Board of Trade, and the hotel lobby, none of
which is a class preserve. They form a group to play golf, but the
golfers include also a couple of the young men, a few otherwise aloof
bachelors, and other outsiders.

Apart from the ill-defined upper class, Oyen is unstratified. Some
of the Ukrainians form a group to themselves. The farmers in the
village do not. The only factor which would cause them to do so
would be the maintenance of close ties with the country, and the
relations of nearly all the villagers with the country are sufficiently

---

[23]There are three groups among the minority who drink. The first includes three
or four men and women who live or work in the hotel, several women who live
in the country but are often in the beer parlour, some farm workers who spend
much time in town, and occasionally a few surveyors and other transient persons.
The transients also drink with a group composed of most of the village's unmarried
clerks and garage mechanics. This group does its drinking on Saturday night
parties, usually in cars. They drink less than they are supposed to, but are always
very hilarious about it. The third group are the town's ex-servicemen, who meet
in the beer parlour every two or three weeks and conduct themselves as they did
in English pubs, drinking little and talking a great deal.

close to prevent the farmers from being very different in this respect. Besides, the former farm women are generally in Oyen the year round—their husbands who farm actively are, of course, not—and are entirely part of the village social circle.

It is for the young people of the farms that the village has most attraction. The people past school age spend as much time as they can in Oyen. It is their accepted meeting-place on Sundays, holidays, days of slack work, and Saturday nights. The young men are in more often than their sisters, probably because they have greater freedom, particularly in the matter of having the car. Several have cheap cars of their own. They come in for dances or shows, for skating and hockey, or just for loafing. They seem to be motivated chiefly by a desire to belong to a group.

For these people and for those of teen age, associations are few and usually shortlived. There have been hockey and baseball teams, and there were young members in the disbanded tennis club, but there has been no athletic association. Most of the young people's activity is under the auspices of the church, and the guidance of the minister or his wife. Boy Scouts, now non-existent, and Canadian Girls in Training fall into this category, as do young people's societies. In 1946 the Roman Catholic priest led one young people's group with about eight regular attendants, and the new United Church minister was organizing another. Almost every unmarried Protestant under twenty-five years of age attended the second meeting of the United Church society. The Pentecostal Church once had a young people's society, but it now has few young people. The Anglican Church has no association for young people partly because it has no resident minister.

In the thirties the school-teachers assumed the role now filled by the ministers, but they relinquished it when the depression lifted and the creation of the larger school division freed them somewhat from local control. One teacher explained:

There was a time when the teachers did all the work in this town. We ran the skating rink—we even moved the thing from the corner across the road to where it is now and badgered the town until they finally put a well in to flood it. We organized this whole inspectorate into an area for musical festivals. Do you know, when the final trials were held here in Oyen we even had to pay the children's parents to bring them in to it. We organized dances and raffles and pie socials to get money. We bought a big radio for the school—it is here yet. And we bought a piano for the school. The board just wasn't interested. Thank heaven those days are over. You know, we did all the work when we were the only ones willing to try raising money, or to go to a lot of trouble over skating rinks and musical festivals. Now everybody's got money. A lot of those old farmers have moved into town. They've got nothing to do so they can take on some of these things. One of them looks after the skating rink. But the thing is that while they won't do anything, really, they've got money for things now. We used to be three and four months behind in our salaries. Now if these people want something that costs $100 they just go ahead. If there's a club, they get something else costing $200. I suppose about 1942 or 1943 would be the last of our shoe-string efforts. Going into the large division had something to do with the change. We went in in 1943 or 1944. Then the teachers weren't so much the slaves of the community any longer. We sensed more freedom whether we actually had it or not. The school sort of drew away from the village too. I mean the local board practically dropped out.

The most interesting and ambitious attempt at organization in recent years was on behalf of young people. Its history is illustrative of many of the problems of all endeavours to form voluntary associations in the village. Alarmed at the inactivity and the "bad reputation" of the young people, a group led by the high-school principal and the two leading clergymen drew up elaborate plans for a club. Its board was to consist of an adult council of three—a director and two assistants—and an executive of young people. Members were to be from thirteen to twenty-three years of age. Programmes, to be held weekly and to last for three hours, were ambitious and varied. The club began with great enthusiasm. Over seventy members joined. It held parties, performed plays, engaged in athletics, and produced an interesting year-book. Then, at the end of one year, it collapsed. The departure of the director was crucial in this, but if the club had been successful it would have survived the crisis. That it did not was said to be owing to the director's over-ambition. A wide range in age was set to secure a large membership, though the boy of thirteen and the young man of twenty-three have little in common. The members were expected to participate in programmes beyond their comprehension. So much time and effort was put into plays and other activities that school work suffered. The antagonism of the Oyen council was aroused when a school building moved into the village at considerable expense by the council to provide a meeting place was rejected as too small. But perhaps the more important cause of the collapse was the director's failure to enlist active adult support and to develop initiative among the young people. The club's council had little real say in the running of affairs; voluntary adult helpers failed to appear. The young people, "crowded into a corner of the club's constitution where they had little to do with the real direction of the club," were abashed by their director's forcefulness. A teacher's account is illuminating:

The whole trouble with the Canada Club was that Mr.——— ran it. He is a man with tremendous drive. He doesn't spare himself a bit. Everything he has a hand in has got to be a polished product, right from the beginning. He's unhappy about it otherwise. And he expects everyone else to feel the same way and be just as good at it as he is. It wasn't that he did all the work. He made the kids do the actual work. And he didn't make the decisions, either. He'd work his head off to get a bunch of kids to make a decision of their own. He'd slave at them. It was just that his tremendous drive was always there. Everyone else was sucked into his wake. Other people would work and he'd force them to make decisions, but they couldn't measure up to his mark. They kept coming along to say "Is this right, Mr.——?" "Will this do, Mr.——?" Nobody really did any thinking. They kept trying things almost at random until something suited him.

The club exemplified the two chief defects of all Oyen youth organizations, dependence upon an adult and lack of continuity in counselling. Wise guidance could probably overcome one of these and make the other less harmful. Meanwhile there are fewer organizations for the youth than for any other section of the population. The young people have parties and sports among themselves, it is true, but much of their time is spent in loitering or mischief. This is a problem of which the village is well aware, and one peculiarly significant for community stability.

It is notable, however, that the village youth and the farm youth react differently to the lack of organized activities. They go to school together, study the same subjects under the same teachers, play together. They do not even recognize the few distinctions their parents do: that is, the children of the Ukrainian ethnic group and of the village upper class mix on equal terms. None the less, the village youth on completing high school leave Oyen "to take courses" and to obtain employment. The farm youth, in numbers astonishing for the drought area, go back to the farms. If their ideal is different from their fathers', it is not to leave the farming community, but rather to have "a decent little house in town with a section or so of leased land either near town or on a good road leading to it." The part that economic opportunity plays in this cannot be ignored. Possibly it is harder for a villager's child to get a job in Oyen than for a farmer's child to get a leasehold. On the other hand in recent years the growing village has attracted a number of young business people from outside.

The village of Oyen makes a vital contribution to the rural community of which it is a part. Although it does not give leadership in any active fashion, it is a convenient meeting-place and its residents give day-to-day support to enterprises only sporadically of aid to the farmers. Oyen does not hold its own young people, but it does make the farm youth who live near it and take part in its life content to stay where they are. The reluctance of other young men to remain on farms in the Hanna area may well be related to the absence of thriving villages for them to visit.

CHAPTER FIVE

Town and Country

ALTHOUGH the village of Oyen is a social centre for the farmers who live near it, as well as a service station, the town of Hanna is only the latter. Hanna supplies more numerous and diverse goods and services than Oyen, but it is not a centre of rural life. It is regarded by the rural communities around as a distinct, and at times a hostile, social entity. Beyond its service-station functions, its only positive contributions have resulted from projects which its residents have, admittedly from self-interest, carried on for the benefit but without the co-operation of the farmers.

Hanna was established three years after homesteading had begun in the area, on August 7, 1912. In a few months it had a population of six or seven hundred people and an impressive number of business enterprises. When the *Hanna Herald* began at the end of 1912, it printed lists headed "What Hanna Has" and "What Hanna Wants" which indicated extraordinary development and high aspirations. The first list included five lumber yards, three barber shops, two meat markets, three banks, four pool rooms, one photographer, one harness shop, two theatres, one laundry (Chinese), two bake shops, one furniture store, a $5,000 post office, five building contractors, two hotels, three real estate offices, three implement agencies, two hardware stores, four general stores, two drug stores, two churches (Presbyterian and Church of the Evangelical Association), one public school (capacity 100 pupils), two grain buyers, one dentist, one medical doctor, one skating rink, four freighting and draying firms, one grist mill, five restaurants, three livery stables, two blacksmiths, one interior woodwork shop, a newspaper, and a population of eight hundred.

The short catalogue of items the town wanted read: laundry (white), music store, tailoress, dressmaker, millinery store, tobacco store, creamery, oil distributing houses, tent and awning dealer, Frost and Wood agency, bowling alley, shooting gallery, garage, saddlery, two more churches (Church of England and Roman Catholic), machine shop, veterinary, brick and tile factory, elevators, boot and shoe store, men's furnishings store, and jeweller.[1] By August, 1913, when the newspaper published another list to indicate the growth of Hanna in its first year, half of the desired enterprises, as well as many not mentioned, had been secured.[2]

From the beginning Hanna seemed equipped to become the focus of wheat-belt life. It made available to the farmers the necessities for everyday existence which their own farms did not provide. It brought to them agricultural supplies, credit, market, storage, and shipping facilities, medical, religious, legal, recreational, and social services. The young business and professional men who composed its population were similar to the homesteaders in cultural background, age, and optimism about the West.

In the eyes of neither the townsmen nor the farmers, however, was Hanna an agricultural centre. Unlike many western towns and villages, including those within its orbit, Hanna was founded not primarily as a country town but as a railroad town. Its site was chosen for its suitability for railroad purposes. It was named after a railroad president. Its first mayor had come to the town as a Canadian National Railways land agent. The *Hanna Herald* indicated the main interest of the town in stating that its aim was to inform "the general public as to events transpiring from week to week and to enlighten the outside districts as to the possibilities of one of the best railroad centres in Alberta."[3] It also devoted much front-page space to exuberant accounts of Hanna's future as a railway centre. Typical was an article appearing in February, 1913, which began:

HANNA TO BE HUB OF THE RAILWAY WEB OF ALBERTA

More Than Seven Different Lines Will Come to Hanna

Hanna To Be Centre of Great Railway Development in Alberta and Will Ere Long Become One of Leading Distributing Points

Hanna the seven-months old town which has already made a name for itself among the investing public of large cities stands in the way of being one of the greatest distributing centres of Alberta, owing to the many roads coming here which are either constructed, under construction, or proposed.

Hanna, nestling in a smooth level stretch between the Hand Hills to the south and Dowling and Sullivan Lakes to the north, is situated in the path

[1]*Hanna Herald*, Jan. 2, 1913.   [2]*Ibid.*, Aug. 7, 1913.
[3]The aim of the paper was printed in every issue for several years.

of any railway running to Calgary. The Hand Hills, some ten miles south of here, are very rough and would prove very hard grading to the construction companies. To the north the lakes make it impossible for any survey to run to the north of here and Hanna is therefore in the gateway of the only practical route from the east to Calgary north of the C.P.R. main line.[4]

The lengthy article was accompanied by a diagram showing Hanna as the meeting-place of a number of lines, one being Grand Trunk Pacific, the others Canadian National. In a circle around the diagram was printed, "All Roads Lead to Hanna."

Although Hanna boasted that it was not a boom town, the rapidity of its establishment and the selling prices of some of its choice lots indicate that it did experience something of a railway boom. At the end of 1912, for example, a corner lot on the chief business street sold for $3,500.[5] Hanna differed from many boom towns in that its railroad hopes did not collapse spectacularly. Rather they slowly waned, without a decrease in the town's population. Only as they dwindled did agricultural interests come to play a significant role in the town's life.[6]

For the rural community, the fact that Hanna was a railroad town had certain advantages. It increased the number of goods and services which the town provided. There were many enterprises of advantage to both townsmen and farmers which could not have been maintained without the aid of the railroaders.

On the other hand, the fact that Hanna was a railroad town made it partially independent of the rural communities. Economically, the independence was more apparent than real. Socially, the very number of the townspeople gave them a certain freedom, in that they could maintain among themselves churches, schools, clubs, and lodges, without aid from either railroaders or farmers. The lack of social contacts, even enforced social contacts, increased the differentiation of rural and town ways of life. Further, the presence of a mobile young male group in the town had a disorganizing effect on the whole life of Hanna. It meant a shifting population, with whom it was neither possible nor profitable for the residents to establish friendly relations. There developed early, therefore, a casual attitude towards strangers not usual either in the rural community or in the small town. As a result, the townspeople did not try to get acquainted with the farmers. This accentuated the effect of the independence of the town.

[4]*Hanna Herald*, Feb. 13, 1913.   [5]*Ibid.*, Jan. 2, 1913.

[6]The foundation of Hanna as a railroad centre may be noted as being similar to the foundation of large numbers of towns in the same area and in the West at large. An account of the establishment of Coronation, a little over thirty miles to the northeast, makes it clear that its beginnings were not too different. See B. Pullen-Burry, *From Halifax to Vancouver*, pp. 232-3.

In such a situation, friction between country and town when it arose resulted in much bitterness. Antagonism between town and country is a common phenomenon on the frontier. The farmers in a recently settled region are cramped by the old economic system, which fails to provide a tolerable means of adjustment to the new environment and to the temporary necessities arising from frontier conditions. The townsmen are slow to make common cause with the farmers for at least two reasons. They are farther removed from the situation for which the old ways are inadequate; they are to a great extent "sheltered from the action of the environment."[7] Moreover, they are functionaries in large economic, religious, political, or educational institutions, control of which, in most matters, lies with people still farther from the frontier than they and still slower to feel the need for adjustment. The lag between the farmer's enlistment in the cause of reform and the townsman's is a fertile field for the development of hostilities.

Even in mature communities, of course, farmers often have a sense of grievance. They feel that they are producers, whereas the townsmen are parasites. Farmers on the frontier are distinguished less by a sense of oppression than by confidence in their own ability to remedy their situation, confidence which springs from the fact that they are engaged in an expanding economic enterprise.

In the Hanna area the farmers were quick to begin to protest against what they considered exploitation. In the economic realm, the small-town business men appeared to control the supply of credit. The merchants could give or withhold credit for food and clothing and other essentials of daily living and for capital goods required for farming, while the banks and loan agents could give or withhold money. The need of the farmer for credit was great. The equipment required for mechanized wheat farming was expensive, the year's income not only fluctuated violently but was almost all received at the same time of year, and agriculture was so specialized that to live on the produce of the farm was difficult, if not impossible. Because of their great need, the farmers felt completely under the control of the townsmen.

In the political field, the small-town business and professional men had control of local patronage. The Liberal party had been in power in the province since 1905, and the residents of the small towns were among its stoutest supporters. In return for their backing they received such perquisites as the party controlled, to the exclusion of the farmers. In addition, the farmers were convinced that the legislation of the

[7]T. B. Veblen, *The Theory of the Leisure Class* (New York, 1934), p. 193.

Liberals was in the interests of the merchants rather than of rural residents.

The feeling of exploitation was expressed at an early date in the first of many acrimonious discussions of mail-order buying to be recorded in the Hanna paper. Mail-order buying has been a cause of dispute in almost every modern rural community. In Hanna the issue was raised by a homesteader who wrote that he had given up the practice of buying by mail. He urged others to follow his example, on the grounds that support of local business men benefited the farmers by establishing goodwill and by developing a market for agricultural produce close at hand.[8] The spirited reply he received showed a different attitude:

In the letter you printed in a recent issue of the Herald in regard to the support of local tradesmen, the sentiments of the writer are very nice, but what does the average homesteader care for sentiment?

When patronizing the local tradesman, we homesteaders are given as an inducement to do so, a twenty-five cent article in exchange for one dollar. I bought a small article in one of the stores of Hanna, and they are all about the same, for seventy-five cents and in a Winnipeg mail order house's catalogue the same article was listed at twenty cents. Allowing ten cents to bring this article to Hanna the local price will still give the dealer 150 per cent profit.

The majority of the homesteaders of this district are at present living a hand-to-mouth existence and require 100 cents value for every dollar spent. Let the local tradesmen give the farmer a square deal and not try to rob him by charging exorbitant prices, and he will surely get the support of the homesteaders and farmers.[9]

The arguments for the local merchant were presented by the newspaper editor, who stressed the fact that the Hanna stores gave credit whereas the mail-order houses demanded cash.[10] Even this point did not convince the farmers, for the controversy was resumed again and again.

In 1915 the farmers voiced their sense of grievance when the Hanna merchants tried to introduce a cash system for their business. Although some farmers were favourable, others were outraged. They looked upon the proposed change as simply another attempt to exploit them. One letter to the paper was especially bitter:

We were very much interested in reading your article in your issue of September 23rd, re the establishment of a compulsory cash system by the merchants of Hanna, in which the statement was made that a fine would be imposed upon any merchant selling for credit. Who is to be the detective to catch the offenders?

[8]*Hanna Herald*, Feb. 6, 1913. [9]*Ibid.*, Feb. 20, 1913.
[10]*Ibid.*

There appears to be a determined and concentrated attempt on the part of dealers of every kind to grab all of the farmers' money that they can get their hands on, and if the farmers are wise they'll fool them. It would be all right to say to the delinquents, "pay up or you get no more," but to insist to a man who has 2000 bushels of grain in his bin that he is holding for a higher price, that he pay cash even though he sacrifice his grain, is an imposition.

Another question to be decided is, how is the farmer to live if the elevators are crammed with grain and the railway cannot supply cars to move it and he comes to town with a load and can't sell it? Must he go home to his hungry family and tell them that they will have to chew the raw wheat to get a living?

Personally I have always combatted the mail order houses, but when this state of affairs comes into effect, I shall cease to do so.

While the war is on some of the best and most highly respected citizens of Hanna frequently have very little cash on hand, even though they have hundreds of dollars owing to them. Will they be refused too!

I am afraid, Mr. Editor, that this act of the merchants of Hanna will so aggravate the farmers that thousands of dollars of grain money which should be spent in Hanna will be spent in adjoining villages and sent to the mail order houses.

Not only will they send their money away, but they will club together and send away their butter and eggs and other produce. Where then will the town people get their butter and eggs?[11]

Significant also was a letter received by the *Hanna Herald* in 1916. In this case the merchants involved were not from Hanna but from villages a few miles west of the town:

I learn from news items of one of your contemporary weeklies that:

1st, some 300 delegates of the Liberal Association are to meet at Hanna shortly;

2nd, that two Craigmyle and one Delia merchants are named as possible candidates.

. . . merchant candidates in a constituency where 90% of our people are on the farm and the remaining 10% dependent on the farmer, where farming is admittedly the basis of industry, is about equivalent to saying to the farmer that he is incapable of representing himself.

I am a farmer, and a U.F.A., and I for one at least shall have very definite assurance that the farmers' interests will not be sacrificed before I vote for any Liberal or Conservative. And other things being equal the farmer candidate shall have my vote every time.[12]

It was in the strong U.F.A. locals that the sentiments of the Hanna farmers could best find expression and reinforcement. The report of a meeting of the Hanna local held in 1918 indicates the manner in which the U.F.A. could be used to reveal the farmers' hostility to the merchants. One of the chief topics before the meeting, that of extend-

[11]*Ibid.*, Oct. 7, 1915.   [12]*Ibid.*, Nov. 16, 1916.

ing telephone services into rural areas, was barely mentioned in the report. Another, having to do with relations between town and country, was fully set forth:

It was stated that merchants of Hanna wanted to join the U.F.A. and a discussion was immediately precipitated on the advisability of their admission. Some contended their presence would hamper free discussion and render the U.F.A. futile in its campaign of educating the farmer in his true economic interests. To the astonishment of some a member stated that on requesting a neighbor farmer to join the U.F.A. he was told he could not as he was in debt at the store where he traded, and he got a strong hint that he need never expect credit again if he joined the local, and as he was a married man and would in all probability need further accommodation, he did not feel free to join, much as he liked to do otherwise.

Farmers have been aware for a long time that they were not getting a square deal, and years ago they formed grain growers' associations to try and get a square deal for their class. They had to fight a long and strenuous battle against grain dealers, manufacturers' associations, wholesale and retail dealers' organizations for every concession they have so far secured and members were afraid that if storekeepers joined the U.F.A. it was not to advance the farmers' interests but rather to protect their own. Would a farmer have any business to join the retail dealers' association? The U.F.A. believes in co-operation but if other interests oppose its just claims, it must be prepared to fight for its rights.

Some members of the Hanna local hold that the farmer, rancher, fisherman and trapper ultimately pay for everything produced on this earth. They do not produce all wealth, but have to pay for all wealth produced whether they use it themselves or some one else uses it. No matter who burns the coal that is mined the farmer and the primary class had to pay for it, and the same holds good with regard to manufactures, whether cloth, iron, paper, food products, or munitions. Even the gigantic debt of the war, if it is ever paid, will have ultimately to be paid by the sweat of the man on the land.

The farmers recognize that they are the lowest—the foundation class upon which our present civilization rests. The different classes of manufacturers and their employees, distributors, inventors, teachers, etc., which make up the present superstructure of our civilization are sustained by them; but they have a just quarrel with present conditions. They consider there are far too many middle men, distributors, agents, personal servants, etc. The cities and towns are altogether too big and are composed largely of nonproducers. They think it is time for a readjustment of society where there will be productive work for everyone and abundance to eat with a chance of self-expression and development and the social amenities which he considers his due, and which will be for the general good. Those who refuse to do some useful social work whether of hand or brain should not eat.

. . . It seemed to be the opinion that though some merchants owned farms, trading was their real business and farming a mere hobby, and it was of slight importance whether it paid or not.[13]

---

[13]*Ibid.*, March 21, 1918.

The editor of the *Hanna Herald* expressed doubt that the report reflected the thought of most U.F.A. members. "To the *Herald,*" he said, "it sounds more like the vaporings of a man, obsessed with a perpetual grouch against everyone in general, but with so much bombast that his betters remain silent in disgust."[14] However, other incidents occurring in the same period leave little doubt of the generality of the sentiments expressed.

One incident was the rebuff administered by a U.F.A. local to the Hanna Board of Trade in 1919. The Board, having just undergone reorganization, invited farmers to become members and gave honorary memberships to the reeves of rural municipalities and the presidents of U.F.A. locals.[15] Lack of a favourable response was soon documented by an editorial, asking the farmers to realize that the Hanna Board of Trade was not "a secret society for the regulation of retail prices." Thereupon the Hanna local U.F.A. passed a resolution which made clear its suspicion of the Board:

Resolved, that the President and Secretary of this Local be instructed to accept the invitation of Hanna Board of Trade to attend their meetings, but as representatives of the Hanna local U.F.A., and not as members of the Board of Trade.

And, be it further resolved, that this local favors having joint meetings with the Board of Trade, to discuss any subjects of mutual benefit to the community, as occasion may arise.[16]

When the editor deplored the resolution as a sign of bad faith, the local affirmed its desire to co-operate, but in such terms as to indicate a real division of interest.

The intense feeling led the U.F.A. to accuse the *Hanna Herald* of unfairness. The grounds were two: first, that the newspaper charged the U.F.A. locals for the insertion of advance notices of their meetings, and second, that it allegedly did not give due space to reports of the meetings. The editor answered the first charge by a detailed statement of the paper's policy, and denied the second. In view of the large number of lengthy accounts of meetings published, the denial seems valid. The whole incident is understandable only in terms of a "chip-on-the-shoulder" attitude on the part of the farmers' groups.[17]

Most striking of all was the attempt of a U.F.A. local to boycott the *Hanna Herald*. This occurred after the election campaign of 1921. It was a bitter campaign, during which the U.F.A. candidate was quoted as saying, "We don't want the support of the town of Hanna." The editor of the *Herald* had fought vigorously against the Farmers' party, maintaining that a political party should not be formed on a

[14]*Ibid.*   [15]*Ibid.*, Jan. 16, 1919.
[16]*Ibid.*, April 3, 1919.   [17]*Ibid.*, Aug. 2, 1917.

class basis, but in print at least he was never vituperative. After the
election, however, he announced on his front page that a U.F.A. local
had resolved to boycott the paper. In the same issue a lengthy editorial
protested against the boycott.[18] It immediately called forth a number
of letters defending the local. Several took particular exception to the
view of the editor that the resolution was the work of only a couple
of disgruntled men.[19] The boycott, although it resulted in no per-
ceptible decrease in the *Herald's* circulation and is now minimized by
local U.F.A. leaders, both indicated and reinforced tension between
town and country.

The U.F.A. not only accentuated this hostility by allowing its expression and reinforcement in group activities, but played a part in
the cutting of two bonds between Hanna merchants and wheat
farmers of the area. One of these was political. Although some poli-
tically active Hanna farmers boast of never having voted Liberal or
Conservative in their lives, many had belonged to one of the old
parties and shared an interest in it with townsmen of the same affiliation. The formation of a farmers' party, from which merchants were
rigorously excluded, destroyed this common interest. One farmer in
1946 made the fact explicit: "I am a U.F.A. life member, mind you,
but the U.F.A. is partly responsible for the cleavage [between farmers
and townsmen]. Before they came along you were either a Grit or a
Tory, and when a town person came along he was either a Grit or a
Tory, and if you were a Grit and he was a Grit, you had something in
common with him. But the U.F.A. stressed that the farmers and the
town people had nothing in common, and they are in large part responsible for the split." Where the 1921 election was bitterly fought,
as it was in the Hanna area, the split involved more than the severing
of a bond of common interest. An active antagonism developed which
cannot be assumed to have vanished altogether so long as participants
in the campaign are still alive.

The second bond between farmer and townsman that the U.F.A.
helped to cut was economic. The U.F.A. played a large part in the
establishment of producers' and consumers' co-operatives. These enabled members to sell and to buy without the intervention of town-
dwelling "middlemen." All the co-operatives in the Hanna region were
sponsored by the U.F.A. or had U.F.A. members among their leading
exponents. Further, the Hanna area—or, more properly, Acadia constituency—pioneered in some types of co-operative action. The Hanna
Consumers' Co-operative was founded by several U.F.A. locals in
1918. Ten years later Acadia and Coronation provincial constituencies

18*Ibid.*, Sept. 1, 1921.   19*Ibid.*, Sept. 15, 22, 1921.

led in the movement to establish district co-operatives and, of the twenty formed, those in Acadia and Coronation districts were two of the three to survive in 1946.

At present the co-operative businesses in Hanna are impressive in number and prosperity. Two of the five elevators are owned by the United Grain Growers. The creamery and egg-grading plant, once owned by Swift's, is now a co-operative. Poultry is marketed through a co-operative. There are a hardware and grocery consumers' co-operative, a gasoline co-operative, and co-operative freezing lockers. Even the telephone company, which has its office in Hanna, extends its services into the rural areas through mutual systems, co-operative arrangements within rural neighbourhoods. These enterprises centre in the town to take advantage of road and rail facilities, but they reduce the dependence of the farmers upon, and the interaction of the farmers with, the townspeople. They are all run for and by farmers. The managers are at least as much rural as urban in their background and character, and the directors are rural. The one co-operative which is a joint town-country project is the municipal hospital.

With the rise of the U.F.A. and co-operative movements in the twenties and thirties there was a marked decline in talk of exploitation and in other symptoms of town-country tension in the Hanna region. The farmers had won freedom from small-town domination. Though their lot was not greatly improved, they could no longer hold the townsmen responsible for the hardships they endured.

Other factors contributed to the change in attitude. Through political and economic activity and through increasing contact with the outside world, the farmers came to see differently their role and that of the townspeople. With the Farmers' party in power, the rural people began to regard their prosperity as closely linked with the goodwill and co-operation of village, town, and city people. In U.F.A. locals and constituency conventions, as well as in provincial conventions, the problem of securing co-operation was much discussed. The radio also played a part in an alteration in attitudes.

Drought and depression, calamitous for townspeople and farmers alike, were even more potent in their effect. Townsmen became keenly aware of their dependence upon the farmers since the railroad payroll did not protect them from hard times when crops failed or wheat prices fell. A mark of recognition of their economic reliance on agriculture was their activity in seeking measures whose direct benefits fell to the rural community. Hanna merchants and professional men, as members of the Hanna Board of Trade, Kiwanis Club, or Chamber of Commerce, took a lead in many such projects. Their persistence

in the face of lack of response on the part of the farmers was notable.
A number of the business men of Hanna extended credit to the farmers.
Several became bankrupt through doing so, some of them more than
once. The newspaper editor who had once been boycotted showed his
recognition of the farmers' plight and of his dependence upon their
welfare by advocacy of their cause. In late 1929 and early 1930 he
vigorously denounced the refusal of loans by the Canadian Farm
Loans Board to farmers in the drought area. The subject received
space in almost every issue of his paper until in May it was announced
that the policy had been altered.[20] A few years later the editor, to
keep up circulation among rural people, accepted wheat in payment
of subscriptions. The rate was 80 cents a bushel for No. 1 Northern,
far above the current market price. The editor gave as his reason for
the action that he considered 80 cents a bushel to be a fair price under
prevailing conditions.[21] For the first year in which the offer was made,
1931, he "sold out" at an average price of 39⅝ cents per bushel.[22] For
the second year, 1932, he probably received considerably less. Of
course, had he not made his offer he would have lost many subscriptions.

It was probably not mere coincidence that in the depths of the
depression a mayor was elected who actively fostered friendship
between farm and town. The man he replaced is said to have made
no attempt to conciliate the rural people. An example given was that
he did not prevent merchants from charging farmers high admission
fees at stampedes and carnivals. The new mayor did so, and in addition
was liked as a person by the farmers, who said with approval that he
had no "side" to him.

The changed attitude and acts of goodwill on the part of Hanna
men decreased the belligerence of the farmers. A business man, asked
about the effect of drought on town-country relations, recognized this:
"I think it has brought the farmers and townspeople closer. In the
spring a farmer would start buying his supplies and maybe by mid-
summer he'd have no money left. The stores would give him credit
when the banks wouldn't give him a loan. Some of the stores in this
town went broke doing it. And the farmers appreciated that." Farmers
and farmers' wives came to talk of kindnesses shown by merchants
rather than of exploitation. They stressed that there was little "fleecing"
of country people by Hanna merchants, and what there was was not
"bad."

The farmers' outlook was affected not only by the changed attitude

[20]*Ibid.*, Nov. 14, 1929–May 22, 1930.   [21]*Ibid.*, Dec. 3, 1931.
[22]*Ibid.*, Aug. 18, 1932.

of the townspeople, but also by a loss of confidence in themselves which arose from drought and depression. In the first years of settlement the frontier farmers trusted their own strength and ability. They felt certain that by their own efforts they could obtain wealth and power. The economic catastrophes of the twenties and thirties, clearly beyond their control, led to a marked change in outlook. It was increasingly apparent that neither as individuals nor in concert could they attain security without the co-operation of townspeople. Realization of this fact strengthened the conciliatory spirit in the rural community.

The role of drought and depression in decreasing town-country antagonisms is indicated by the fact that the occasional revivals of talk of exploitation in the last twenty years have taken place in good times. It was in 1928, for example, a good year, that the *Hanna Herald* printed a poem in which exploitation seems to be charged against even the church:

> When the wheat looks good 'round Hanna,
> And prospects all are fine,
> There's a general stir in business;
> Folks are busy all the time.
>
> Oh, they say, you'll need a tractor,
> And you'll need a combine, too,
> And of course you'll need a new car
> Your old one will never do.
>
> Then you'll need a truck for hauling
> And for marketing your wheat,
> And, "Dear sir, you should buy this one
> For you'll find it can't be beat."
>
> Oh, they'll run the wheels off one car
> Selling implements galore;
> Later when they come collecting,
> They'll run wheels off of two more.
>
> It's funny how they swarm in
> When the wheat is looking good.
> "Madame, you should buy this washer;
> Really now, you know you should."
>
> "Then your stove is getting worn out,
> And you really need more light,
> Now just let us sell you this one;
> You'll find it quite all right."
>
> "Books and papers you are needing,
> Magazines that you should try.
> If you have no cash we'll take some
> Eggs or chickens we could fry."

Why, they run the women crazy,
  Always calling come and buy,
And the men can't work for talking
  To the agents wise and sly.

Then of course there's hail insurance
  They would sell if they could,
And the merchants even say "Mister,"
  When the wheat is looking good.

Then we can't forget the preachers
  Who say a tenth belongs to God.
Oh, let's not forget the Giver
  When our wheat is looking good.[23]

Again, it was in 1939, when prosperity was apparently well on its way back in the Hanna area, that an issue almost as recurrent as that of mail-order buying brought bitter railing from a few farmers' wives. The issue was the provision of rest-room facilities for rural women. From early days outbursts occurred in Hanna against hotel owners for not allowing rural women the use of their facilities while they and their fellows grasped avidly at the farmers' trade. On several occasions special accommodation was provided under the supervision of the Women's Christian Temperance Union, the Women's Institute, or other organizations, but the projects were always of short duration. In the late thirties there was a rest room but it was extremely ill kept. The refusals of the hotels to accommodate the rural women brought two militant letters. The first challenged:

What can the farm population of our surrounding district think of a town that offers us no better service and hotel managers who are not sports enough to open their door to the women and children whose husbands and fathers are in many cases downstairs spending hard-earned money in the beer parlor.
What can we think of the Mayor and Council and members of the Board of Trade. Are they dozing? If so, it is high time they wake up and take in the serious situation or else we can go to other towns not so far away that do offer us first class accommodation both in hotels and rest rooms.[24]

The second was even sharper:

Kindly remember such tactics are unkind and quite distasteful, and incline us to regard the sales people as vultures who consider us easy prey. . . .
Keep in mind the fact that when a farm family comes to town it is to spend money, hard earned money too. Of course, it would be easier to write out mail orders and have satisfaction guaranteed.[25]

[23]*Ibid.*, Sept. 6, 1928.   [24]*Ibid.*, Nov. 9, 1939.
[25]*Ibid.*, Nov. 16, 1939.

The improved relations between town and country were reflected in politics. The townsmen could hardly be expected to become U.F.A. supporters, although in villages near Hanna the merchants are said to have done so. Their attitude, however, became conciliatory. The newspaper frequently lauded the Government's policy, and gave full and friendly publicity to U.F.A. conventions and to prominent local participants. The attitude of the U.F.A. was shown in its taking the lead in 1932 in the formation of the C.C.F. which, instead of being a farmers' party, tried to enlist both town and country. A Hanna farmer was active in drawing up the plans for the new party.

The most spectacular manifestation of the change in outlook was the support of the Social Credit movement by both farmers and towns-people in 1935. This represented a breaking-away of the farmers from the political party that they had helped to form, to join a party that cut across the town-country line. In the Hanna area the leaders of the Social Credit group included doctors, an implement dealer, two evangelical preachers, and other townsmen, as well as a few farmers. The candidates in the provincial and federal elections for the consti-tuencies in which Hanna lies were a professional man and a farmer.

While the hostility between townsman and countryman has waned, several factors have hindered the establishment of genuinely friendly relations. One is the changing ethnic composition of the rural popula-tion. The preponderance of the German-speaking farm group in the im-mediate vicinity of Hanna might have been expected to draw together Anglo-Saxon farm and town-dwelling people, especially since the Anglo-Saxon farmers separated themselves so decidedly from the German-Russians. It does not operate thus; indeed, the ethnic char-acter of the majority of the farm people has served to rationalize and to increase the already existing gulf between town and country. This is latent in one man's reply to the question, "What part, if any, do the farmers play in the social life of the town?" He said, "Most of the farmers around here are Dutchies, so of course we don't do things together."

At the same time the constant growth of Hanna has made it in-creasingly difficult for the farmers and townsmen to know one another. In the frontier days, through dealings in town, the farmer became acquainted by sight with a large number of the townsmen. As the population of the town has increased, especially since it has continued to include the large and mobile railroad group, such relations have become attenuated.

Moreover, both farmers and townsmen are rapidly aging. The Anglo-Saxon farmers of the area for the most part came into the district between 1909 and 1912. The German-Russians came during the twenties. The business men also are old-timers: many as youths bought town lots at the original sale. The increasing age is linked with a preoccupation with individual and with family affairs which leaves little time for casual visiting. Especially is the preoccupation great when special economic hardships are added to the more usual cares.

As yet many farms and businesses are still in the hands of the men who established them, and acquaintances formed years ago are re-called. But where there has been a change of ownership, the relationship is much more formal, even if the new owner is the son of the previous one. Sometimes the distance is expressed by a farmer in such terms as, "Bill's not the man his father was. George had the farmer's interests at heart, but young Bill—I don't know him. He's a townsman."

The result has been that a social cleavage has remained between country and town. The claim is made that the rural areas of North America are being urbanized. The Hanna area has many of the traits that give rise to the claim. Its agriculture is highly mechanized, highly specialized, and closely integrated into a cash economy. Its farmers are mobile, individualistic, and materialistic. But the ways of life of Hanna farmers and townspeople are still very different.

The distinction has its visible signs. The townsman or the railroader can be distinguished from the farmer at a glance. The farmer wears durable, drab, and loose-fitting work clothes and clumsy, dark, and usually unfashionable "good clothes" which contrast strongly with the business suits or sport suits of the business and professional men and even with the workaday overalls of the railroader. His wife, while she may buy her dresses at the same store as the town woman and have her hair permanent-waved at the same beauty parlour, also tends to wear looser and less stylish clothes, and to have her hair "set" less often. Both stand and walk differently from the town people. Even when they choose their food at the restaurants differences are marked: in mid-morning or afternoon or in the evening the farm person prefers ice-cream dishes to the standard coffee or "coke" of the town person.

In community organization the distinction is no less clear. Hanna has remained an important service station for the rural communities around, although it has no vital role of leadership in their activities. It has big implement and automobile dealers, garages, two egg-grading plants, a liquor store, a jewelry store, a shoe store and a shoe-repair shop, beauty shops, bakeries, specialized dress stores, a bank, a Special Areas office, a courthouse—many facilities used by the farmers and not to be found anywhere else in the area. The farmers crowd its streets and stores on week-ends. But even the economic services do not bring close relations, and in other areas contacts are few and categorical.

The co-operatives exert one form of limitation upon contact, but others are probably equally effective. Mail-order concerns still receive a large share of business, and their catalogues are found even in the homes of the German-speaking settlers. The city stores of Calgary and Edmonton have become increasingly accessible through the development of motor transportation. Further, in cases where the farmers have contact with town merchants they frequently do not meet any townspeople other than the store personnel. Some enterprises serve farmers almost exclusively, such as the farm-implement agencies and the elevators. In others although both town and farm people require the service supplied, there is a tendency for them to go to different establishments. Eating-places furnish an example of this. A farmer who eats in the dining-room of the National Hotel is considered to be trying to identify himself with the town. In speaking of a farmer who said himself that he did not enjoy associating with other farmers, a store clerk made this clear. She said, "He always raised his children so that they weren't like farm kids. He'd bring them into town every Saturday, and they used to be nicely dressed, and they'd have dinner at the National." Instances are also common in which the town and country people patronize the same stores at different times. Town housewives do not shop on Saturdays if it can be avoided, particularly in the afternoon. Several spoke of not having been down town on Saturday for several years, and did not know the closing hours of the stores on Saturday nights.

In other respects the importance of the town for the rural community is even more limited. Hanna has a vast number of associations of various kinds. It has such an array of churches, clubs, lodges, athletic associations, and other more or less formally organized groups that they are difficult to count, especially since they form and disband frequently with the fluctuations in the town's economy. In this respect Hanna offers a striking contrast to Oyen, with its few associations. The town differs from Oyen also in the lack of joint participation of farmers and townspeople in the groups.

Most churches make the town their centre. The governing bodies of the churches assume that the minister located in Hanna serves an area extending half-way to the Saskatchewan border and for many miles north and south, and that the Hanna church serves an area including a considerable farm population as well as the town. Except for the Roman Catholic church, the assumption is almost completely false. The German churches serve retired farmers living in Hanna and also the farm families living within ten or fifteen miles of the town, but the orientation of the town-dwelling Germans is so largely rural that the religious ordinances cannot be said to bring together farm and town people, and the ministers are really members of the German rural group rather than the town. The United Church minister located in Hanna had only two farm families coming to his town church and gave little evidence of fulfilling any liaison function when he visited his rural charges. The Church of England minister reported only one farm family attending his church. The Hanna officers of the Salvation Army mentioned giving clothing to a burnt-out farm family, but otherwise had no contact with the rural community. Asked whether the Army served the farmers, the captain replied: "No, we don't. Several have promised to come in and attend our meetings, but they never get around to filling their promise. Of course we see them when they come in Saturdays, but we have no way of getting out. And of course we really have no time to visit them as well. We're responsible for the smaller towns around in our spring drive for funds, but otherwise we don't have any connection with them either." The minister of the Calvary Tabernacle asserted that his people were all from Hanna; the minister of the Church of Christ, that two farm families, from a half-mile and one mile away, belonged to his church and another occasionally attended. The small Seventh Day Adventist and Pentecostal congregations are also largely urban.[26]

The schools of the town provide little contact, especially since the growth of rural high schools. There is no association of town and country people upon school boards, as there is of village and country people elsewhere in the region, since the town boards are quite separate. On the other hand, the dormitory provides facilities for a number of young people from farms who attend the town schools, and the inadequacies of the rural school afford a considerable stimulus for parents to send their children in to town.

[26]That the situation has lasted a long time or at least been intermittent is suggested by a letter to the *Hanna Herald*, Dec. 21, 1922: "Some time ago you were criticizing in *The Herald* the addition of another religious body, to the already well supplied town and to a certain extent I quite agree with you, when one takes into consideration the number of people on the prairies that never or seldom get any religious services and the multitudes of children that are growing up in complete ignorance of any religious influences whatever.

"One would think that some of the energy that is going to waste in Hanna and the various other towns along the lines could be used to great advantage through the outlying districts. It would not be much for some of those people that have cars running around all day long doing no good to arrange to drive some of the Ministers or their assistant out into the country to give the people out of reach of civilization a chance to hear the gospel."

Among the voluntary associations, the Board of Trade has constantly tried to promote closer town-country relations. In 1919 and in the early 1920's it agitated for the extension of telephone services into the rural areas and the inauguration of irrigation projects, and sponsored meetings at which farmers could learn about a promising new system of dry farming. When the Board of Trade passed into decline, and was replaced in activity by the Kiwanis, existing in Hanna from 1924 to 1931, agricultural projects were even more frequent. A farmer sometimes was appointed to the board of directors; speakers on agricultural topics were imported; banquets were held to which farmers were invited; crop competitions, with liberal prizes and full publicity, were held; successful agitation to have a District Agriculturist located in Hanna was carried on. In the thirties the Board of Trade took up the task again, with Farmers' Nights, agricultural short courses, and other activities. In 1946 it had a farmer as vice-president. It has, however, failed consistently to secure farmer members; and it has even had difficulty in getting farmers to attend special events it has sponsored. Once when the Kiwanis Club arranged a Farmers' Night, with a winner of the world wheat championship as the chief speaker, the editor of the *Hanna Herald* had to plead: "It is true, Mr. Farmer, that this authority on seed wheat is being brought to Hanna by the 'townsman,'—the Kiwanian. But the direct benefit of his visit will accrue to the man on the soil, if he accepts the opportunity."[27] The farmer vice-president was regarded as being an exceptional case. In talking about him, other members of the executive hinted that he was elected because of his role in the larger community rather than in the Hanna district alone.

In other voluntary associations farmers are only nominal members. They do not come into town for the meetings of lodges or of recreational clubs. The Curling Club, the most active of the latter, has an annual Farmers' Bonspiel, in which townsmen act as skips for rinks composed of farmers, but it is a formal gesture of friendliness rather than a sign of genuine mutual regard.

Cliques and friendships seldom cut across the town-country lines. This is almost a corollary to the sparseness of formal relations. Merchants and professional men, the latter of whom have an excellent basis for friendship with rural clients, have almost no informal associations with farmers. A young business man, a Hanna booster by reason of both occupation and office in the Board of Trade, could make only a slight and unconvincing case to the contrary. Asked if there was any social life between town and country, he was eager to prove that there was, but as his only evidence offered, "We go out to visit farmers

[27]*Ibid.*, March 3, 1927.

on Sunday and have a bucket of beer with them. When we had a car we used to make a custom of going to a different place in the country each Sunday." A prominent woman, the wife of a town official, made a revealing answer to a similar query. She said she did know a few farmers around: "For example, there is the woman who brings me my butter and cream. She is very nice." Townspeople excused their lack of knowledge on the grounds that the farmers were for the most part German.

Even the few English-speaking farmers who have retired into town do not form friendships with town people. One tried to stress town-country solidarity, making statements concerning the participation of farmers in the Curling Club which disagreed with all other evidence. The record of an interview showed that his wife at least felt very isolated:

When we were alone, Mrs.——— at once volunteered in her diffident manner, "You know more people in town than I do."

"Oh, is that so?"

"I don't know anyone very much—except the people we used to know who always call when they come in town."

"You don't play bridge, I take it, or go to teas?"

Mrs.——— gave a deprecatory little grimace: "I think it's a waste of time." Plainly she was lonely, and nostalgic for her country neighbours.

The former farmers who have become members and senior employees of the Special Areas Board and the School Division Board are also cut off. They and their wives form cliques among themselves. Frequently they substitute intense church activity either in an established denomination or in an evangelical sect for friendship relations.

In contrast to these two groups a few former farmers do participate in town life. These are grain buyers and Dominion government employees under the Prairie Farm Rehabilitation Act (P.F.R.A.). They are socially mobile in a marked if not fully conscious way, and sever all bonds with the farm group, except necessary economic ones, with alacrity, skill, and despatch. Grain buying in particular functions as a channel of mobility from the rural to the town society.

It is often remarked, in Hanna as elsewhere, that the young people do not pay as much attention to social distinctions as their elders. There is nevertheless little evidence of the mingling of rural and town children. Farm young people come in to the town to attend high school, but they live together at the dormitory and whenever possible return home for week-ends. Intermarriage of Hanna farmers and townspeople is infrequent.[28]

The separation of town and country is continually being reinforced

[28]This statement is based upon marriage records in the *Hanna Herald* and the *Register of Marriages*, Hanna District, as well as upon interviews.

by misunderstandings which could not occur if the townspeople and farmers had more common ground. The townspeople may, for business reasons, try sincerely to please the farmers, but lack of insight is so great that their best-meant efforts may merely widen the breach. They have spent money to arrange an Old Timer's Day, for example, which is free for the farm people. As its chief attraction they import shows from the large cities. The farmers say, however, that they prefer informal gatherings, and that they resent being robbed of the occasion for a picnic.

Resentment against the townsmen by the farmers on the grounds that the former have a more pleasant and easier way of life is also related to lack of contact as both effect and cause. The farmers believe that the townsmen need not work so long nor so hard as they, that they receive greater rewards for their work, that they are always able to indulge in the forms of recreation most highly regarded by the farmers. While there is a basis for some of their beliefs, their view is in part based on unfamiliarity with the lives of the Hanna business men. Not knowing how the latter actually live, the farmers attribute to them a much more desirable form of existence, pictured from casual contacts with town and city life, from movies, radio programmes, and books. It is probable also that the conception of farm life contrasted with this is not accurate, but a stereotype minimizing the advantages of wheat farming and giving its disadvantages full weight.

The general evaluation of the difference between town and country traits contributes to the farmers' resentment. In modern society urban ways are ranked as superior to rural ways. This means that small-town people are eager to increase their resemblances to city people and their dissimilarities to farmers. With modern communication facilities it means also that the farmers, aware of the general value system, are keenly sensitive to any imputation of their inferiority. This is reinforced by the farmers' unconscious acceptance of the ranking and their tendency to avoid the townsmen or to be submissive to them.

Hanna and the rural regions around it are so sharply separate that the contributions of the town to the farming community are minimal. The town may even detract from the stability of the rural regions, in so far as contrasting the rural way of life with their picture of the urban and feeling the scorn of townsmen makes the farmers less satisfied with their lot and less eager to have their children follow them in their occupation. That this occurs is suggested by an account of an interview with a farmer's wife:

Mrs. ——— said out of a blue sky after lunch: "Oh, I was disappointed when Mary married a farmer. She had a good job, and she was getting

$133 a month, and she had a good future in office work, and she gave it all up. I kinda think she was sorry to go back [after her last visit here]—like she was when she first went away."

"Why didn't you want her to marry?"

"Oh, it wasn't that, but farm life—I don't think a woman has it easy on a farm, and I don't like the idea of her marrying a farmer. I didn't expect her to marry, somehow. She had lots of dates in Calgary, and she went bowling, and skating, and to ball games and things like that. But there was no nonsense about her, until she fell in love with this farmer and married him."

Town and country are economically interdependent but socially distinct. In spite of the cash economy and the highly specialized and mechanized methods of farming of the Hanna wheat farmers, their interests and activities are still unlike those of the town. Wheat farming bears many resemblances to a business or industry, but it retains basic differences. A lack of understanding and a lack of contact between the Hanna farmers and townsmen results. This perpetuates some of the effects of frontier antagonisms, although the antagonisms themselves have died. It negates the effects of a political alliance of town and country in the Social Credit party, an alliance against an outside enemy —the eastern financier—which might have been expected to complete the betterment of relations which depression forces began. The farmer and the small-town man are not members of the same community. They may unite for expediency at certain junctures, but they remain fundamentally distinct.

CHAPTER SIX

Class and Clique in the Town

THE SOCIAL distance between Hanna and the rural areas around is fully understandable only in the light of the social organization of the town. The cleavage between townsmen and farmers is not more marked than the cleavage between various groups within the town. Division into classes and cliques is one of the outstanding characteristics of Hanna. Because of it, not only does leadership devolve upon a small number of citizens but also the ability of these citizens to give wise and effective guidance is severely limited.

Far from denying the division of Hanna into groups, Hanna residents describe the town as cliquish, or, with reference to the attitudes of people above them in the social scale, as "snooty." Those who do not aspire to rise socially boast of the friendliness of Hanna, but their comments, as well as the bitter strictures of the ambitious, make it clear that the friendliness is limited by class and clique lines. Asked if the town has a group who think themselves better than anyone else, they reply, "What town hasn't?"[1]

The most important division is between those who are and those who are not considered townspeople. The first group includes the merchants, professional men and women, clerical workers, and labourers who live in Hanna and supply goods and services to the Hanna area. The second includes the members of the farm community

[1]The organization of the Women's Association of the United Church is pointed out as an excellent accommodation to Hanna's social structure. A few years ago the Association, which has about ninety members, was divided into a number of groups. The basis of the division was originally that of neighbourhood. Shortly it became that of clique. The manner in which the groups are designated suggests this. There is the active "old Ladies' Aid," "the lazy group," "the business girls," and so forth. When new groups are projected it is because some clique, not some neighbourhood, is not accommodated by existing ones.

whether or not they live in town, the travellers who visit the town regularly, and the railroaders.

The railroaders are the most numerous and important of the outsiders. They and their families form about a third of the population of the town. The merchants and professional people are to a large extent dependent upon them. None the less they are regarded as separate from and subordinate to the townspeople proper.

The Hanna railroaders are recruited by a somewhat haphazard process from diverse backgrounds. Few are sons of railroaders.[2] Most have drifted in from other occupations. One was a musician, another a bank clerk, a third a law student, and a fourth a farmer. The former musician described how he entered railroading:

> [After the First World War] I came back to my home town and played in an orchestra there. It didn't bring in enough and we heard there was a pianist needed in Hanna so my wife came here. I followed and played with the dance band. At that time they needed men on the railroad and it seemed to fit in with the other so I started. That's the way most railroaders get started. They just drift in without ever thinking much about it. The rate for new men is high. The C.N. pays you high for learning. There are lads out on the yard now who have only taken one run who are getting seven dollars a day.

A man who had worked at no other occupation than railroading mentioned the fact with pride. He said that he considered his case almost unique. The workers do not even come from the same region. They rarely start their railroad career in Hanna. Rather they are hired in Winnipeg or other centres and sent to Hanna, either directly or after work elsewhere.

Once hired, they are assigned positions in a very complex structure. Of the main functional divisions in railroading, four are represented in Hanna. There are half a dozen station employees, over a score of train crews, sixty or seventy section men, and a number of shop men, varying from fifty to over seventy in winter and from twenty-five to thirty-five in summer. The men in the different divisions achieve different degrees of integration into the railroad culture and have different degrees of prestige. The station employees, for example, are virtual outsiders, and the section men, while within the cultural group, have low status. Each division, moreover, has within itself an elaborate hierarchy, in which advancement and prestige are closely related to seniority.

His background and the place he occupies within the railroad group vitally affect the railroader's view of himself and the world, but

[2]Cf. W. F. Cottrell, *The Railroader*, pp. 8-11.

there is little to apprise the Hanna citizen of the differences among railroaders. He regards them as all the same except on the rare occasions when divisions among them are brought to his attention.[3]

The strength of most railroaders' identification with their occupational group and their separation from the rest of the community account for the outsider's lumping of them all together. So dependent upon their work are they that, as in other occupations bound up with a whole way of life, retirement frequently brings personal disorganization. The railroaders are somewhat boastful of this. One said:

Have you ever met retired railway men? They never last more than three and a half years on the average. There's figures down at the office to prove it. Some of course last even less than that. They'd have to make up the average. Sixty-five's the retiring age. And they put down a little every year on some little farm, usually out at the coast, or Victoria. There are a lot of retired railway men out there. But they don't last long. No matter how active they were, they just die when they have nothing to do with their work. I remember one guy, who was so strong that he ran everywhere, over box-cars, around the yard, never saw anything like him. Well, he retired to Edmonton but for the next year and a half he spent his life riding the trains out from Edmonton and back again. He was as strong as a horse still when he retired, but within a year and a half he was dead.

The separation of the railroaders from the townsmen was shown by the comments of a professional man who has wide contacts and, since he is a farmer's son and his wife a railroader's daughter, is unusually free from occupational group prejudices. He said that he talked with railroaders and called them by their first names, but he had never entered their homes, nor they his. Of a railroader who lived next door, he knew little but that he liked the writings of Somerset Maugham. This had been discovered through the exchange of books while the railroader was bed-ridden.

The mobility of the railroaders both strengthens their occupational identification and increases their separation from the town. They are attracted to railroading because they are mobile and they are made more so by the nature of their work. Many railroaders are stationed at Hanna only temporarily. Until they have seniority, they have little choice in the matter of their location. If employees of higher ranks than theirs die, retire, or are promoted they may on application move up in the hierarchy. Frequently going from Hanna to other places is entailed. Also, in slack times, Hanna railroaders may be "bumped." That is, they may be "let off the end" in favour of men of greater

[3]One of these occasions occurred in 1934, when a railroader tried to bring public pressure to bear against the rigid seniority rules of the railway. *Hanna Herald,* Jan. 18, Feb. 8, 22, 1934.

seniority, who have applied at Hanna after being released somewhere else.

Few men refuse to accept posts elsewhere for which they are eligible. Hanna is not a popular town because of the status of rail-roaders there and the dry-belt situation. The limited rainfall and high winds make it difficult for trees and flowers to grow and the town tends to have a dreary appearance. It is also unattractive to rail-roaders whose hobby is gardening or fishing. On the other hand, in depression many men from elsewhere come to Hanna. The town has a reputation of always providing some work because Drumheller coal is hauled by Hanna workers and because the shops usually have repair work to do.

The prospect of moving in six or nine months keeps railroaders from "growing roots" in Hanna. Many stay at the less luxurious of the town's two hotels, at rooming houses, or in shabby shacks unsuitable for permanent residence. At these places they are in contact with their fellow workmen rather than with townspeople, and have less incentive than property owners to interest themselves in town affairs. Their mobility is an impediment to family life, and to an interest in schools and churches.

Moreover many of those stationed in Hanna for long periods travel in the course of their work. They are in town for only part of the time, sometimes briefly. Thus they too are prevented from being active in the associations of the town. The mayor believes that the railroaders should be represented on the council, but has found that many of them cannot attend the council meetings. The Board of Trade has courted the railroaders as it has the farmers, but has failed to enlist them partly because of the difficulty they have in being in town on meeting nights.

The railroaders' unusual and irregular work hours increase their separation. Shift work and the necessity of being on call for un-scheduled work serve as does travelling to prevent participation in regularly scheduled town activities. A reason for the prevalence of gardening and fishing among railroaders is that they are individualistic forms of recreation. A popular man whose wife is active in town organizations has been in Hanna since 1924, but for most of the time has worked from three in the afternoon till eleven at night. He has not been able to go to the Board of Trade or other meetings.

The amount of the income of the railroaders and the manner in which it is received also hinder integration into town life. The rail-roaders are usually well paid, but they do not receive the same sum on each pay-day. Their work week varies from season to season and year to year, and their cheques vary with it. The irregularity is conducive to free spending and lack of foresight. A railroader pointed out that the mechanics and other more steady workers budget carefully and always seem to have money, but the people who receive different amounts each pay-day, although their income is often much higher, never have money. It is a case, he said, of "easy get, easy spend." Conductors receive higher wages than any other railroaders, but there are more collections for the funerals of conductors who die in poverty than there are for any other category of railway workers. Along with the careless attitude towards money goes a materialistic philosophy which holds that everything worth while has its price.

The outward signs of the railroad culture include a distinctive language and dress. The group has an argot which is useful and even necessary on the job. This serves also to identify members and strengthen their in-group relationships, and to set up a barrier between railroaders and townsmen. Modes of dress function similarly. Even a man of high occupational rank, whose salary exceeds that of many business men, who is very precise in manner, and whose friends and interests indicate refinement, can be identified at a glance as a railroad employee by his greasy trousers and open-necked shirt.

Finally, the scorn of Hanna townspeople for the railroaders contributes to their isolation. It makes the railroaders reluctant to participate in the life of the town, and the townspeople unwilling to have them participate. The townspeople are said to go so far as to refuse to employ the sons and daughters of railroaders. Whether or not this is true, belief that the practice exists leads the young people to leave the town to seek work.

In the early days the railroaders were given more prestige. The C.N.R. was expected to be the basis of Hanna's growth in numbers and prosperity. The employees of the railway had prominent and respected places in the town. Disappointment about railroad expansion led to a gradual change during the 1910's. The business and professional people came to consider themselves economically dependent, not upon the railroaders alone, but upon the railroaders and the farmers. Whenever it seemed advisable, they could deny their debt to one group in favour of the other. The railroaders thus lost much power. The loss was confirmed during the depression. The railroad did not protect Hanna from the fluctuations of the wheat economy. The number of people the C.N.R. employed and the wages it paid shrank greatly, both in the early twenties and in the thirties. Many railroaders had to seek relief from the town. Their poverty weakened their claim to consideration as the mainstay of Hanna's economic position.

If the railroaders were looked down upon everywhere as they are in Hanna, they would not gain by moving to similar jobs in other towns. They are not. The daughter of a railroader who came to Hanna ten years ago said that in her home town, not far from Hanna, railroaders were the *élite*. She concluded, "When I came here I was proud of being a railroad person coming into a railroad town, but after a while I stopped saying I was railroad." The fact that their status is lower in Hanna than in some other places contributes to the town's unpopularity with railroaders and to their reluctance to regard it as a permanent place of residence.

Instead of taking part in town organizations, the railroaders form their own. In these are strengthened in leisure hours the bonds woven on the job. The chief formal organizations are the railroad brotherhoods. There are locals of each of the Big Four in Hanna, the Order of Railway Conductors, the Brotherhood of Railway Trainmen, the Brotherhood of Locomotive Engineers, and the Brotherhood of Locomotive Firemen and Engineers. There are also members of the Order of Railway Telegraphers, but no local organization. A prominent member of the Brotherhood of Railway Trainmen placed strong emphasis on the economic activity of the organizations, and minimized the purely social functions. After he had explained the insurance plans in force in the unions, he was asked specifically what functions they fulfilled. His reply was:

"We always believe in trying to get higher pay. At the same time we often make 'sympathy' motions that we are in favour of something that has been done by the Government, for example, keeping down prices. Of course we know that higher pay for us doesn't jibe with keeping prices down, but we move them both just the same. If there has been compensation to a railroad man that seems unfair, we send it down to Winnipeg and if need be on to our man at Ottawa. But if there is something we don't like about the way things are being run around the yard, we don't go to the superintendent—although I'll go and speak to him any day—we do it through the local chairman of the Brotherhood and he takes it up."

"What connection have superintendents with you?"

"It's this way, the superintendents and their assistants are 'the company,' that's the C.N., and everything else is 'the men.' We work through our local unions for what we want, and all the rules of working and promotion are union rules."

"Is there a social side to your clubs?"

"No, there is no need of any. We do give a 'do' if anyone retires. We are allowed twenty-five dollars toward a banquet. But our motto includes 'no drinking' so we cannot as an official group have a party. Almost everyone who retires is a member of some other group as well, Oddfellows, Legion, or such. They usually go in with us. The last man to retire was a Legion chap and that only cost us ten dollars for we had the hall free. I have forgotten how many came to the reception. It was a lot, though, and we gave him a purse that came to—I think it was $178."

The social activities include large dances. The B.L.F.E. held its first ball in 1914, and the newspaper reports show that it and its many successors were very successful.[4] There used to be clubs among the railway men, of a semi-commercial character. Some of their activities, notably gambling, were illegal. These clubs have either disappeared or gone underground.

On the informal level there are gatherings in the beer parlours and restaurants and in private homes, as well as in the roundhouse and on other parts of railroad property. A railroader described these: "Of course, we see a lot of each other outside of the Lodge [the Brotherhood of Railway Trainmen]. A bunch of us sometimes get together and go down and wreck a guy's house. In spite of the rules it's done a lot. Anytime I want to see a guy on his day off I just have to go down to the ten cent store [beer parlour] to find him. That's where you should go if you want to meet people in this town. You hear all the news at the roundhouse. Once it's out there, there is no holding a story."

The women have only one organization, the Women's Auxiliary of the Brotherhood of Railway Trainmen. Of the many wives of railroad employees in Hanna, twenty belong. These women have the characteristics ascribed by W. L. Warner to the lower middle class.[5] They are frequently active church workers, especially in the evangelical churches. They do not drink; certainly they do not go to beer parlours. They rarely smoke. They are proud of their families and although they seldom have had much education are eager for their children to do well in school. Their club is chiefly social, although it provides insurance benefits and raises money for philanthropic purposes.

Wives of lower status than the Auxiliary members sometimes frequent the beer parlours. One young woman explained:

There's a lot of drinking done here and it's because there's nothing to do. If there's nothing to do you go down town to see who's there, and you go to the bar, or if you're looking for someone you go in there. When I'm away from Hanna in a busy place I don't go to the bar for months on end because I don't want to and there's no need for it. Before the dances here, nearly everyone goes to the bar because there's simply nothing else to do. You can have fun watching people at the bar, especially if some of the silly cowboys decide to fight over which is their girl. When that happens I like to sit up against the wall and watch.

4*Ibid.*, March 5, 1914.
5W. L. Warner and P. S. Lunt, *The Social Life of a Modern Community* (New Haven, 1941) and *The Status System of a Modern Community* (New Haven, 1942).

The number of railroaders' wives who spend time in the beer parlour is large, although not so large as the townspeople contend. Some of the women of low social position work as waitresses.

Ranking above the members of the Auxiliary are certain women who are concerned with respectability as a means of distinguishing themselves not from the frequenters of beer parlours but from the town's social leaders, who "do nothing but play bridge and drink—stay up till three and four in the morning and then don't get up till noon." They are usually dependent for their social relationships upon a few congenial friends, whose husbands are also railroaders. Others more or less openly want acceptance by the social leaders. They seek it by such methods as participation in the I.O.D.E.

A distinction exists between "railroader" and "C.N.R. employee" in Hanna as in other places.[6] The holders of certain C.N.R. jobs, such as the chief telegrapher and the station agent, are not railroaders. Their jobs provide greater stability and more regular hours than is usual on the railroad, and involve "white-collar" work. The personality and background of the man in such a position and of his wife determine their social participation. One man is an extreme "lone wolf." He spends most of his leisure in a solitary hobby. His isolation is increased by his wife's being a semi-invalid. Another man is a member of the town's socially superior group. He said that he never talks railroading when he is off work: he has enough of his job while on duty. No railroaders visit him, and when he passes groups of them "talking shop" on the streets he greets them but does not stop. His friends are business and professional men. His wife is a leader in the "best" cliques and clubs, in part by virtue of vivacity and great good humour.

Other C.N.R. employees who are not railroaders are "particular individuals who fail to qualify as brothers in the blood,"[7] or who refuse to identify themselves with the railroaders. Like the telegrapher and station agent, these may be either "lone wolves" or members of the town society, but if the latter their identification with the town

[6]Cottrell describes this distinction: "To the layman, 'railroader' usually means any employee of a railroad. When 'railroad labor' is talked about in the press, it is safe to infer that the 'Big Four' brotherhoods of the train service are meant. Among railroaders the word has a refined meaning: not all employees of a railroad are 'Railroaders.' Many employees are definitely excluded from the category, and the basis of this exclusion is extremely significant. Those excluded include groups of employees and also particular individuals who fail to qualify as brothers in the blood. Almost any railroader will be able to say who is included and who excluded, but the criteria on which his feelings are based are hazy and indefinite, and difficult or impossible for him to state. But that classification is highly significant, and once a person is identified as 'belonging' or 'not belonging,' a whole set of attitudes come into play." *The Railroader*, p. 4.

[7]*Ibid.*

is likely to be resented by the railroaders. The outstanding instance in Hanna was a "car knocker." During a long stay in town he was a leader in the Board of Trade and other associations and in politics, wrote editorials for the paper, and served as magistrate. The townspeople accepted him: they considered him radical, but admired his brilliance of intellect. The railroaders disliked him for taking the viewpoint of the town.

There are a few people who make a liaison between the townspeople and the railroaders. These are not integral members of either the town or the railroad group, but enjoy the friendship and trust of both. One is a conductor who has lived in Hanna for over twenty years, and held office in many organizations. He mediates not only informally between town and railroad but also, as a union officeholder, between the "men" and the C.N.R. His wife is socially skilled, and a member of the highest Hanna circles. Another mediator is a railroader whose wife is a musician, allowed entrance into the top strata on the basis of her talent.

The relation of the townspeople to the railroaders resembles the relation of the townspeople to the farmers. Both railroaders and farmers are cut off from the Hanna people, although they have vital economic dealings with them. Both are considered subordinate, and in spite of resentment unconsciously accept the judgment in part. The similarities are not coincidental. In comparison to the town merchants, both railwaymen and dry-belt wheat farmers are mobile, receive their income irregularly and in large amounts, are free spenders, wear clothing considered inferior, have irregular working hours, and are so discontented in their occupations that they want their children to choose others.

Nevertheless there is no link between railroaders and farmers. Sometimes farmers or farmers' sons, especially during depression, become temporary railroad workers; occasionally they become railroaders, but only by breaking all ties with the agricultural workers. Farmers' daughters or widows doing domestic or restaurant work in town may meet railroaders, through railroaders' wives doing similar work, and marry them. At election times, some railroaders work with farmers in the interests of the C.C.F. party. Otherwise, contacts are few. Even in old age, there is no mingling: the railroaders on retirement move north or to the coast, often, oddly enough, to farms, and the farmers, except the Germans, do not leave their land. In short, the railroaders are even more remote from the farmers than the town merchants are, since they lack business contacts with the farmers.

Lack of contact breeds lack of understanding and sympathy, and even antipathy. A farmer's daughter who had married a railroader expressed the view that the welfare of everyone in Hanna depended on the farmers. She was asked if this attitude was common among railroad women. She replied that it was very rare, that "in fact some of the railroad women say it [the drought] serves them right." Railroaders often say that they envy the farmers' wealth. One, at the beginning of an interview, volunteered: "Well, there is one thing I can tell you about this place. If I had just part of the bank account of some of the farmers around here I'd be happy. They gripe about the drought. Sure, there's drought, but it's good chicken country because it is dry. Chickens and turkeys need dry weather, and I know those guys make lots of money raising chickens out here."[8]

Like the railroaders and the farmers, the commercial travellers who make regular and frequent stopovers in Hanna have an important influence on the town's social structure. They are mainly salesmen and accountants, employed by Calgary firms. They make their homes in the city, and travel out from it to the towns and villages of southern and central Alberta and western Saskatchewan. On trips to east-central Alberta they stay at the better of Hanna's hotels on Monday night and, since there is no comparable accommodation for miles around, return to it on Tuesday night. On Thursday or Friday they pass through again on their way back to their base. The travellers may go east only once in two or three weeks, but schedules are so regular that they claim they can predict whom they will meet during their stay. They are so important to the business of the hotel that many of its practices are suited to their needs, even if the casual guest is inconvenienced.

A class division among the townspeople is as clear as the split between those who are and those who are not considered townspeople. The socially superior class includes the main business and professional men, a few government and railway employees, and their wives. The first citizen of Hanna in prestige has a large and prosperous retail store. Others who rank high are a merchant who retired recently and has not yet left town although he intends to do so, Hanna's two doctors and two lawyers, the high-school principal, the school inspector, the P.F.R.A. inspector, the theatre owner, the bank manager, and an insurance agent. The two druggists who after many years in Hanna

---

[8]This statement may be contrasted with an instance of warm sympathy. In the drought of the twenties an engineer was so moved by the plight of the farmers he had met along the Wardlow line that he appealed in the *Hanna Herald* for aid for them, and with a fellow worker distributed the toys and clothing collected. *Hanna Herald*, Dec. 29, 1921, Jan. 26, 1922. Such cases, however, seldom occur.

left in 1946 were in the top group, and one of their successors, sponsored socially by the man he replaced, quickly entered it. Usually the managers of the liquor store and of the larger of the two hotels belong. The late newspaper editor and a late implement dealer were prominent members.

The men are mostly "old-timers" who came to Hanna or nearby communities in the frontier days. Several bought their lots at the original sale of the townsite in 1912. Others entered in the next few years, or at the end of the First World War. Young on their arrival, they are now in their fifties and sixties. New-comers to the town who are accepted into the top class, such as the bank manager, are in the same age group. A professional man and an insurance agent in their early forties are exceptional.

The members of the upper class are fairly well-to-do, although to be wealthy is not so important as in some other communities. To have been rich for a long time is quite unimportant. A few people may boast that they "have always had a bath tub," only about a dozen prosperous families having had bath tubs and toilets with running water before the installation of the town water system in 1941. But men who have gone bankrupt have not sunk in the social scale, especially if their failure was due to giving credit during the depression, and men who came to town with little capital are proud rather than ashamed of their humble start. In 1946, however, money is essential to maintain the way of life of the top class.

The social leaders have well-built and attractive homes, those put up in early boom years being particularly large and imposing. The houses are mostly within a few blocks of the main business street because the sidewalks, the water supply, and the sewage disposal systems do not extend far beyond the centre of the town.

Activity in Hanna's leading organizations is characteristic of members of the top class. The organizations include the town council, the school board, the Board of Trade or Chamber of Commerce, the Kiwanis, the East Central Irrigation Association, the Masons and perhaps the Oddfellows and Elks, the Curling Club, and the churches.

The mayor has always been in the socially superior class. The present mayor who has held office since 1934 is a prominent business man.[9] The mayor from 1922 to 1934 was a doctor. His predecessors were the business man who is now the town's leading citizen, the present town secretary-treasurer and clerk, and a railway land agent.

[9]He and his wife are very active socially. It is remarkable that well-informed country people, with whom the mayor is popular, are unaware of this. On learning of his presence at a fashionable wedding reception, a farmer's wife expressed astonishment, on the grounds that the mayor "doesn't go in for that sort of thing."

At the moment only one of six councillors is of high social rank, but in the past more have been.

The school board is more clearly a preserve of the social leaders. It has shown even more continuity in its composition than the mayoralty. Two esteemed business men have been on it for many years, one for over thirty.

The local organizations of the Liberal and Conservative parties are led by socially prominent men and women and have been throughout the history of the town. These organizations spring into activity at election times although neither party has been successful in the constituency since 1917. All members of the top class belong to the "old" parties, while lesser business people are Social Credit stalwarts. Frequent mention is made of the fact that one lawyer is Liberal and one Conservative, and one doctor is Liberal and one Conservative. The fact that the mayor and some councillors, members of the socially superior class, are Liberal or Conservative whereas the bulk of the electorate is Social Credit is said to have occasioned some difficulty in the past. Now party lines are of little significance in the municipal field. At least three parties are represented on the council but it is by chance rather than design.

The Board of Trade, although it is sometimes at loggerheads with the council, also draws its leadership from the upper class. The Board was organized in 1912 and has had a varied career. It has lapsed several times, to be reorganized a few years later. Usually hard times have been associated with its cessation. The last eleven years of the Board of Trade, since its reorganization in 1935, have coincided with prosperity. The Board when active has been the outstanding economic and social organization of the town. Its extension through the social and economic strata has varied: at present it is wide both horizontally, since it includes such people as the high-school principal, and vertically, since it includes the small business men such as garagemen, as well as the more substantial. Its executives have almost invariably been drawn from the town's highest ranks. There are signs of a trend toward younger and less firmly established men, but it is not clearly marked as yet.

The Masonic Order has been dominated by the business and professional people since its organization in Hanna early in 1913. Almost all of the social leaders belong, except the Roman Catholics. The chief office has been held by the leading merchant, a bank manager, a doctor, and the newspaper editor. No other lodge has been so largely composed of the upper class, although the Hanna unit of the Elks included many prominent men both Roman Catholic and

Protestant. This unit was organized in 1926 with 72 members; its membership increased in five months to 112 active members, who ranged from the top to the bottom of the social scale.

The Curling Club is the leading recreational association. Its membership is usually well over a hundred, embracing many social and economic strata and age grades. Men from neighbouring villages take part in bonspiels, but except on special occasions few farmers curl. Examination of degrees of participation, of the selection of skips and rinks, and of scores might be as revealing of Hanna community structure as bowling games were of Whyte's street-corner gangs.[10] Such an examination would almost certainly show a high degree of participation by the members of the prestige groups.

The three churches which the socially superior attend are the United Church, the Church of England, and the Roman Catholic Church. The men are active in church affairs. In the United Church, one is a faithful attendant, usher, and chairman of the Board of Stewards. Like several others, he goes to church regularly without his wife. It is said that formerly the town was run by church people as now it is run by social leaders. The role of prominent men in church affairs may be a survival. Religious differences are not stressed, except for the fact that one doctor and one lawyer are occasionally referred to as the Roman Catholic doctor and the Roman Catholic lawyer and that there are Masonic and Orange Lodges.

The high-ranking business and professional men often get together informally. Those who can take time off gather to drink coffee in mid-morning and mid-afternoon in the bigger Chinese café. Small groups also meet for crap-shooting or simply for conversation during the day.

The women of the upper class are wives or widows of men who "belong."[11] Although marriage to a member usually indicates pos-session of the requisite traits, in at least one instance a wife is not accepted because of her shrewish disposition. In other cases, a wife's social skills and characteristics strengthen the position of a man who would otherwise not be considered eligible.

The women must have the desire and the ability to attend and give teas and bridge parties in the approved manner. The teas are elaborate "spreads," with attractive and well-served food. Their prepa-ration takes much time: in the absence of adequate bakery and cater-ing facilities the hostess does most of the cooking herself. Gossip is the chief entertainment. Often three or more teas are given in one week,

[10]W. F. Whyte, *Street Corner Society: The Social Structure of an Italian Slum* (Chicago, 1943), pp. 14-25.

[11]There were in 1946 no bachelors or widows in the socially superior class.

with almost the same people at all of them. Teas are used to introduce guests or new Hanna residents or to honour departing townspeople, but many are held without any such reason.

Bridge is important and time consuming. At some winter parties the women meet for bridge while the men curl at the rink. The permanent bridge groups are small, and show a nice appreciation not only of friendships but of social ranking, although women not in the top circle are admitted. The bridge clubs are not an accurate index of present position, however, since new-comers or women who are rising socially cannot join until a member moves from town or withdraws from the club. In summer poker sometimes replaces bridge while regular players are on vacation.

The social round of members of the socially superior class is dizzying. Some people spoke of playing bridge five nights a week and attending teas on as many afternoons. According to one informant, in 1945 four teas were held between September and Christmas. After the fourth there was a lull, except for regular bridge-club meetings, and "people were getting restless." In the New Year, a hostess had "tea-bridges" on two successive nights in order to entertain all her friends. From then until May such two-night affairs were held two or three times a week. The people who attended, about thirty in number, were "always the same."

Afternoon coca-cola or coffee drinking by the women corresponds to the coffee-drinking by the men. To have a "coke" or coffee with friends while down town shopping is a regular rite with many, except when teas interfere. Cigarette-smoking is an accompaniment. The smoking marks the "smart set" off both from some other town groups and from the farm women.

The formal associations in which the women take part are few. The Roman Catholics are active in church groups. The other women are not. Those who belong to the United Church are members of the group in the Women's Association called "the lazy group." The I.O.D.E. is led by members of the socially superior class, although it includes women of lower rank as well. So was the Red Cross during the war, when many Hanna women belonged.

A book club is made up of fifteen of the top-ranking women. The members undertake to buy a book each every year, and to rotate the books among themselves. The club was organized by the only university-trained woman in the topmost circle, possibly the only one in town except for a pharmacist and a teacher or two. The woman, wife of a professional man, gives some direction through circulating reviews from the *New York Times*, the *New Yorker*, and other papers and magazines to which she and her husband have the only subscriptions in town. This book club, another emulative one among women of lower socio-economic rating, and such organizations as the Book-of-the-Month-Club, which is much patronized in Hanna, are the only sources of books other than the drug stores. That relatively little book-reading is done is owing to the fact that magazines are heavily subscribed to and that teas and bridges are frequent.

Having a job does not bar a woman from the socially superior class, although it does keep her away from teas and bridges.[12] Many women do work, probably because of the shortage of labour in frontier days and of money during the depression. The wives of most merchants with stores on the town's chief street either help their husbands regularly or have businesses of their own.

The men and women of the top class take part jointly in bridge clubs, bridge and poker parties, and cocktail parties. There are also "At Homes," which though nominally open are actually attended on invitation. One of these is held at Christmas by a leading citizen and his wife. Of it the hostess remarked that it was not really open to the public since she telephoned people and asked them to drop in. She had thought of putting a notice in the paper making it official open house but, she said, she could not quite stand the thought of everyone tramping through her house. Wedding receptions for children of people in the upper social stratum are other occasions for gatherings.

The socially superior class carries on few group activities out of town. Formerly there were within reach two resorts: Clear Lake, to which the members could go for an afternoon or evening, and Buffalo Lake, where many had cottages and where week-end parties were held. The drought made both unattractive by the early thirties. Since then there has been no convenient holiday resort.

There are a few people who want to belong to the upper class but because of personality, behaviour, or background are not acceptable. These are sometimes regarded as "belonging" by people lower in the social scale: if so, they are likely to be thought to be far more snobbish than the real members of the socially superior class. They for their part think the socially superior very snobbish. One used the graphic term "poof-poofs" to describe people of the top rank.

[12]The wife of the leading citizen is her husband's bookkeeper. She belongs to one of the "best" bridge clubs, attends some teas, but does not entertain much. Once or twice a year she pays off social obligations by lavish entertainments. The wife of a druggist who had recently left town worked in his store and belonged to the upper class, though she and her two closest friends were less active than most members. Two women, the co-editor of the paper and the owner of a dress shop, could have joined in the activities of the top group, but did not wish to do so.

People who are acceptable but by choice do not join the top circle are more numerous than those who strive to be admitted. They include business and professional families with a "middle-class code" of behaviour. They look askance upon many activities of the social leaders: they disapprove of drinking and smoking, and consider teas and bridge parties a waste of time. They are frequently active in local government, church work, and a lodge. A garden may receive much of their time. Their great preoccupation, beyond their work, is almost invariably their children. Whereas the few grown children of members of the upper class have not gone further than high school, the children of these people have usually gone to university and taken prestige-giving positions away from Hanna.

A few individuals are too lax rather than too strict in their observance of moral rules and of etiquette to be accepted by the social leaders. The latter drink, but they do so in homes rather than beer parlours and on conventional occasions rather than at will. They gamble, but in homes rather than "joints." Their practical jokes and coarse humour are also restricted as to time and place, and generally hidden from their fellow townsmen. Several business men, one of them wealthy, refuse to subject themselves to the discipline involved in upper class behaviour. They are regarded by their townsmen as lovable eccentrics, and their exploits are related with amusement and pride.

The members of the lower classes are relatively few, since the town lacks industries and its businesses are mostly small and family operated. Large firms, with employees not related to the owner, seem poorly adapted to the violent economic fluctuations of the area. The men of low social position are truckers, draymen, odd-job men, and workers on the road. They are of varying degrees of respectability. Some are pious church attendants; others are ne'er-do-wells, to whom are attributed idleness, sexual irregularities, alcoholism, and theft. Few are destitute: in 1946, the Salvation Army, the chief welfare agency in Hanna, could name only four families who were considered as "down and out" and in need of more than temporary aid.

Among the younger adults, class and clique divisions are less clear than among the older. The young people select their companions less in terms of social rank than of personal qualities. The groupings that exist are allied to occupation. The young business and professional men are united by social as well as economic bonds; so are the nurses, the school teachers, the clerks, stenographers, and telephone operators, the beauty-parlour operators and their assistants, the waitresses, and the truckers and labourers. The groups are ranked, with the business men at the top and the waitresses, truckers, and labourers at the bottom. The women clerks, stenographers, and telephone operators are hardest to place. As children and potential wives of business and professional men they are in some respects superior, in others subordinate to the teachers and nurses. Neither the lines between the groups nor their ranking are in any case clear cut.

Young people are generally less "cliquey" than their seniors, and they are especially so in Hanna. They are socially mobile in so far as personal qualities and achievements affect social rank. These factors are more effective on the frontier than in older societies because on the frontier birth and unearned wealth are not convenient determinants of position. Since the population is recruited from outside, an individual's lineage is unknown, and in the expanding economy the will and ability to work avail more than wealth.

"Democratic" behaviour among the young people of Hanna is influenced also by the age composition of the population. In the town there are few people in their twenties and thirties. Unless they are to go around with much older men and women, therefore, members of these age groups cannot draw fine social distinctions.

Moreover, young business and professional men and children of the members of the socially superior class cannot join the top circle. When the members of it were young, there were few persons in the frontier town who were older or more secure economically. They, by their public interest, activity, and ability, attained economic and social leadership. They have held it ever since. Able younger men have not come to, or stayed in, the town because of drought and depression conditions. During the twenties and thirties new enterprises could not be established, and the people willing to take over the management of older businesses were not young men. They were pioneers of the Hanna area who were being forced westward from hard-stricken villages. Thus for a long time no younger men joined the top class. The social organization of the town adjusted itself to the leadership of a particular aging group of men.

In the forties the children of the social leaders were reaching adulthood, but they did not become members of the socially superior class. They found little economic opportunity in Hanna, for although the first generation were reaching old age economic conditions prevented their retirement. Probably also the children "are not the men their fathers were." The men who left older communities to take advantage of western expansion, who were leaders in establishing a new town, and who in face of hardship achieved economic security, have undergone a rigorous selection. Their sons have not been subjected to like tests nor, having spent their lives in a single new community, have they had as good a chance as their fathers to develop their interests and abilities.

Only one young person is both a leading business man and the son of a member of the socially superior class. His father, an invalid for many years, died in the thirties at the age of forty-five. The business thus passed on to the son while he was still youthful. He does some things with the top class, but is not thought of as belonging to it. Like other young business men who are not yet firmly established, he serves beer instead of cocktails at parties and is not extravagant in his card-playing. The townspeople do not accept him as his father's equal. Frequently his name is prefixed by "young" to indicate his junior status.

Because of class and clique divisions the duties and privileges of leadership devolve upon a small portion of Hanna's population. The town has eighteen hundred or two thousand people, and its services in local government, education, religion, and recreation must meet the needs of these people and some needs of the farmers, commercial travellers, and casual visitors. The railroaders and the rank and file of the townspeople give only financial aid in the provision of services. None but the members of the socially superior class and some aspirants to it are willing to take office and are trusted to do so by their fellow citizens.

The comments of certain residents about Hanna suggest that the multifarious activities of the town are led and participated in by a mere handful. People in the lower social strata, including those whose junior position is due to youth, express dislike of the town because "there's nothing to do here." Often they use the same words as dissatisfied railroad employees and their wives. One young woman, when an interviewer said she liked Hanna, complained at length: "Well, I don't, because there's nothing to do here. Of course there are the movies, and I go to most of them. But there's nothing else. There's no place for picnics or anything. In the evenings I mostly just stay home and iron. I read, of course. . . . Books cost quite a bit, but it's as good a use as any for your money as long as you're stuck here." People in the top social stratum have no such feeling, however. Many stress as characteristic of Hanna the very qualities the lack of which other residents deplore. "There's lots to do," or "There's lots of fun here," they say. Undoubtedly their words reflect a booster spirit. The belief that it is wrong as well as unwise for business reasons not to praise the town is strong in Hanna.[13] On the other hand, accounts of the activities

[13]The columns of the *Hanna Herald* and the remarks of members of the "Five Hundred" have sometimes been strongly reminiscent of Sinclair Lewis's novels about small-town boosters. See especially *Main Street* (New York, 1920).

of the social leaders leave no doubt that both the men and the women are busy and contented.

That only the socially superior class are active participants in the town's associations decreases the stability of the town and its contribution to the country region around. The business and professional people are probably able enough, but they are too busy, too fun-loving, too removed from and too disliked by the rest of the town to give wise and constructive leadership.

The ability of the professional men is open to question.[14] The doctors, lawyers, clergymen, and high-school teachers are the most highly educated people in the community, having attended university, while the merchants have had only grade-school and high-school training. But they are not otherwise outstandingly well qualified. Some are in Hanna because they cannot measure up or feel they cannot measure up to urban competition, perhaps because of too long a stay in small towns early in their careers. They cling to Hanna as a "safe berth," contributing less and less to its life. Others are presumably competent but personally ill qualified in health, appearance, or conduct. Still others are both incompetent and personally ill qualified.

Some of the professional men in Hanna are quite able,[15] but even they tend to become frustrated and bitter if they are there because of fortuitous circumstances such as the health of a dependent or because of lack of capital or opportunity to set themselves up somewhere else. Those preferring small-town life or practice are exceptional. The attraction of the big city is strong. It lies in part in the living conditions, including opportunities for attending concerts and art galleries and associating with people of similar tastes and outlook, in part in the professional advantages of libraries, equipment, and colleagues at hand, in part in the greater prestige and greater income of the big city professional.[16]

Unlike the professionals, the business men seem to be well equipped to act as leaders. While few of the professional men came to town

[14]The statements made are based on newspaper accounts and interviews concerning Hanna professional men and the professional men from other areas in the dry belt who have taken part in the activities of the town's upper circle in the course of the town's history.

[15]Among the able professional men in Hanna are highly qualified ministers serving the German-Russians. These are not, however, members of the socially superior group.

[16]People tend to assume that the city teacher, preacher, doctor, or lawyer is more able than the small-town practitioner. A person from the Hanna area in 1927 stated at a convention of the Alberta Municipal Districts: "Small town solicitors are not much good or they would not be in small towns. They are incompetent, inefficient and untrustworthy." Hanna Herald, Dec. 1, 1927.

before 1920, many of the merchants were pioneers and have shown willingness to co-operate and initiative from the beginning. At the sale of the townsite in 1912, land speculators bought up the lots along the intended main street of the town. The merchants, rather than pay the high prices asked, located their shops along another street. Their manœuvre succeeded so well that Second Avenue rather than Main Street is still the business street of Hanna.[17]

Enterprise was also evident in the early years in the rapid establishment of a full complement of institutions. Under the leadership of the business men a village council, a Board of Trade, several lodges, recreational associations, religious organizations, and political clubs were set up during the town's first six months; a policeman was hired and plans for a hospital begun shortly after. A year from Hanna's founding the editor of the *Hanna Herald* could write: "Today, Hanna, only one year old, is undoubtedly the most progressive prosperous and promising town in Canada for its age. There is no misrepresentation connected with the publicity given this town for facts are better than imagination and it has been the rock bottom facts connected with this town that have brought it to where it is today and which will continue to push it onward."[18]

Over the succeeding years, the merchants of Hanna experienced great fluctuations in business. The town's prosperity showed a striking correspondence to that of the rural community. The effects of drought and crop failure were mitigated by the railroad payroll, but the effects of depression, in both the twenties and thirties, were if anything magnified.

Hard times resulted in the departure of many business men and the suicide of at least one. It cannot be assumed that those who left were inferior to those who remained. Many of the able and ambitious moved from the drought area to more promising fields. But certainly, in the light of their subsequent careers, the failure of the others to move cannot be explained in terms of lack of enterprise or timidity. To have not only survived the economic depression but to have built up or maintained flourishing businesses suggests ability as well.

The business men have also on the whole conformed to moral and legal standards. They have not become involved in scandals. Almost the only charge of chicanery laid against a prominent merchant had to do with shrewd but legal turning of bankruptcy laws to personal advantage in the early years. Even farmers had few tales to tell of trickery by leading merchants.

[17]*Hanna Herald*, July 29, 1937.
[18]*Ibid.*, Aug. 7, 1913. Another editorial similar in tone appeared Jan. 1, 1914.

But however well qualified people in the socially superior class may be, frequently they have no time to give constructive leadership. In addition to their vast number of avocational duties, all the male and several of the female members are still active in business or a profession. The upper stratum is not a leisure class. It is composed of people who are too busy to embark upon new ventures of long-range benefit to town and region.

Except for the Germans, there are no retired men in Hanna. The town is so young that some of its pioneer business men are not yet old. Hard times have deprived others of the means to retire. Further, Hanna has not held those of its citizens who have been able to retire. Only one prominent retired merchant was living in Hanna in 1946, and he planned to move "as soon as things got settled." Most have gone to Calgary and Edmonton or to the west coast. An annual picnic of former Hanna residents and summer visitors from Hanna was instituted at Vancouver in 1927.[19] Three years later the first of many reunions was held at Long Beach, California.[20] By 1934, seventeen families who formerly lived in the Hanna district had organized a Hanna Club at Chilliwack, British Columbia.[21] Chilliwack has been the goal of retiring Hanna people ever since. At a recent picnic there, eighty-five families were present, including visitors from Hanna. The possibility of owning a small farm or selling insurance to supplement their income, as well as nearness to Hanna and to old friends, leads people to prefer Chilliwack to other sections of the coast.

The people able to retire have often been those who had taken an active part in town life. Moreover they retire when in their sixties, that is, while still vigorous. The town suffers from the loss of their experienced leadership and participation. The loss is particularly noticeable in such fields as social welfare. The retired merchant who has stayed in Hanna temporarily has done outstanding work in War Loan and Red Cross campaigns and in other areas of public service.

Of course, the pressure of work is not the sole reason for the failure of the Hanna upper class in the field of leadership. It spends much time in teas, bridge, poker, and curling. In many mature societies an *élite* has developed a sense of stewardship and responsibility, which has led to an emphasis on public service. Its members have had "the essential, undeviating discipline of background"[22] pressing them to play a leading role in community affairs. Such discipline has not yet developed in Hanna.

[19]*Ibid.*, Sept. 1, 1927.   [20]*Ibid.*, July 7, 1938.
[21]*Ibid.*, Dec. 20, 1934.
[22]J. P. Marquand, *The Late George Apley* (Pocket Books ed.; New York, 1944), p. 4.

The general atmosphere of the town is of rather reckless enjoy-ment of life. Several times the prevalence of drunkenness has been discussed in the local paper. In 1928, for example, a councillor asserted that no woman could walk down the street without receiving insults from intoxicated persons and that cars were being recklessly used by drunken drivers.[23] In 1929 the assertions of a visitor caused an amusing show of indignation in an editorial entitled "Naughty Hanna":

> Extravagant statements made in the heat of enthusiasm are often pardoned with a smile when they are heard during the course of ordinary conversation, and are forgotten almost in the next breath, but statements reported to have been made by an Alsask lawyer recently anent the de-praved conditions existing in this town must be met with a frown.
>
> Speaking from the pulpit of a church in the town of Eatonia a week ago last Sunday, in support of a temperance campaign having for its objective the influencing of public opinion against the sale of beer in that town, the speaker launched upon a fantastic state of inebriety allegedly existing here. Hanna was held to be a horrible example of the debasing effects resulting from the sale of liquor. It was "a city of drunkenness—bottles were to be found on every doorstep, while beer was in everyone's cellar." In short, it is the drunkard's "Rock Candy Mountain."
>
> The speaker based his wild assertions on the evidence he "discovered" (?) whilst attending the bonspiel held here a year ago. Hanna is justly famous for the genial hospitality extended to the visiting bonspieler—a measure of hospitality so generously given that lovers of the "roarin' game" make it a point to compete on the local rinks year following year. That this hospitality should be repaid by slanderous statements publicly made by a member of an honoured profession is neither becoming to the individual uttering them nor likely to enhance the weight and prestige the words of the learned legal gentleman carry in his community. The statements made regarding the liquor conditions existing in this town are so absurdly ridiculous that they refute themselves. Great causes are more often hindered than helped by the vaporings of over-enthusiastic zealots.[24]

Shortly afterward another editorial outburst on the subject was called forth by the remark of a local minister at a convention of the Alberta Prohibition Association, that the town of Hanna was "probably the wettest in Alberta." The editor of the *Hanna Herald* tried to show, by the returns of the Alberta Liquor Control Board for 1929, that the statement was false.[25] The minister replied, however, "Mr. Editor, come, now, $142,000 spent in the Hanna Liquor Store is a huge sum to be spent in a community like this. There is enough hard stuff con-sumed in this town to make it a little wet, just a little, eh?"[26] State-ments similar to the minister's are still current among both residents of the town and outsiders. Gambling is also extensive, in spite of news-

[23]*Hanna Herald*, Aug. 16, 1928.
[25]*Ibid.*, Feb. 27, 1930.

[24]*Ibid.*, Dec. 5, 1929.
[26]*Ibid.*, March 6, 1930.

paper campaigns against it,[27] and riotous parties are much discussed. While officially these things are denied or minimized, they are frequently spoken of with some pride, as evidence of gaiety.

Its youth contributes to the amusement-loving and carefree atmosphere of the town. Hanna is not long past its frontier phase. Its residents are the first generation to have settled in the region. They still have some of the instability and the disrespect for convention of frontiersmen.

The commercial travellers and railroaders also contribute to Hanna's spirit of undisciplined enjoyment of life. These free-spending, mobile young men have hedonistic standards which are easily copied by the townspeople. They help support forms of amusement which otherwise could not survive.[28] Moreover, their presence weakens the informal social controls customary in small towns. The travellers and railroaders, being cut off from the townspeople, are themselves free of the controls and by making the town less cohesive free Hanna residents also.[29]

Hanna's economic vicissitudes are another factor promoting the light-hearted pursuit of pleasure. A code concerning the use of wealth has never developed. Sudden reversals of fortune continually throw the town into a state of social disorganization. The rates of immorality, crime, and suicide have varied greatly in correlation with economic fluctuations. A resident of the town shrewdly said that when the people of Hanna got money after a depression they did not know what to do with it and each put on a wilder party than the other in

[27]*Ibid., passim.* An intensive *Herald* campaign took place in November and December, 1926.

[28]The farmers also support some recreational institutions which are disapproved of by certain of the townspeople. Cf. W. H. Wilson, *The Evolution of the Country Community*, p. 85: "Just as the lumberman or cowboy or sailor when he comes to town 'tears loose and paints the town red,' so, in a milder degree, the farmer's son or hired man, because he has at home no recreations supplied by his church or school, patronizes in the town or small city a cheaper and nastier theater than one would expect to find either in that town or in his home community."

[29]The lack of cohesion is seen in the treatment of strangers in Hanna. Whereas in many towns of the same size a stranger arouses great interest, in Hanna little notice is taken of a new-comer for at least a week. Little effort is made to enlist new arrivals in town activities. Three months after a young professional man, his wife, and his parents moved to town, both his wife and his mother complained of loneliness. They had been invited to only one house in the town, that of an employee. The only friends of the young couple were two other couples who had come to Hanna at the same time. One of these found it equally hard to become acquainted with townspeople. The other was sponsored by the business couple it succeeded, and was aggressively friendly. The woman in particular "went more than half way" to establish cordial relations with people she met. People remarked that they felt they ought to try to get to know the new-comers, but so many stayed only a short time that it was neither easy nor "worth while."

an effort to excel. Others stated that drought-area towns had to have hectic pleasures to offset their economic hardships: "Towns have their own personalities. Vermilion was run by church people, Taber always turned out for a serious lecture, but in Hanna they're all out for amusement. At any serious lecture put on here you'll get just a handful. But maybe when there is drought you have to have amusement."

For the socially superior class there is an additional factor making for absence of restraint. Being at the top of the social scale, its members are free from some of the controls to which other ranks are subject. A person vehement in her denunciation of the "Five Hundred" suggested this:

> "What makes a Five Hundred then?"
> She shrugged her shoulders and said bitterly, "They're just above everybody else. They live in another world. All they do is talk about the terrible things everyone else in town does. . . . I was at one of their parties around Christmas—I don't know how I got mixed up in it—and I saw things there that are never done and wouldn't be put up with in our own crowd. Yet they talk about us!"
> "Do you talk about them?"
> "They just can't be talked about. They're just out of this world!"

The result is devotion to having a good time, which not only leaves little time for public affairs but decreases the influence of the upper class over people who have a sterner code, notably the people near the middle of the town's social ladder and the "respectable" rural residents.

The width of the breach between the social leaders and other Hanna people makes the leaders, even when they wish to do so, unable to understand and to implement the interests of the others or to secure their co-operation. The members of the top group cannot know the point of view of people with whom they have almost no contact. They meet one another frequently but other townspeople only occasionally and casually. They do not even know most of the residents of Hanna. The mayor's wife, whose circle of acquaintances is wider than that of most of the social leaders, estimated that she did not know more than a quarter of the people in town. Others confessed staying within their own groups almost entirely, although they felt they should try to meet people and especially to call on new-comers.

The breach between the socially superior class and the rank and file gives rise to a hostility toward the top class. The hostility sometimes seems to be a reflection of the split between the "respectable people" and the socially prominent. That it is something more is shown by the fact that it is expressed by many who themselves defy convention and love amusement. Indeed, the insinuations against the morals of the upper class may proceed from, rather than contribute to, the hostility.

Hanna is singularly lacking in cohesion. A substantial portion of its residents, the railroaders, neither identify themselves with the town nor are considered by the rest of the people as genuine townsmen. They add to the number of people whom the institutions of the community must serve, but not to the stock of office-holders and leaders. Moreover, like the many transients who visit the town, the railroaders impair the efficient functioning of the town's social structure by contributing to an attitude of irresponsibility and by decreasing the knowledge which the other townsmen have of one another. Among the people who think of themselves and are regarded by others as genuine townsmen, the absence of cohesion is seen in age and class divisions, the placing of the privileges and obligations of leadership upon one small group, and the inability of that group to give wise and effective guidance. The inability proceeds from the small size of the group, the lack of close contact with other people in the town, and the hostility with which it is regarded. Galpin has suggested that the rural community sustains loss in that urban business agents become urban social leaders, that is, that small-town merchants and professional men, "half-made by the farmer," are called upon to devote all of their surplus time and energy to the political, religious, educational and social institutions of the town.[30] Part of the weakness of the Hanna community is accountable to such a loss; part arises from the fact that the agents give only limited social leadership in the town itself.

[30]C. J. Galpin, *Rural Life*, pp. 95-6.

CHAPTER SEVEN

The Problem of the Rural Community

IN THE face of a fluctuating and declining economy, sparse population, low standards of living, ethnic invasion, and lack of leadership from villages and towns, old patterns of rural living have failed in the Hanna area. At first the ways of life developed in the eastern parts of Canada and in the United States appeared to have been successfully transplanted to the prairie. Then, with startling suddenness, their inadequacies were revealed and attempts had to be made to replace them.

The history of the Hanna area, except as it has to do with the Plains Indians and the cattlemen, began in 1909 and 1910. Settlement had been delayed by the reports of Captain John Palliser and other surveyors that the south and central parts of eastern Alberta and the adjacent parts of Saskatchewan were unfit for agricultural development.[1] However, by the early twentieth century the absence of alternative lands, the extension of railroad facilities, a few years of good wheat prices and of adequate rainfall for wheat, and the development of dry farming techniques led to the opening up of the dry belt. The territory was peopled with amazing speed. The whole of the Northern Plains was settled quickly: students have asserted that "nowhere in the world has so vast an area been opened to human settlement in so short a space of time."[2] The Canadian portion of the Plains was filled much more rapidly than the American. Stephen Leacock concluded a description of the development of Alberta with the sentence, "Thus grew Alberta, or rather thus was it raised like a circus tent in the shouting years before the War."[3] His terms are apt for the east-

[1]Cf. W. A. Mackintosh, *Prairie Settlement: The Geographical Setting*, chap. II.
[2]C. F. Kraenzel, W. Thomson, and G. H. Craig, *The Northern Plains in a World of Change*, p. 49.
[3]S. Leacock, "Social and Other Credit in Alberta," *Fortnightly*, CXLIV, Nov., 1936, p. 526.

central region. In a few years there was someone on every half-section.[4]

No less remarkable than the speed of settlement was the rapidity with which thriving rural communities were organized. The homesteaders were young and energetic and most of them, although they had received little formal education, had had sound training in the organizations and ways of life of rural communities and the broadening experience of migration. Except for a few who intended "to make a million" and move on, they aimed at setting up homes for themselves and their children. They were convinced that farming was important and profitable. Here and there remittance men and "gentlemen farmers" wore gloves to milk cows and in other ways earned ridicule but there were not many of these. The backgrounds of the settlers were similar enough to make for harmony. Such factors are behind the statements of Hanna pioneers that "when you go into a new country you find the finest people on earth," and that the dry-belt homesteaders were "the best type of settler that ever put plough into sod on the North American continent."

The character of the people was not the only factor making for the rapid development of rural communities. The level land, the absence of trees, and after 1912 the railroad made it easy for people to assemble. Many tasks on the farm, such as threshing, required the co-operation of several households. Early bumper crops and abundant credit facilities meant that there was more capital available than is usual on farming frontiers. There were none of the barriers to the full employment of talent which a class system may create.[5] All these things were conducive to pleasant and progressive community life.

On the informal level there was a wealth of activity—visiting, bees, plays, concerts, dances, picnics, and charivaris. Gatherings, which people sometimes endured great hardship to attend, lasted a long time and were very hilarious. They created the possibility among the dry-belt farmers "of accepting a common purpose, of communicating, and of attaining a state of mind under which there is a willingness to co-operate."[6] Out of them grew formal structures, which in turn strengthened the informal relations. Prominent among the formal structures were organs of self-government, educational and religious organizations, and, most important, farmers' groups which came to dominate almost every area of rural life.

[4]Cf. A. S. Morton and C. Martin, *History of Prairie Settlement and "Dominion Lands" Policy.*

[5]A few families of lofty social pretensions who attempted to farm associated almost wholly with town residents. They usually soon moved to a town.

[6]C. I. Barnard, *The Functions of the Executive* (Cambridge, Mass., 1946), p. 117.

The units of local self-government were rural municipalities, consisting of about nine to twelve townships.[7] Although their functions were, as in most parts of North America, limited to looking after the local roads, straying animals, pests, and so forth, the councils of the municipalities were active and shrewd. In them settlers gained training and experience in, and reputation for, political leadership.

School districts were set up rapidly. Most of the settlers were about the same age, and raised their families at the same time. A few years after the opening up of the district came a sudden heavy demand for schools. This, coupled with experience in other rural communities, led to the creation of numerous school districts. Such school districts conformed to eastern precedent even in size. They usually were only four miles square.

The school boards, like the councils of the rural municipalities, gave the people a chance to change things to suit the Hanna environment. They also gave many people a means of displaying qualities of leadership and of rising from local offices to offices in the larger community. The school buildings provided meeting-places for community members, centres for their social life. Often they were the first buildings erected that were large enough to do so. Dances, plays, concerts, church services, educational and political meetings could be held in them. They were a vital integrating force in community life. In some cases also schools attracted teachers who, by experience and education, a different work schedule from the farmers, and their position of prestige, could take an important role in community affairs. The women teachers were a chief source of brides, and when they married and stayed in a district they continued to take an active part in its affairs.[8]

Even the churches seemed to be developing satisfactorily. The chief religious denominations sent ordained men, students, or lay preachers into the field, and even the smaller sects held services. A Presbyterian congregation began to meet in May, 1910, on a farm a mile east of the site of the town.[9] Its minister was a student who remained in charge until 1912, and was succeeded by an ordained preacher. The church included Methodists as well as Presbyterians, and in time became the First United Church, the largest in Hanna in

[7]As in other parts of the province, some of the rural municipalities were formed voluntarily, and some under government pressure.

[8]The teachers frequently came from older Canadian communities, as was the case in other parts of the West. Several excellently trained women from Nova Scotia were among them. Cf. E. B. Mitchell, *In Western Canada before the War*, pp. 68-73.

[9]See the *Hanna Herald*, Jan. 30, 1913, July 29, 1937, Jan. 20, 1938.

1946. The Church of England, considered usually to be slow in adapting to frontier conditions,[10] sent out itinerant lay preachers who went about the country on horseback, spending the night and holding services where they could. The same church also had railroad missionaries, who preached at various places along the railway lines. Although it was not customary for any one denomination to have regular weekly meetings in a particular neighbourhood, some kind of service was provided with fair regularity, and was well attended. In a number of cases ministers took a lively part in community activities, organizing entertainments, trying to secure needed enterprises, and spreading local news both through personal contacts and through the columns of the weekly newspapers. Even students, in the community for only a few months of the year, played important roles. One popular young man before he left wrote and produced a play concerning life in his rural charge.[11]

However the churches never became so firmly established as the other forms of organization. The largely male population, the pressure of work at various seasons of the year, the prevalence of a materialistic point of view—such factors as these were obstacles to the progress of churches. The centring of the services in Hanna and in villages when the town and even many of the villages were regarded by the farmers with hostility also impeded advance. But the inadequacies of the churches seemed likely to be of short duration. It appeared that the area would soon be rich enough to support religious establishments and that churches would then begin to thrive.

The most notable rural organizations were the locals of the United Farmers of Alberta and the United Farm Women of Alberta. Locals were established almost as soon as the Hanna area was settled: several preceded the association centring in the town itself which began in 1915. They did not have unvarying success, but they did in many cases carry on extensive programmes in which the population of the farming communities participated with benefit. Some of their primary aims and achievements were economic. Co-operative buying and selling, for example, were attempted at an early date. The U.F.A. and U.F.W.A. also promoted and channelled the discussion of economic and political questions, and educated the farm population along various other lines. As for social life, one reason for the appeal of the U.F.A. was that its meetings were festive occasions for men, women, and children. Usually held in the schoolhouse, the business meeting, lecture, and discussion would be followed by a substantial lunch and a lively square dance,

[10]Cf. E. B. Mitchell, *In Western Canada before the War*, pp. 83-7.
[11]*Hanna Herald*, Sept. 18, 1924.

which often continued till sunrise. Within the organization a strong
stress on democratic procedure and on local initiative made the locals
the more effective in community organization.

The U.F.A. in part replaced or at least competed with religious
organizations. It held Sunday meetings and an annual U.F.A. Sunday.
This indicates both the weakness of the church and the vigour of the
U.F.A.

In the entrance of the U.F.A. into politics and its attainment of
political power, Hanna farmers played an energetic part. Several were
elected to the provincial and the federal legislatures and to prominent
positions in the U.F.A. organization. That the U.F.A. could organize
effectively for political action, gain political power, and embark upon
activities which earned the praise even of one-time opponents, attests
to the strength and the co-operative spirit of the farm communities.

All of the organizations faced some difficulties of finance and of
personnel, especially in years when crops were poor. Early in 1914
a movement arose within a rural municipality near Hanna to have the
area revert to the status of a local improvement district.[12] The "booster"
spirit of the *Hanna Herald* led it to print a vigorous denunciatory
editorial:

It has been reported that a movement is on foot at present to disorganize
the Rural Municipality of Dowling Lake. At this enlightened age, this seems
to us to be reverting to the mediaeval times and that the residents of the
Dowling Lake municipality, or rather a few of them, are trying to follow
the customs of their forefathers instead of trying to build up their country
and make it to resemble a prosperous modern municipality. A petition has
been prepared and circulated by a ratepayer who himself says that he does
not know what benefit the ratepayers will derive by having the municipality
disorganized. This man has been asked by a number of the ratepayers to
circulate a petition and is doing his duty in good faith, but he does not
appear to understand what the result will be. It is said that a large majority
of the Dowling Lake ratepayers want the municipality disorganized. What
for? If there is anything being done by the Council of Dowling Lake municipality that does not meet with the approval of the ratepayers, the best and
only remedy is to meet the council, tell the council what the ratepayers
want and we feel sure that the body of men now in power in that municipality would not intentionally go directly against the wishes of the people.
Instead of trying to do the impossible, it would be much better for the
ratepayers of that municipality to hold a mass meeting in some convenient
place and ask the members of the council to attend. The trouble can then
be remedied very easily.[13]

[12]Improvement districts enjoy fewer services than rural municipalities and are
not self-governing. The provincial government provides the services to these areas
and levies and collects the necessary taxes.
[13]*Hanna Herald*, March 26, 1914.

Some of the savings which it was hoped the change would achieve
were indicated in a letter sent as a reply:

> I see the question is asked, "Why disorganize Dowling Lake Muni-
> cipality?"
> Being a ratepayer of that municipality, I should like to answer that
> question for myself and the majority of the ratepayers of my neighbour-
> hood.
> Were we not compelled to pay to the extent of $2,000 or thereabout for
> Council fees, Secretary-Treasurer special election expenses, sundries and
> other unpaid accounts, besides about $300 for office furniture (a sum I
> dare say many of us have not invested in our own homes for the comfort
> of our families).
> We probably would be able to have just as much road work done as
> we have had since the organization of the municipality, and in addition
> would be more able to meet our school debts, instead of being told "There
> is no money for us."
> Let us form Local Improvement Districts and dispense with some of
> these unnecessary taxes until such time as our land is developed into a
> paying proposition and the R.R. brings markets for our produce.[14]

At the end of the same year the *Herald* urged the electors of the
rural municipalities to select able men to fill the places of those not
running for re-election. It stressed that intelligence and foresight would
be much needed in the year to come, and that it was in the power of
the ratepayers to nominate and to elect competent men.[15] Again a
response came from Dowling Lake, this time accusing the councillors
of representing the interests of particular individuals who had nomi-
nated them.[16] The letter was followed by others, revealing bitter
factional strife. Other incidents, some of them amusing, showed that
Dowling Lake was not alone in its difficulties.

A number of school districts near the town of Hanna experienced
trouble in 1915. An editorial stated that the outstanding causes were
misunderstandings as to the length of the school term and disagree-
ments concerning teachers. In no case was the trouble serious: it
usually started from a trivial source and was heightened as people
gave free rein to their emotions. Two illustrations were given:

> In one district the teacher engaged did not suit a few of the members
> of the school board. In order that she might become discouraged with the
> school, the children were kept home, no assistance was given by the parents,
> and in every conceivable way her efforts on behalf of the district were
> hampered by the ratepayers who were anxious to see her discharged. The
> attention of the inspector was directed to the matter and it was necessary
> for him to take the management of the district out of the hands of the

[14]*Ibid.*, April 16, 1914.   [15]*Ibid.*, Nov. 5, 1914.
[16]*Ibid.*, Nov. 12, 1914.

trustees, in order that the affair might be settled with justice. Since then things have gone much more smoothly, and the new board of trustees will be expected to carry on the school work in a manner which should do them credit.

In another district, which lies south and west from Hanna, school has been closed, and the trustees have given out the statement that they will not re-open until they see fit. This is a pretty autocratic way for a handful of farmers to handle the school question in a free country like Canada. That their little attempt to keep the school closed will be foiled, is certain. No liberty-loving citizens are going to allow three or four individuals, who have a misconception of the method of educating children, to close the school without a word of objection. In this same school there are twenty-six children, and one boy of fourteen years is only in the first grade. With few exceptions, every child is old enough to attend school through the most rigid weather.

The editorial went on to say that petty squabbles in the school districts might be easily averted if the members of the school board or the ratepayers read the School Act or consulted with the inspector before matters got out of hand. The concluding remarks of the *Herald* writer were that if local boards did not function efficiently and amicably the provincial Board of Education could and would replace them by "official trustees."[17]

News items from the rural districts revealed that the editorial was timely and that it by no means exaggerated. Not quite a year before it appeared, a man wrote to the *Hanna Herald*:

The ratepayers of the Solon S.D. met at the annual meeting recently for election of trustees. Our worthy secretary was absent as usual, which meant that we had to do without his report. It looks as though the children of this district were doomed to be without schooling for another year, unless it happens to be a dance-hall education, and some are not quite willing to take what is offered. As the meeting could not come to any agreement in regard to the length of the school term, the meeting broke up with the decision to try to finish wearing out the school floor with the customary dances.[18]

In July, 1916, the report came that the school in another district had been opened at last, after having been a bone of contention between opposing factions for four years.[19]

The U.F.A. locals also had problems. In January, 1915, a member of the Hanna local wrote to the paper:

The word "United" seems a little misplaced when applied to our Local. We are only "United" in our determination to stay away from the Union meetings.

At the annual meeting not a quarter of the members were present, and there were less at the last meeting. This is not as it should be. Anyone

[17]*Ibid.*, Dec. 30, 1915.   [18]*Ibid.*, Jan. 28, 1915.
[19]*Ibid.*, July 20, 1916.

treating a trades union in the way we farmers treat our union, would get into trouble, yet the trades union would cost five or six times as much and would not bring any more benefits. Why is it that farmers are the only body of men who find it hard to work together? The U.F.A. has already done much to improve the conditions of farming and if we would only give it our loyal support, it would be able to do much more. The farmer is generally a busy man and sometimes finds it hard to attend a meeting, but at this time of the year we have not that excuse.

A sale, social or dance would likely bring more of us out. Although the fee is only a dollar, it may be that money is scarce with some of us but it will be scarcer if the U.F.A. should go under. Let us see if we can make a better showing this year. We must not think that when we have paid our dollar we have done all. Our presence at the meetings is necessary if we are to get the best out of our Union. Any farmer may attend the meeting, whether a member or not, and if he does not want to join, no one is going to make him.[20]

But on the whole by 1920 the rural communities around Hanna seemed to be thriving. Most needs of the population were being taken care of within some form of organization. Participation in local associations led to participation and leadership in organizations of wider scope. Such participation and assumption of tasks of leadership were important in making life seem worth while, in both material and non-material respects, and in creating optimism about the future.

The long droughts of the 1920's and 1930's had disastrous repercussions, however. Financial stringencies made people over-cautious in their daily activities and in their plans for the future. Many people left the area. This made it hard for those who stayed to get together, and depleted the human resources of the organizations as well as the financial resources. Informal social life was crippled. As a direct result of drought, the lake which had been a pleasant resort for picnics, sports, and dances, dried up. Cars and telephones could not be operated. Knowledge of the embarrassment which hostesses felt when they had no food to offer made people diffident about visiting. Lack of suitable clothing kept both men and women at home. Rural municipalities could not collect taxes because of the abandonment of land and the extreme poverty of the people who remained. School districts were similarly handicapped. School houses closed. Churches foundered. Even U.F.A. locals lapsed, in spite of a few energetic supporters who held that "now, more than at any time, it is necessary for the farmers to stand together and fight for their rights, which they have been denied."[21] The good crops of 1923 and of 1927 and 1928 interrupted the decline only slightly. The improved morale and

---

[20]*Ibid.*, Jan. 28, 1915.
[21]*Ibid.*, Jan. 2, 1919. See also *ibid.*, Jan. 16, 1919.

improved circumstances of some residents and a backsurge of migration were offset by the departure of people who, though thoroughly disillusioned, previously could not afford to move. It was also offset by the increasing numbers and the segregation of the German-Russians.

Many who left were able people, whose departure was a great loss to the rural communities. Although in the early bad years it was the people unsuited for settlement, the "crackpots" and the unstable, who moved, in the late twenties and the thirties it was the young people, especially the single men and the married couples with growing families. Talking of the thirties, a pioneer said:

Well now, the big things to make men move out was the young people. And the wives, too. Bachelors stayed, or at least a lot of them. It gets a man in the end, mind, to hear his wife and children always nagging at him to leave. It wasn't just the poor crops, or even the prices going down to nineteen and a half cents or twenty cents a bushel for wheat. With help from the government a man could last through the bad years. But the young people couldn't see any future here, and the women—well, hard times were hard for them to bear.

Parents encouraged their children to leave, because they were discontented with dry-belt life and aware that to pass on a drought-afflicted farm to a son was not to provide him with the means for earning a good living, or because they felt that farming was "no life for a woman." Whereas in an earlier day the most active young people migrated to the frontier, now they went from the prairie West to the cities or to other rural regions.[22] Of those who stayed behind, few had the breadth of outlook of the first settlers. Some were completely uninterested in community affairs.

In the upper age groups many capable men stayed on. Sheer hopelessness and inability to meet the expense of moving were not the only reasons for remaining. Some men had family ties in the area. Some were reluctant to leave the country they had pioneered. Others were

[22]Marjory Harrison felt sure this was true generally: "Canada is facing what has been described as a farm problem of the first magnitude, and one that is of the greatest importance from the standpoint of the whole nation. Already the effects of the bad conditions are being seen. Agriculture generally does not provide a living satisfactory to young Canadians. The best of the young men and women brought up on the farms realize that there are other callings that will pay them far better. In the old days it was the best and finest who faced the hardship and dangers of the early settlements, hoping for reasonable gain for themselves and their children. Today their children and grandchildren are realizing that the game has not been worth the candle. They are of the same fine type, possessing as much courage and capacity for hard work as their forbears. But the spirit of adventure, which is the will to success, is drawing them to the cities, and all too frequently to the cities of the United States. This is an incalculable loss to Canadian farming." Harrison, Go West—Go Wise! pp. 130-1.

less destitute than their neighbours because they happened to have slightly better land, or could foresee the possibility of large-scale farming and sheep-raising. A few stayed because they were in positions which made them responsible for getting aid for their fellow-farmers. The problem then was not altogether that the community leaders moved. It was that since there were few fit successors for these men they had to continue their activities as they grew older or see the community organizations lapse, and that some, embittered by repeated failures, became unwilling to work for improvements they might not live to see.

The rural municipalities suffered greatly from the occurrence of factional disputes, the reluctance of able men to run for office, and the apathy of ratepayers. A farmer explained:

> The truth of the matter is that there are a lot of petty personalities in local politics. Able men don't get nominated because somebody's always a little bit envious, or because they lose interest in what seems just a lot of squabbling. There's always someone who hasn't any ability but who likes the idea of office—I don't know why, I suppose it makes him feel important or something—and he's willing to flatter a lot of other fools, so they'll elect him. They don't feel envious of him, and he makes them feel important. And if a local man is elected he gets sick of a lot of complaints from people, and won't run a second time.

As their difficulties of personnel and of finance increased the municipalities restricted their activities as much as possible, sought government aid, or were reduced to local improvement districts. Then, at the end of the twenties, a radical innovation was made in the administration of the drought-stricken parts of Alberta. In 1927 the Special Area of Tilley East was formed, to the south of Hanna. The innovation proved successful, and in the thirties additional Special Areas were created, which included all of the rural parts of the Hanna area.

The special municipal areas are large units, including several rural municipalities or local improvement districts, administered by appointees of the provincial Government rather than by elected local councils. At first there were four Special Areas in the Hanna region, in each of which there was a field man who had the rights and duties of the municipal district councils, including some policy-making powers. A Special Areas Board at Hanna to whom the men were responsible also had wide powers, though nominally it was controlled by the Department of Municipal Affairs. In 1939 the powers of the field men and the Board were somewhat decreased. The municipal districts within the areas were abolished, and the former four areas in the Hanna district reduced to two—the Sullivan Lake–Berry Creek Special Area and the Sounding Creek–Neutral Hills Area. The Special

Areas Board was retained, and offices were set up at Hanna and Oyen, each with a field man and a chief clerk. Nominal supervision by the Department of Municipal Affairs was replaced by actual control by the Department of Lands and Mines.

Under the Special Areas Board local government in the Hanna area has been more solvent. The Board has improved the financial situation by the use of funds not available to the old municipalities, by economies resulting from centralization, and by measures for the rehabilitation of the individual farmer. The last, by improving the farmer's financial status, enable him to contribute to the costs of local government. An old settler said of what had been done: "The Special Areas did great work in this country, great work. People came here to farm just like they'd been used to farming. Some of 'em had never farmed. Anyway, they farmed the wrong way for this country. The Special Areas took over after the country had pretty well gone broke, that's what happened—and they took over with the people remaining here." Another farmer echoed his words, giving an extreme instance of over-grazing which the Special Areas Board had remedied and adding that the Board "did a lot for water conservation."

Of course, outside forces as well as Board policies have led to improvement in the financial condition of the area. The war has brought a substantial increase in the price of wheat. Some people argue that the effect of the war has far outweighed the effect of administrative changes. A farmer strongly in favour of local self-government asserted:

The old field men were efficient but the Special Areas Board is as muddle-headed as anyone can be. The truth of the matter is that it has no power. I'm not belittling the Special Areas Board at all when I say that the world situation put us back on our feet. It's nothing but the war. A farmer today has got to pay attention to what's happening in Ottawa, and not just Ottawa. Don't think I'm not stretching this bald head of mine in the attempt to figure what's going on in the world. I think it's important. Why, people in Europe will be starving next winter because we had two weeks without rain. Every farmer around here will tell you that. What the blamed fools won't see is that things happening in Europe affect them.

To the degree that improvements are due to the war, they may be temporary.

However successful the Special Areas Board has been financially, it has accentuated certain social problems. One of its aims is to diminish the population to the numbers that can subsist in the area, and in carrying out that aim it has weakened local community organization. The rural communities have been made less stable both indirectly and directly by Board action. The indirect effect of the

Special Areas Board policies has been to lessen the security which farmers feel in land ownership. The Board's insistence on leasing rather than selling land, on making short rather than long-term leases, and on breaking up very large holdings has weakened the bonds of the farmer with the community. This has increased mobility and decreased interest in local affairs.

The Special Areas Board has more directly decreased the stability of the local community by taking from the farmers control of their own affairs. The only function assigned to elected representatives within the Special Areas is advisory. On a recommendation made by delegates of municipal units just before the units were dissolved, an elected advisory committee was set up in 1939 to meet with the Special Areas Board.[23] The committee is usually deprecated as powerless.[24] It can only advise the Board which in turn can only make recommendations to the Department of Lands and Mines. The farmers therefore have no real self-government.

Loss of local control means at some point inefficiencies through failure to take into account the peculiarities of a particular area. The farmers cannot make themselves heard by men who feel that their primary responsibilities are to the provincial Government. One farmer said:

I said something a while ago about representatives getting too far away—I don't mean just physically—from the people they are supposed to represent. I said that to a field man at a meeting once and he had to

[23]*Hanna Herald*, March 30, 1939.

[24]The District Agriculturist located in the drought area, who attends the joint sessions of the Board and committee, gave one of the few opinions received to the contrary: "The suggestions the advisory committee makes are usually pretty good. There's some shrewd heads on that committee. They're not afraid to ask for what they want, either. They think up, oh, things about roads in certain places. I remember one meeting that was a real row. It was about a big lease in the Bow West Area. A fellow'd had a big lease for a number of years and he'd put a lot of improvements on it. Anyway, his lease expired and instead of renewing it they broke it up into a couple of smaller ones—well, still pretty big ones. He raised a squawk, naturally, and the advisory committee were expected to either support the Minister's decision or recommend that the lease be continued for the original lease. Well, there was a row over that. One chap from up north of here, he was all for the big lease being continued. He's got a lease himself with a few improvements—he's paid for dugout, one or two things—and he was starting to worry a little about the idea of leases expiring and not being renewed after improvements had been put in. So he was dead against changing that Bow West lease. The Deputy Minister of Municipal Affairs got so excited he was voting with the committee-men. It's only the committee-men who can vote—you see, the others can discuss, but they're not supposed to vote. The Minister sat there listening to it all, and when they were voting he said, 'Mr. Chairman, there are people here that have no business voting.' The Deputy Minister remembered himself then."

agree with me, that although he thought of himself as working for the farmers, he was really responsible to the Department of Lands and Mines, and so far from the farmers they didn't have any voice in his work. He can take advice from them, but what good is that when the government has to O.K. everything before he can do it?

The loss of control also means a feeling of insecurity. The people are afraid that Special Areas Board funds will be diverted to other purposes than those for which they are intended. The general opinion was expressed by a farmer:

The people in the Special Areas aren't secure. They haven't any protection from the government at all. Now, in the municipality the provincial government is prevented by law from interfering. The people have protection. But in the Special Areas they're just simply at the mercy of the government, if it has any mercy. The only way they can get back at all is at elections. The members from around the Special Areas are Social Credit members—cabinet members, too—and they know they have to look after their votes. If the members from here weren't cabinet members, and weren't Social Credit, the people would really be on the spot in the Special Areas.

Further, the dissolution of the municipal councils has closed channels through which local leaders could be developed to help the community to adjust to crises. The present form of administration gives no such chance for either participation or well-informed observation as the old municipalities gave. Even in the advisory committee, farmers are asked by the Board merely to criticize a policy which is drawn up and ready to be put into practice, or one already carried out. They do not really have political freedom and responsibility. The present members of the advisory committee gained experience in the rural municipalities; the committee can probably secure and maintain influence only while its members come to it with such experience.

A farmer summed up the problem, in discussing the larger school divisions as well as the special municipal areas. It was a loss to democracy, he said, whenever control of their own affairs was taken from the people, and vested in the state. With local self-government, people were selected and trained in small units for service in wider spheres. The units of local government were the proving-grounds for leaders in a community. Centralization destroyed democracy. This was especially true since civil servants constantly tried to extend their powers at the expense of local officials. To abolish the self-governing bodies was to threaten the whole democracy.

Special Areas residents submit to the present arrangement more gracefully than they otherwise would because some of them believe that it is a temporary measure. They are convinced that self-government will ultimately be restored.

Already slackening interest and decreasing ability in local government can be noted. A dry-belt lawyer said of the farmers that "the government has to wipe their noses for them now," and a farmer remarked: "I tell you, it's made me sick to see the people just leave everything to the Special Areas [Board]. They don't realize that they ought to be helping themselves. Their initiative has simply died from lack of use. The older men forget, and the young ones aren't learning to run their own local affairs. There's absolutely no training for the young people. If this keeps up for long we'll all be like sheep."

But apathy was one reason for the creation of the Special Areas administration, and hence cannot be considered to be wholly a consequence of the abolition of local self-government. Beyond this, the limited power of local councils leads to lack of interest in them in many communities. Also in the dried-out wheat-farming lands economic problems get more attention than political problems. Concern with government is largely concern with its economic aspects. Therefore the Dominion government, which can regulate freight rates, wheat prices, and tariffs on machinery is of more interest than local government. But the Special Areas Board has played a part in increasing the indifference.

The problem of education was more difficult than that of local government. In the small school districts, interested and able trustees became hard to obtain as people grew poor and moved away in the 1920's and 1930's. Of the first annual convention of school trustees of the Hanna Inspectorate, held in 1926, the newspaper reported:

School trustees of the Hanna Inspectorate are in convention here today. While there are 159 school districts within this inspectorate, there were approximately only 40 delegates present, which is somewhat disappointing to those who are responsible for bringing the convention into being.

However, the delegates who attended today are the leaders in educational work. It is regrettable that more of the school districts could not see their way clear to send one delegate. But perhaps the forty odd who were here this week can do as much as the one hundred and fifty-nine.[25]

The next year the headline for the report announced that the attendance was even lower than in 1926.[26]

The apathy in the community generally is shown by two items of local news from a district northeast of Hanna, which appeared less than a month apart early in 1930:

January opens up the question of rural schools and the usual train of difficulties that follows such a system. Within the next few days, between now and Wednesday, January 15, Hiram alone will have to elect about seventeen trustees, and even at that there will still be twice as many holding

---

[25]*Hanna Herald*, Nov. 18, 1926.   [26]*Ibid.*, Nov. 10, 1927.

office. Is it possible to find in our district fifty men who will specialize in education and its needs? Is it not more probable that it would be easier to get a quarter as many who will have the necessary qualities that go to make up the good trustee? The season permits of the different factions bringing on their favorite candidate for office, and saying the very least for the times, it provides an interest, even if it does leave a tinge of antagonism on its trail. Boarding the teacher—hauling the coal—teaching the higher grades— and the school commencement—all suggest real items for thought, that can be forgotten after the fifteenth.[27]

The Peace Valley School District Trustees are the same as last year. At the annual meeting there were only four residents in attendance—three trustees and one other.[28]

There also occurred in the school districts the sort of friction frequent in a small community, where feuds between neighbours over a straying cow or a broken fence can lead to deadlocks over school business. Such difficulties, added to financial straits, sometimes led to the dissolution of the local boards and their replacement by official trustees, appointed by the provincial Department of Education. The official trustee was frequently the school inspector. If so, he would not then be checked and guided in his chief duties by representatives of the community.

It became impossible to collect school taxes. In 1931 forty schools in the Hanna Inspectorate required special government aid to remain open.[29] There was a great deterioration in the quality of school build- ings and equipment. The annual report of the Alberta Department of Education for 1935 quoted the inspector located at Hanna as saying, of the schools in the eastern half of his area: "The majority of these schools present the appearance of weather beaten desertion. The teacher has nothing to work with except a scarred and cracked black- board, some chalk and what material her ingenuity can improvise."[30] Libraries and other facilities became fewer and fewer, and so low in calibre as to be of little use.

Capable teachers also were hard to secure and hold when salaries were cut perilously low, and frequently went unpaid for long periods. Teacherages, which increasingly had to be provided as population declined, were obtained as cheaply as possible. Usually they were small, crude, and almost unfurnished. At the same time living condi- tions generally in the dry belt were becoming less and less attractive to young adults. The consequence was a decline in the quality of teachers and in the continuity of teacher service.

[27]Ibid., Jan. 16, 1930.   [28]Ibid., Feb. 6, 1930.
[29]Ibid., Oct. 29, 1931.
[30]Thirtieth Annual Report of the Department of Education of the Province of Alberta, 1935, p. 49.

The financial difficulties regarding equipment and staff had grievous effects upon the quality of education. Schools began to teach fewer grades, to shorten the school year, and to close down. At the same time, the demands made upon teachers and equipment increased. The need for high schools grew acute as the first native generation completed grade school.[31] The task of educating increasing numbers of students from homes where the English language was not spoken nor English ways known was especially heavy.[32] In addition, soon after the immigration of the German-Russians in the late twenties epidemics of disease apparently brought from overseas occurred in the schools.

The sparseness of the population made the maintenance of schools within walking distance of the children's homes difficult. Having no school near was particularly burdensome for younger children and for those in poor health. At least one death was attributed to the strain of a long journey to school.[33] Many could not attend school until they

[31]Mrs. Strange, living northwest of the drought area, said in a newspaper article that there were enough public schools in the province, although some children had to travel long distances to school, but that the shortage of high schools was serious. When children completed the eighth grade, they had either to leave school altogether or to go to high school in a near-by town. The former course was frequently taken, because the country people could not meet the expense and inconvenience of sending the child away. There were in the province sixty-eight consolidated schools and one or two rural high schools, but these were far too few to meet the need. She wrote: "There are some high priced, though excellent, boarding schools in the west to which the more prosperous farmer may send his children, but the great majority of farmers cannot stand the 'racket' and have to compromise by sending them into town, to board with strangers, in order that they may attend the nearest high school. I have found from experience that the lack of parental discipline and home associations have far more disastrous results than has the lack of an education." Hanna Herald, Aug. 27, 1925. Cf. ibid., Aug. 18, 1927.

[32]The extent of the problem was noted in the Hanna Herald, July 16, 1931: "In a survey of the children examined in the rural schools of the Hanna Municipal Hospital District, during the recent clinic, it was ascertained that a very large percentage of these children were of foreign extraction. In fact, it may be of some interest and the cause of some surprise to note that MORE THAN ONE OUT OF EVERY THREE children in the rural schools has been born on foreign soil.

"Not including those from the United States as being 'foreign,' the following figures show the proportion of foreign children attending rural, village and town schools in the Hanna Municipal Hospital District.

Schools	Enrolment	Foreign
Rural	1503	581
Craigmyle	101	14
Hanna	436	27

"These figures indicate a real responsibility upon this community, in order that this large percentage of foreign blood may be properly assimilated and educated to become true promoters and defenders of Canadian ideals, and not merely 'foreigners' whose domicile is in the Dominion."

[33]Ibid., April 12, 1945.

were past the usual age for starting, or could attend only irregularly. The hardships were especially great in winter. In severely cold weather, even children who were driven to school suffered greatly.

Remedy was sought through enlargement of the administrative unit. Consolidation of schools was discussed, and even attempted, at an early date. It was commented upon in the Hanna paper in 1914. The most outstanding and long-lived consolidated school in the drought area is one established in 1916. In spite of several periods of severe financial distress and an ebbing of the consolidation movement throughout the province, it has survived and in recent years bettered its position. The setting-up of centralized rural high schools, through the co-operation of three or four districts which retained separate elementary schools under the jurisdiction of local boards, was also tried.

The major innovation in the field of educational organization was the larger school unit or "division," introduced throughout Alberta in the thirties. In the Hanna area most of the rural high schools and centralized schools developed within the large divisions.

The plan for the introduction of the larger units was first expounded by the Hon. Perrin Baker, Minister of Education, in the late twenties. A newspaper account of his address at a convention of the trustees of the Hanna Inspectorate indicates the nature of the innovation, the situation it was devised to meet, and the expected consequences. Mr. Baker claimed that the problem of rural education was threefold: the provision of enough schools, the division of the financial burden of supporting them, and the improvement of the training provided in them. Both elementary and high school training had to be provided, and the schools had to be open for a full term. Equalization grants were inadequate to meet the problem. What was needed was the formation of larger units of administration, in which the existing school districts would be retained, but grouped into 20 divisions of about 150 districts each. A divisional board, divided into five wards, would be elected by the same people who chose school trustees, at the annual meetings of the school districts. The old districts would retain all powers except the placing of teachers and the setting of salary schedules. The divisional board would engage the teachers and a superintendent for each division, with possibly two assistants. The superintendent would make recommendations for the staffing of the schools, and dissatisfied teachers or school districts would be able to appeal to the divisional board. Each board would have its own budget. The taxing unit might be either the division or the province as a whole. If the division was the unit, the divisional board would set salary schedules; if the province as a whole, a general provincial board would perform this task. Mr. Baker felt that the province as a whole should be made the taxing unit in order to equalize salaries, to give stronger borrowing powers to each division, and to prevent local conditions such as drought or crop failure from seriously affecting the schools. He summed up the advantages to accrue from the larger unit: "There will be no short term schools, teachers' salaries will be regular, a salary schedule will be possible, which will recognize scholarship, experience and efficiency, the burden of the costs will be equalized, secondary education will be developed by the erection of further high schools at the in-between points, and teaching will be made a better job. The proposed system will respond to measures designed to improve conditions."[34]

The larger unit encountered strenuous opposition. Although Department of Education officials carried on an intensive campaign, the Hanna Trustees' Association rejected the proposals for innovation repeatedly, after acrimonious disputes, from 1926 onward. The resolutions passed at the 1929 convention suggested the chief objections. It stated that "the proposed new School Act would, in its operation, entail the creation of much unnecessary and expensive machinery, and . . . would be a curtailment in the democratic control of the rural schools."[35] The U.F.A. locals also opposed Mr. Baker's plan, although the Acadia federal constituency convention endorsed it in 1929.[36]

In 1933, in spite of lack of support not only in the east-central area but throughout the province, the Department of Education set up a large unit as an experiment. The region chosen was in the Hanna Inspectorate, south of the town of Hanna. Of sixty-seven school districts brought into the unit, only twenty-one had been able to operate.[37] The financial success of the scheme was immediate. For the district involved, the cost of operation of schools for the fiscal year 1933, during which the new programme was in effect for only the last four months, was $37,000. In 1934 the cost, including extraordinary expenses for the moving of schools and the setting up of dormitories, was $23,395. The estimate for 1935 was $21,000.[38] Within a few years, and before public opinion had fully accepted the measure, the provincial Department of Education felt warranted in introducing the larger unit on a wide scale. In the Hanna area Acadia School Division No. 8 and Sullivan Lake School Division No. 9 were functioning by 1937, and Neutral Hills School Division No. 16 began operation the following year.

[34]*Ibid.*, Nov. 15, 1928.   [35]*Ibid.*, Oct. 31, 1929.
[36]*Ibid.*, July 25, 1929.   [37]*Ibid.*, April 27, 1933.
[38]*Ibid.*, Jan. 31, 1935.

The larger division had advantages in economy and in freedom from local feuds and local apathy. An early comment of the *Hanna Herald* on the larger units was:

Editor Horton, of the Vegreville Observer, devotes a column to criticism of the new educational policy as it is being presented to the people of Alberta by Hon. Perrin E. Baker, Minister of Education, and doesn't think that "the multiplying of boards will tend to simplicity." Don't worry. When the Divisional Board gets started exercising its jurisdiction the local boards will make about as much noise as a Jew's harp in a jazz band. It's about time the most of them were muzzled, anyway, and no one realizes this better than the present Minister, who has also served his apprenticeship on these small units of the present system. There is a great deal to be said about this matter, but it is of little use to say it. The mills are grinding—slowly, but surely. More power to the Minister.[39]

The prophecy proved correct. In many school districts in the Hanna area an official trustee has been appointed to replace the local board, and regulations were in prospect in 1946 to make it possible for the boards to consist of only one man. Where the small boards remain, they have little prestige or work. The remarks of an inspector are suggestive. Asked about a certain man, he said:

He's on the local board here. Most people haven't any use for him. He wasn't on the school board before the division was formed. He's just been on it lately. He never got into anything before. When the school board was of some importance, nobody would elect him. Now he's got an office at last and he makes himself obnoxious. He's just a busybody. He's no leader. He hasn't anybody's support at all—he isn't worth it. He comes into the office now and then to peer over my shoulder. It's not because there's something he wants to do. It's just inquisitiveness. . . .

You know, in most of these districts there isn't a local board—the kind he's on—any longer. The people just don't bother to elect members because there isn't anything for the local board to do. I'm sole trustee in most cases. That's because in quite a few school districts—this was before the division— the small board just gave up. They couldn't collect enough money in taxes to carry on with. In those cases the provincial government financed the school, and the inspector was made trustee with the responsibility of operating the school again. When the division was formed quite a number of the districts had the inspector for their trustee. Since then others have done that, and more have just stopped having a trustee at all.

The bringing in of the larger unit has reduced the number of elected administrators in the field of education, but on the other hand, unlike the Special Areas Board, the board for the school division is elected. The new arrangement therefore does not remove self-government, but merely increases the size of the unit of self-government.[40]

[39]*Ibid.*, Nov. 22, 1928.

[40]The counterpart of the larger school division in local government is not the Special Area but the larger municipal unit which has been established throughout Alberta except in the Special Areas.

That its advantages outweigh its disadvantages in this respect is seen in the discussion of an ardent exponent of local self-government. After stating that the big school division meant a loss of control over the trustees, he admitted:

But there is one good thing, the men who act as trustees aren't bothered with small complaints that haven't any real basis. And the men who ran for trustee here all were able men, I think. The jobs got too big for those trustees who used to get on the small boards sometimes. I think probably there are more good men to choose from, so membership on the board isn't likely to be a vested interest, like it used to be sometimes. Then there are other things to be said for the divisional board. They have a full time secretary, which I think is a good idea. They can work with the school inspector, too. Of course they may just tag along with him but I don't believe it's likely to happen. For one thing there's sure to be a man with the ability to do his own thinking on the board. Besides the viewpoint of the board is generally so different from the inspector's viewpoint, that while they can co-operate, the board isn't likely to run in leading strings.

A member of the divisional board pointed out that "in a little district the secretary is just some joe, but this way the secretary and the inspector are sort of experts like a civil service and we correspond to the legislature."

The advantages and disadvantages of the larger unit may be gauged by comparing a consolidated school district within the drought area and the school division to which the country around it belongs. A consolidated school district was founded by an agreement among five rural school districts and the village of Chinook. The three-room school is in the village, and the children are brought in to it by vans. The school district collects its own taxes, and in addition receives a provincial grant. Although at one point it had a debt of $14,000, it has recovered from the depression well. It has no trouble in collecting the taxes on private lands although the rate is higher than in the school division. The difficulty is in collecting the taxes on the land— 180 quarters out of a total of 270—which has reverted to the Special Areas Board and is leased for grazing or for cultivating. The school board receives a percentage of the amount paid by the leaseholder to the government, but when the crop is under five bushels per acre nothing is paid. The teaching in the school is excellent, in part at least because the school district pays the teachers regularly. The inspector has lauded the work of the pupils. They have done well on departmental examinations and at university. The equipment is better than average, especially in the science department.[41]

[41]The high-school principal wrote a thesis on the teaching of science, including the devising and use of laboratory equipment, and directed the making of much of the apparatus in the school.

The people are proud of the school. Some childless farmers object to the taxes, but those with children are unwilling to exchange their school system for the less costly one of the division. A resident of the district explained:

We think we have an excellent school here. The vans are one of the best features of the consolidated, I would say. The children can go to a good school, a larger school, and still be home every night. We like that because it means that our children aren't away from home in dormitories where the supervision is often not good, and if they are needed to help at home it means they can help and go to school as well. You see the advantages.

We like to think that this is our school. We run it ourselves and we can make changes. It's under our own control. Now if there was a dormitory here we wouldn't be in such close touch with the school. The children would simply be gone for the winter, and school would never seem to have anything to do with us old folks, but with the consolidated we make the school our business.

The weakness in the consolidated school district is that much of its merit depends on the whole-hearted devotion of its secretary. He is a former school-teacher who homesteaded in the area in order to pay for a university course. He did not go to university, but has retained his zeal for education. He spends much time on school business, while his sons manage his large farm. In a report of a meeting of the school board, an observer wrote of him:

Throughout the meeting he entirely dominated the trustees. The creakiness in his voice, the nervousness, and the obvious care in choosing words which had characterized him in conversation the night before were gone. His voice was clear, his manner confident, his speech fluent. Chinook Consolidated School District No. 16 is the darling of his heart. He has all the statistics off by heart and is delighted at a chance to reel them off. He is on an advisory committee to the Special Areas Board and is secretary of Chinook village, yet neither of these things rank in his affections with the consolidated school.[42]

His neighbours corroborate the impression that it is he who is responsible for the welfare of the consolidated school. An interviewer remarked to a teacher concerning another man, who had been active on the school board, "I've got an idea that he's one of the reasons why the consolidated school has continued to survive." The reply was, "I guess he is. Of course the real reason is the secretary. He's the driving force behind everything. The other chap's one of the few who has helped instead of just folding up and letting him do it all." The board member, when interviewed, also emphasized the part that the secretary played: "You listen to the secretary or the school principal

[42]Field notes.

and they'll tell you all about what a wonderful school it is and how the whole community is behind it. Well, that's all very well as far as it goes. But if ——— didn't put most of his time into seeing that the service was good nobody would support the school. They aren't sold on education here any more than anywhere else."

In the larger school unit, Acadia School Division No. 8, the taxes are lower and the service, for many regions, poorer. In Oyen the schools are good, but there has been difficulty in securing suitable supervisors for the dormitory. The rural schools are frequently small, crowded, and ill equipped. One was described in these terms:

> The school proved to be a tiny white building with a barn and teacherage in the yard and another school building which had been moved perched on skids beside it, waiting to be painted, put on a foundation, and generally made fit to use. The little building in use was absolutely packed with thirteen pupils. There was not enough room between the seats or before the blackboard. The stove was right in a corner with a desk catching its ashes. The walls were covered with a few maps, a couple of pictures, and the children's jackets hung from nails. The door opened inward unless someone was using the pencil sharpener: then it did not open. The library was off in one corner. It consisted of three shelves, half of it industrial pamphlets and such-like. About one-third of the books were along the line of Botsford's *History of England* and the *Book of Knowledge*, of which latter there were two volumes. The only new books were a few elementary textbooks.

Teachers, or even people to aid the children in completing correspondence courses, are hard to find. In some cases, the only possible helpers are young girls who cannot control the children. In others, the helpers belong to families which are on bad terms with others in the community, and their appointment leads to the attempted withdrawal of youngsters from school.

On the other hand, at meetings of the division board the members deal ably with the problems that face them. They are capable, sincere, and conscientious, subject to the domination of no single man. Theirs is a bigger job than that of the consolidated school board, and they are equal to it. This is not because interest is keener in the division than in the consolidated school district but because the division has a larger constituency from which to draw its board members.

The larger school unit is more effective in coping with the educational problems in the drought area than the small school district, but it does not solve them. In 1946 the secretary of one of the large divisions indicated that the apathy which was partly responsible for the change in policy has not decreased. He told of travelling forty miles to a scheduled meeting and having no one turn up, and of having only eight present at another meeting, four of them trustees. In at least three instances in his division, official trustees had recently been appointed to replace the local board of three because of lack of interest. It may even be that as in rural municipal government the innovations in educational organization have increased the apathy. One thoughtful farmer argued that the large division took school management farther away from the people, so that they were inclined to take it for granted. "People have to be made to do their own thinking," he said. "They won't consider a problem their own if it isn't dumped on their doorstep."

The larger school unit has also not solved the problem of securing fit teachers. As the units have become solvent, the salaries offered have increased, but at the same time other occupations than teaching have become more remunerative. The division has merely been able to place the short supply of teachers, many of whom are inadequately trained, to better advantage than was possible under the old system.

It was frequently said before the larger divisions were formed that they might solve certain community problems by placing in the schools teachers able to give community leadership. This has not been the case. The typical rural school teacher since the depression has been a young girl recently out of Normal School. Possibly she came from a farm, possibly from a city high school; in either case her range of experience is not wide. She moves frequently, with matrimony or a town school as her goal. She is often isolated, living in a teacherage because no farmhouse is near enough or large enough to give her a room. Less usual are the young men using teaching as a stepping-stone to the university, housewives who formerly taught and resume the occupation so that a local school need not be closed, and elderly men with English university degrees. Some teachers do take a leading part in the community, organizing plays and dances, picnics, and Red Cross groups. Others are active, but in a manner not to the liking of the "respectable" part of the community. For example, one high-school teacher encouraged parties in the school at which there was much drinking, and staged plays the practices for which took up a large amount of school time, although the students received no credits for participation. The majority of the teachers do not afford leadership. The assistant secretary-treasurer of a school division, asked if teachers played a part in community affairs, replied: "Some of them do. It just depends. You know if a young girl is put away out there, where you have to drive forty miles to a dance, it's pretty hard on her, and she can't do much. But some of them, where people are closer together, do quite a bit. It depends on where they are."[43]

[43]The experiences of a woman who boarded the teacher for a school near Hanna in the thirties indicate how completely some teachers failed to provide

Nor does the larger unit solve fully the problem created by the closing of school houses during the depression. It can aid only by moving schools to the most convenient locations and by installing dormitory and van systems. It has even been said that the distance between the trustees and the community served has resulted in closures which might otherwise not have occurred. The closing of schools has been a factor in the migration of people for whom education is an important value, either to towns and cities or to agricultural regions which had better school facilities. It has also weakened local community integration by removing community centres. The dwindling population no longer has a place for frequent friendly intercourse. Even when meetings continue to be held, they are frequently held at a greater distance, and in a trading centre, where they must compete with stores, movies, pool halls, and dance halls. Thus there are no longer so many gatherings in which almost the whole community takes part. The closing of local schools has contributed to the decline, though it is not the sole cause.

Religious organizations collapsed during the drought and depression years. The activities of the churches in the rural communities were seriously curtailed, though to some extent the social welfare services were expanded. Churches were closed or reduced to mission status. Ministers were withdrawn or forced to extend their field of service widely. In the denominations which became the United Church of Canada there were in 1920 seven ordained ministers between Hanna and the Saskatchewan border, as well as the Hanna minister and two students in the summer, whereas in 1946 there was only one ordained United Church minister besides the Hanna man and one student.[44]

leadership. Four had stayed with her. The first she described as "very nice." The second, an eighteen-year-old, "got in with a very tough crowd" as soon as she arrived, the tough crowd including a farmer whom the girl eventually married, a single farm woman who was "going with" a married man, and a married woman who was "going with" a single man. The third teacher was "man-crazy": "She wanted to have people think all the men were after her, so she'd have them all come over on Sunday afternoons." The fourth was miserly, and kept protesting at having to pay twenty dollars a month for her room and board. Regarding the teachers at the rural high school in the same district, another farmer's wife, a former teacher, had only slightly more favourable comments to make.

[44]The Superintendent of Home Missions for the Alberta Conference of the United Church, who had charges in east-central Alberta for many years, wrote: "We wanted the church to stay with these people and, although it was no easy job, there were men prepared to do this, and the church strained the resources of the Board of Home Missions to help them stay. The people who moved out were very often those who supported the church with their presence and their gifts so that the local support in the bad years was very small and the scattered families made it difficult to gather a congregation of any size. With the reduction

Sometimes the student ministers, coming from the East, had difficulty in adjusting. An occurrence in Saskatchewan was cited in the Hanna paper, indicating local interest in such incidents and antagonism both to the church and the East:

A young student minister from Victoria College, Toronto, was assigned by the United Church to a district in Southern Saskatchewan for the summer months. The . . . town he was located in . . . is right in the heart of the drought area. Two weeks after arriving there the young man was on his way back east. He said nobody wanted him except maybe a Chinese restaurant keeper and that the people seemed to have lost faith and were not much interested in "hearing the gospel from a new man."

We would like to be fair to young Mr. ――― but we are inclined to the belief that prairie people even in the heart of the dried-out area in southern Saskatchewan, are not the irreligious infidels which he pictures. The prairie country is a tough land to live in. Nature is hard and cruel and people get somewhat hardened and fibres coarsened as a consequence. Our country isn't all "dolled up" like the east, with trees and foliage and flowers. We have to face the sweep of the elements and the vicissitudes of the weather.

But in the hearts of prairie people still live those enduring faiths taught in childhood days. The exteriors may be hardened and calloused but who is there to tell what is going on in that hazy region we call the soul? We like our people as they are but to a stranger, nurtured in a milder clime and with more of the nicer things of life, they may seem uncouth and forbidding.

Two weeks is a mighty short time within which to gauge a people's feeling. The explorers in the Arctic don't measure up the Eskimos in such a brief period of time. It is impossible to get a close contact with any person in a brief fortnight. It isn't fair.

Of course it is easier to be a Christian when life is soft and easy. It is hard to be so constantly frustrated as our prairie farmers' families have been for so long. It tends to discouragement and bitterness. Just the same we don't believe that conditions are as bad from a religious standpoint, among the prairie people, as portrayed by the young minister who came to . . . Saskatchewan, and stayed two weeks.[45]

People who had formerly attended churches "got out of the way of it" because their clothing did not seem suitable, and because they were unable to contribute as they once had or as they thought

---

in the church funds it was impossible to keep all the men there so that men worked two or three fields, spreading themselves out and doing what they could to bring some cheer and hope into the lives of the people. The population in the towns fell off as well so that the whole outlook was discouraging and, in many cases, the only man with hope in his speech was the minister. He was trying to run a car and feed and clothe a family on a salary that often did not total $1,000, although the Board of Home Missions tried to make it $1,250." Letter from Rev. Thomas Hart, Superintendent of Home Missions, Alberta Conference of the United Church of Canada, Aug. 23, 1946.

[45]*Hanna Herald,* July 22, 1937.

proper. A resident of Hanna who had grown up in a near-by rural area stressed lack of money as preventing her from attending church. "You don't like to belong to a church unless you can give as much as the others do, and in the church it's nothing but give, give all the time," she said. Since coming to town the woman has been one of the staunchest workers in the congregation to which she belongs. Even the Roman Catholic Church lost its hold on rural members. The Roman Catholics became almost as lax in church attendance as the Protestants. They were neither punctual nor regular in their church-going.

The most acceptable religious services were those of the evangelical sects, who sent representatives through the district and held camp meetings, and of radio evangelists. The latter could be heard in the home, and listening in cost less than driving to services. Moreover, while few rural districts had regular services, radio sermons could be heard every Sunday and even on week-days, and they were usually ably delivered: the most eminent and successful of the radio evangelists, William Aberhart of the Calgary Prophetic Bible Institute, was highly skilled as a speaker. The response to the radio services was extraordinary. Dried-out farmers went hungry so that they might send in contributions.

In recent years the radio church services and the sectarian groups have been falling off. Some of the sects moved into the town or village as they gained in strength, and thereby lost rural support. But even in the towns and villages they have declined with the falling off in the numbers of the jobless young men who made up part of their membership. There has been no revival of the older churches to compensate, and as a result the rural communities of the Hanna area are almost without religious organization. The immigrant communities are an exception. The importance of the church and the minister among the German-Russians brings out clearly the gap which the collapse of religious organization has left in the Anglo-Saxon districts.[46]

The U.F.A. during the worst depression years was in political office, and was economically active. This did not protect the locals in the Hanna area. Some stopped meeting. Others continued to meet but only through the activity and for the sake of a few individuals.

The breakdown of the locals coincided with a general weakening of the U.F.A. organization. A gulf developed between the leaders and the rank and file. The leaders had almost all been active farmers and

[46]Concerning Sublette, Kansas, E. H. Bell asserts that the churches "retain great importance" but later qualifies this: "Interviewing people in the country, one finds that the family attending at all regularly is rather rare. It is certain that the churches are not well supported financially." *Culture of a Contemporary Rural Community—Sublette, Kansas*, pp. 77, 86.

outstanding people in their communities. Now they were so busy with organizational work and other special tasks that they lost touch with their constituents. Some became members of Edmonton and Ottawa communities, rather than those of rural Alberta.

The economic field was the only one in which U.F.A. success was continuous. The co-operatives, apart from the wheat pools, were little injured by the depression, and they became the U.F.A.'s chief strength. Because of them the locals in the Hanna area kept more members than any other locals in the province. However, the economic activities to a certain extent hindered the social and political activities. They attracted people not genuinely interested in, or in some cases actively opposed to, the U.F.A.'s political programme, and they required a disproportionate share of the time and energy of the U.F.A. leaders.

The most spectacular result of the weakening of the U.F.A. was the withdrawal of support from it as a political party. Many farmers deserted in favour of Social Credit. As Aberhart, heading up the Social Credit crusade, moved into politics, he enlisted all the members of many rural communities in his audience. A district nurse located eighteen or twenty miles east of Hanna reported of the period from 1934 to 1937: "The whole countryside was composed of Prophetic Bible Institute fans. Those who did not believe in Aberhart listened out of curiosity to hear what he had to say next. This was during the time that he was promising twenty-five dollars a month to everybody and even the people who realized it was impossible would listen in order to hear his arguments. I think a few people would listen for the religious message that was given, but the majority listened for the political aspect or just curiosity."

Social Credit study groups between 1933 and 1935 quickly replaced the U.F.A. and U.F.W.A. groups on which they were modelled. They represented no reassertion of strength by the rank and file of the farming communities, however. Shortly after the election of August, 1935, most of the groups dissolved, except where a strong individual gave leadership. At the same time the U.F.A., having withdrawn from politics, became partly re-established as an educative and social organization. But its strength was gone, and the split between it and Social Credit accentuated the deterioration of rural community organization. The only organization which benefited from the split was the Women's Institute, which gained at the expense of the U.F.W.A. but did not come to equal it.

Informal social activities reflected the cleavage. U.F.A. and Social Credit partisanship was so strong that people of different allegiance, even if on adjacent farms in the sparsely settled countryside, stopped speaking to one another and "neighbouring." A farmer told of a man living near by who until 1935 had telephoned him several times a week and visited him frequently, but in eleven years after the rise of Social Credit telephoned only once, that time on urgent business. The split speeded the decline of the rural community so much that residents frequently use 1935 to mark the collapse of social organization. One man stated:

Nineteen thirty-five was the death of social and community organization. When Social Credit came to the fore in 1935 it destroyed social and community life. Today [1946] it is just beginning to come back. I do not mean to say that social organization was completely destroyed. There were a few places that weren't affected. They are places so isolated and self-contained that they're still as the others used to be. They have no movies, the mail comes in only once a week, and on mail day everybody comes into town. But almost everywhere there was a definite breakdown in 1935. There was a split, and it's just beginning to heal now.

Whereas in economic life, municipal government, and school organization a measure of readjustment to the Hanna area has been made, the replacement of the U.F.A. by Social Credit cannot be termed a successful adjustment. The only sign that adjustment may be near is a recent decline in bitterness between the two factions, and a willingness to resume personal relations interrupted in the early thirties.

Disorganization in the rural communities in the drought and depression years did not show itself only in the division between the U.F.A. and Social Credit. Something resembling class division developed. A few families of wealth, educational aspiration and achievement, and superior standards of housing came to stand apart from the rest of the community. Of sons of these families who went to university, a farmer said, "Oh, they come back and they talk to the people, they say hello and how are you, but that is all." Much came to be heard about members of the community who drank too much or took part in irregular sex behaviour. The weakness of rural organization was seen in the number of these people, and the degree to which they were tolerated though disapproved of. In general, drought and depression made interaction among people more difficult at the same time as the passing of the frontier made it less necessary, and the result was a much more loosely knit social fabric.

The high incidence of personal disorganization is the most grievous result of the breakdown of the rural community. Some of the cases have probably occurred among people who were unstable when they went west. The frontier attracts a disproportionate number of such people. However, social conditions also played a part.

Excessive drinking has been one form disorganization has taken.[47] Newspaper records indicate the prevalence of drunkenness and the unwritten lore of the district corroborates the records in rich detail. A minister said that he left wedding parties early because of the over-consumption of liquor at them. A large number of recipes for home brew are current.

More distressing is "prairie madness" or mental disease.[48] Many cases are reported in the newspapers and in travel books, and attributed to isolation, a lack of physical comforts, and drastic changes in living conditions.[49] Whereas excessive drinking is largely confined to the men, the reports suggest that the mental disease rate is especially high for the women.

Suicide, or suicide accompanied by murder, also has a high incidence. It is a striking indication of the weakness of group organization and of the violent fluctuations in economic conditions. Throughout the history of the Hanna area it has occurred or been attempted again and again. Many times members of the family or neighbours of the person who took his own life professed to recall extreme anxiety over financial affairs prior to the suicide. Typical extracts from newspaper accounts, between 1929 and 1939, read:

Deceased who was highly respected, and who had countless friends throughout the Richdale district, had been worrying over the crop failure which he sustained last season and the terrible deed which culminated in his death is attributed to a fit of despondency over financial matters.[50]

[Deceased was] worried over crop failure and recent rains which threatened what crop remained. . . .[51]

The question of renewing the lease [of his farm] is believed to have caused him [the deceased] considerable anxiety, and for the past several weeks the young man had apparently been in a despondent mood and his actions seemed rather peculiar at times.[52]

[47]It has given rise in dry-belt fiction to such types of men as Ben, in W. O. Mitchell's *Who Has Seen the Wind*, and Uncle Pete in R. R. Annett's *Especially Babe*. The former is a completely demoralized married man who does no work beyond running his still and telling stories in return for drinks. The latter, a bachelor, is equally disreputable: "He might just as well have been a hermit, so utterly solitary was his life. Nobody bothered about him or talked to him. He seemed less human than the mongrel dog that slunk hungrily about the place— just an old soak, with his mottled, shapeless face and his clothes that had been nondescript in their best days and were now rags." (p. 4)

[48]Like drunkenness, it has caught the attention of many writers about life on the Northern Plains. Cf. O. E. Rölvaag, *Giants in the Earth*; J. Bojer, *The Emigrants*; M. Radcliffe, "Sigrid," *American Folk Plays*, ed. F. H. Koch (New York, 1939); G. Pharis, "Still Stands the House," *ibid.*; W. O. Mitchell, *Who Has Seen the Wind*.

[49]Cf. *Hanna Herald*, June 5, 1913.   [50]*Ibid.*, Jan. 17, 1929.
[51]*Ibid.*, Sept. 24, 1931.   [52]*Ibid.*, Dec. 7, 1939.

Leaving the Hanna area is an obvious solution to the problems of the individual. During the thirties, however, there was an important curb on migration. Almost every part of North America was suffering severely from depression and unemployment. Dry-belt youth, lacking in training and capital, had no alternative to the farm, except drifting across the country as hoboes or tramps. Some young men accepted this alternative. Many, discontented though they were, stayed at home. With better times, the rural communities have failed to meet the competition of the army and of the cities. The young men and women have joined the armed services or gone to work in industries. The result has been that the age structure of the rural communities is highly unbalanced. There are large numbers of people from forty-five to sixty years of age, and from ten to twenty-five, but small numbers between twenty-five and forty and below ten.

At present the decline seems likely to continue. The older farmers are sometimes in spite of disaster still imbued with a sense of the importance and security of agriculture in general and of dry-belt wheat farming in particular. They have a stake in their farms. They are attached to the area and the way of life which they know well. On the other hand, the young people are looking outward. They do not feel that agriculture is worth while and profitable, because they grew up during the drought and depression years and because since the West was opened Canada has become increasingly urban in outlook. They have little sense of security[53] and little affection for dry-belt living.

Thus in 1946 the rural communities of the Hanna area give no promise of continuing through the years. Thirty years ago they appeared to have developed an adequate institutional system. Their local councils, schools, churches, and farm organizations were flourishing, their informal social activities were numerous and diverse. The members of the communities were content with the present and optimistic about the future. Drought and depression, coupled with technological change, have made the communities crumble. Their formal and informal groupings have disintegrated, their members have left or have stayed on more in grim determination than in hope. The sociological problems of settlement are unsolved.

[53]The oldest son of one of the most able and successful farmers near the town of Hanna illustrated this. He was a logical heir to his aging parent. Of his three brothers, one had been killed in the war, another had established himself as a trucker, and the third was a youngster in high school. He had no definite alternative occupation. He was of an unaggressive disposition which led community members to feel him unsuited to urban life. Nevertheless, he said that he couldn't make up his mind about farming. He liked it, but "it was too uncertain."

CHAPTER EIGHT

Conclusion

THE RURAL community of the Hanna area has not achieved a stable adaptation to its physical and socio-economic environment. For a time the ways of life developed elsewhere appeared to meet the requirements of the dry belt, but they were adequate only on a short-run basis. This lack of adjustment has been one reason why people have moved away; among those who have remained, it has contributed both to personal disorganization and to social unrest.

Two chief ways of life have been brought to the Hanna area. The first and more important was that worked out in other parts of the continent, and more particularly in other parts of the Northern Plains, by predominantly Northern European peoples. The second was the peasant pattern as developed in Europe, brought to Hanna by German-Russian immigrants. Each for a time appeared to afford the possibility of successful adjustment. Although the picture of community life in the first ten years of settlement painted by men who homesteaded in the dry belt is probably idealized, there can be little doubt that before the first long drought there seemed to be a tolerable adaptation of the North American rural culture to the local situation. The protests of the United Farmers of Alberta around 1920 were not those of a weak and disillusioned group. The farmers did not look to the U.F.A. movement, as twenty-five years later they looked to the Social Credit movement, as a last hope. The outbursts of the United Farmers were rather those of vigorous and optimistic people, who interpreted their difficulties as easily remediable by their own efforts. The instability of the rural cultural system was revealed only with the onset of drought and depression. Then breakdown was rapid.

The peasant culture was able to invade the area while the other was disintegrating, and contributed to the disintegration. The German-

Russian way of life, like the North American, established itself with seeming ease, even in the difficult thirties. Before completely supplanting the American culture, however, the peasant way of life has begun to show signs of disruption. The signs are the more notable since they are appearing in years of prosperity rather than economic hardship.

Neither pattern of social organization could persist under the conditions which prevail in the Hanna area. Both physical and economic factors on the one hand suggest wheat growing as the most profitable form of economic enterprise, and on the other hand prevent wheat growing from providing either a high or a steady income and from supporting more than a sparse and scattered population. This situation offered a challenge to the settlers which they were unable to meet by means of their old customs.

In terms of social organization, a familial society would have seemed a likely adaptation to the isolation of the household groups within the area. Inter-household groupings for social purposes are difficult to form, and the household suffices for the work of the farm. But the economy of the region has in it factors which weaken the family unit. The fact that cash-crop rather than subsistence agriculture is carried on acts strongly against a familial system in that it accentuates the patriarchal character of the family form brought into the area, while at the same time other factors render a patriarchal family unstable. The abundance and necessity of communication with the outside world counteract the effects on the household of its isolation within the local community. Hence a familial system has not developed, and the German-Russian familial system which was imported is not likely to survive.

A social organization based upon agricultural towns and villages, somewhat according to European patterns, is another solution to the problems of the Hanna area which has frequently been suggested. In the opinion of many people the drought area could best be farmed by men who lived in population centres and went out from them daily for work. The farmers would thus resemble city workers in having their homes and work-places separate.[1] There are indications of the spontaneous adoption of this solution in the Oyen area, where some farmers have moved into the village and where their sons voice the hope of farming from the village. The results have been favourable for community stability.

But it must be recognized that the pattern of town- and village-centred farming communities has its limitations. The fashion in Ameri-

[1] Cf. K. Liepmann, *The Journey to Work: Its Significance for Industrial and Community Life* (London, 1944).

can sociology is to look on most villages and small towns as the nuclei of rural communities. Galpin's formulations have had widespread and uncritical acceptance. Indeed, in their study of 140 agricultural communities, made in the 1930's, Brunner and Lorge state:

Those who have worked on this series of studies believe that the facts revealed demonstrate that the village or town center has become the capital of rural America. The crossroads neighborhood is no longer the chief integrating social factor in rural life. Despite fluctuations, farmers are steadily increasing their use of the village or town center for education, especially on the high-school level; for the ministries of religion; for social life; for professional service of various sorts; and for the purchasing of daily necessities.[2]

The case of Oyen substantiates the view expressed, but the study of Hanna suggests the need for amplification and modification. Oyen is a part of the rural community and contributes to its well-being. Hanna is a distinct social entity, and perhaps has adverse effects on the social organization of the farming communities around it. To ignore the difference between the two is to imply that there are far greater resources available for the solution of community problems than is actually the case.

It is not by virtue of the number and quality of its formal associations that Oyen is the centre of a rural community, for these are few and weak. The village is important rather in relation to informal social contacts. Indeed, the scarcity of formal associations, which stems from the sparseness and lack of wealth of the population, may contribute to the richness of informal intercourse available to the farmers. Oyen serves as a community centre because it provides a convenient place of assembly and because its citizens, though their way of life differs from that of the farmers, must co-operate with them if the facilities for an adequate existence are to be maintained.

On the other hand the town of Hanna is not the centre of a rural community. It makes available moving pictures, beer parlours, specialized stores—the facilities farmers mention first as attracting them to population centres. But these advantages do not outweigh its disadvantages. Its residents not only have a different way of life but also a minimum of personal contacts with the farmers, because the townsmen are numerous enough to have a reasonably complete and self-sufficient community structure among themselves. This has been most apparent in times of rapid social change, when the different ways of life of farmers and the townspeople have involved a difference in response to it. Even when drought and depression quickened the

[2]E. de S. Brunner and I. Lorge, *Rural Trends in Depression Years*, p. 83.

townspeople's enlistment on the side of reform alongside of the
farmers, the alliance was merely opportunistic and not based on common understandings.

Hanna's case, though it has exceptional elements in it, may be
more normal than would appear from current theory. It is frequently
said that the distinction between a village and a town is obsolete.
Certainly the distinction is vague in political administration, in popular
and literary and even in sociological usage. But the two terms are not
altogether synonymous. The town has more nearly urban organizations
and attitudes and usually a larger population, while the village is more
intimately bound to the surrounding rural region and has a smaller
population. From this it follows that the town tends to be a distinct
social entity, whereas the village tends to be a part of the functioning
social system which includes as integral parts the farming regions
around.

This generalization may need to be qualified in terms of the stage
of development and the economic base of the village or town. In
east-central Alberta in the frontier days small villages had an urban
outlook, and were regarded by the farmers much as Hanna is. Only
in the twenties and thirties were the surviving villages knit into the
rural community structure. It may be the general rule for agricultural
villages to be distinct from and hostile to the rural regions in the
frontier and to be allied with them in the more mature area. For
example, Moe and Taylor write of Irwin, Iowa:

Early village-country relations were somewhat strained. Farmers disliked the merchants, and the merchants disliked the farmers. The farmers
hoped that the railroad would bring good prices. The railroad didn't. The
farmers believed their soil was the richest on earth but that the combination
of eastern bankers and railroad companies kept their corn from bringing
what it was intrinsically worth; furthermore, that what little they did get
was taken away by high prices for the things they had to buy.[3]

The community in many ways is much more a community now than
it was 50 years ago. The village has become the centre of the activities of
the farmers, and the differences between the villagers and farm dwellers
have declined. They meet together in the work and programs of the
churches, and fraternal orders, and the school. The farmers' business relations in the village are on a much friendlier basis. There is general recognition that the farm and nonfarm groups are dependent on each other. In
athletic competitions between the local high school and the neighboring
high schools, particularly Harlan and Kirkman, the prestige of the community is felt to be at stake. The competition of trades and services in
Harlan, which has developed in the last 40 years, is resented and the

    [3]E. O. Moe and C. C. Taylor, *Culture of a Contemporary Rural Community—
Irwin, Iowa*, p. 8.

numbers of people who come into Irwin village on Wednesday and Saturday evenings are closely watched. Any increase or decrease is thought to be a measure of the success of the village in its competition for trade with other villages and towns. Irwin is praised and supported, whereas the disadvantages and failures of competing communities are emphasized.[4]

The influence of the centre's economic base is suggested by the fact that Hanna's role as a railway town has apparently accentuated its separateness from the farming regions. It is suggested also by the fact that the mining town of Drumheller plays a negligible part even as a trading centre in the life of the farmers who are as near to it as they are to Hanna.

The normality of cleavage between town and country is indicated by the major place given by rural sociologists to town-country antagonism and conflict. Most rural sociology text-books devote considerable attention to this phenomenon, and almost every study in the field touches upon it to some degree. The bulk of the explanations echo in milder terms the trenchant views of Thorstein Veblen:

> The American country town . . . is a business community; that is to say it lives for and by business traffic, primarily of a merchandising sort. It is often spoken of as a center or sub-center for the distribution of goods to the country population, and for the receipt and transmission of country produce; but this is definition by enumeration of mechanical facts only. The reason of its being is the gain to be got by doing business in this particular place. The nucleus of its population is the local business men, whose interests constitute its municipal policy and control its municipal administration. These local business men are such as the local bankers, merchants of many kinds and degrees, real estate promoters, local lawyers, local clergymen. In the typical town all these have something of a hand in municipal politics, which is conducted as in some sort a public or overt extension of that private or covert organization of local interests that watches over the joint pecuniary benefit of the local business men. It is a means of rewarding serviceable local politicians with salaries and perquisites, especially the latter, and of safeguarding the local business community against interlopers and against any evasive tactics on the part of the country population that serves as host to this businesslike growth. This politico-pecuniary enterprise in municipal perquisites is a case of joint action rather than of collective action, since each and several of the participants, overt and covert, takes part as a strategist or diplomatic agent for his own pecuniary interest.

Veblen related the nature of the country town to its genesis, as a product and exponent of the American land system. The town, he claimed, is located and developed as an enterprise of speculation in land values, as an attempt to get something for nothing by engrossing as much as possible of the increment of land values caused by the

[4]*Ibid.*, p. 72.

increase of population and the settlement and cultivation of the surrounding farm lands. It never loses the character of a real-estate speculation. The merchants, lawyers, ministers, and the like commonly begin with a share in the speculation. This affords a common bond and a common ground of pecuniary interest, which so frequently and consistently masquerades as public spirit that most of the men come to believe that they are altruistic rather than selfish. It follows that the farmers have cause for hostility and distrust of townsmen.[5]

But even the theorists who adopt Veblen's view are prone to treat town-country antagonisms as accidental, and to consider the town as not only a part of the rural community but its centre. Those who do consider the antagonisms as a natural social phenomenon usually make the geographical isolation of the farmers the chief factor in their explanations. A corollary to their hypotheses is that town-country hostilities disappear as communication and transportation improve. That active antagonism wanes seems to be borne out by the example of Hanna, but better communication and transportation facilities, the so-called urbanization of farm life, and the impact of drought and depression have all failed to lead to the development of new intimacies and understandings between rural and urban people. Both farmers and townsmen have gained a new conception of their interests as interdependent. Conflict between them has ceased. None the less, their ways of life are distinct, their relationships specific in scope, their few united efforts a result of expediency rather than a sense of community.

The town, being distinct from the country, not merely makes little positive contribution to but even detracts from the stability of the rural community. Hanna's way of life appears easier to the farmers than their own, and its residents seem to scorn the rural people. Both these factors make the farmers discontented, and reluctant to consider agriculture as a permanent occupation for themselves and their children.

Cities likewise have adverse effects. Through their abundant contacts beyond the local community, the farmers are constantly made aware of the urban formula for living as an alternative to their own rural formula. The authors of *The Northern Plains in a World of Change* write:

Because the Plains is an area of recent settlement and because it has failed to develop its own large dominant cities, it has struggled ineffectually against the influences from the outside. Cities are centers of communi-

[5]T. B. Veblen, *Imperial Germany and the Industrial Revolution*, pp. 316-18. Cf. Veblen, "The Country Town," *Absentee Ownership and Business Enterprise in Recent Times: The Case of America* and "Farm Labor for the Period of the War," *Essays in Our Changing Order*.

cation, invention and change. Without any large cities of its own, the Plains has looked outside to Denver and Winnipeg, Chicago and Toronto for many of its ideas. These urban centers tend to have cultural arrogance, by means of which they force their preconceived ideas upon the outside without tolerating mutual exchange of ideas. Such a process is not conscious on the part of these city centers but nevertheless real.[6]

Thus the question of the balance of the rural and the urban ways of life, vexing in almost every region, is very acute in the Plains.

Perhaps the Hanna area can never become the home of a permanent self-sustaining population. The economic and social problems may be so severe that neither spectacular attempts at change such as the social movements in which residents of the Hanna area have already taken part nor more gradual efforts can bring about adjustment. Moving away may be the only solution for community members. However, such is not necessarily the case. Men have displayed great ingenuity in moulding their culture and institutions to meet the demands of inhospitable environments. Webb has shown graphically how the North American rural system has been altered in some respects to provide an adjustment to the Great Plains[7] and there is little doubt that it may prove to be adaptable in others.

The Hanna area is not wholly unique. While certain problems of the wheat-growing dry belt are peculiar in kind or in intensity, many are found throughout rural society. The integration and combination of "the industrial, the urban and the mechanical" with the "agricultural, the rural and the natural"[8] is a problem facing the residents of almost all modern communities. It has spread with Western culture into the remote parts of the world. No community is so self-sufficient and so isolated as to be able long to avoid it. Other areas may not have so unpredictably variable a physical environment as Hanna, but they must accommodate to the unpredictably variable industrial-capitalist order. Other peoples may not have to face the problem of erecting an entirely new rural society, but they must be ready to change many parts of their socio-cultural system to meet new challenges. The wheat farmer of the North American Plains is not alone as he confronts the task of devising a new rural way of life.

[6]C. F. Kraenzel, W. Thomson, and G. H. Craig, *The Northern Plains in a World of Change*, p. 169.

[7]W. P. Webb, *The Great Plains, passim.*

[8]Kraenzel, Thomson, and Craig, *The Northern Plains in a World of Change*, p. 185.

APPENDIX OF TABLES

TABLE I

FARM AREA AND CONDITIONS OF OCCUPIED FARM LAND
CENSUS DIVISION No. 5, ALBERTA, 1921-1941*
(In acres)

	1921	1926	1931	1936	1941
Total land area	4,915,886	4,915,886	4,915,840	4,915,840	4,915,840
Area in farms	3,290,450	3,045,975	3,615,373	3,010,868	3,491,776
Improved land	1,600,651	1,529,811	1,800,085	1,469,402	1,378,036
Field crops	1,063,796	948,209	1,086,507	812,927	688,819
Pasture	13,704	28,188	49,820	89,564	75,793
Fallow	} 497,074	} 539,451	545,339	427,575	444,661
Idle			Not given	133,298	Not given
Unimproved land	1,689,799	1,516,164	1,815,288	1,541,466	2,113,740
Woodland	8,571	10,962	13,003	3,510	5,064
Prairie or natural pasture	1,608,347	1,463,286	1,759,762	1,439,491	2,024,635
Marsh or waste land	72,881	41,916	42,523	98,465	84,041

*Compiled from Dominion Bureau of Statistics, *Eighth Census of Canada, 1941*, vol. VIII, and preceding censuses of Canada and of the Prairie Provinces.

TABLE II

LIVESTOCK AND ACREAGE UNDER FIELD CROPS
CENSUS DIVISION NO. 5, ALBERTA, 1936-1941*

Domestic animals	1936	1941
	(nos.)	
Horses	39,075	37,006
Cattle		
Cows in milk or in calf	28,469	14,315
Other cattle	41,054	48,427
Cows milked	12,687	9,836
Sheep	36,459	21,010
Swine	9,622	17,705
Poultry		
Hens and chickens	263,754	264,536
Others	22,797	25,355

Field crops	(acres)	
Wheat	653,617	502,431
Barley	3,835	17,368
Oats	105,294	99,876
Rye	26,617	23,523
Flaxseed	2,357	15,749
Other grains	1,264	367
Cultivated hay	12,142	16,699
Other fodder crops	6,675	11,032
Potatoes	1,112	663
Other field roots	11	
Other field crops	3	5
Total field crops	812,927	687,713

*Compiled from Dominion Bureau of Statistics, *Eighth Census of Canada, 1941*, vol. VIII, and *Census of the Prairie Provinces, 1936*, vol. II.

TABLE III

VALUE OF FARM PRODUCTS
CENSUS DIVISION NO. 5, ALBERTA, 1920-1940*

	1920	1925	1930	1935	1940
Field crops	$16,694,742	$15,585,999	$3,064,058	$4,395,996	$6,380,248
Farm and market gardens	73,433	123,612	56,928	77,262	56,176
Forest products	553	1,545	1,087	1,035	2,466
Stock sold alive	936,499	771,441	526,832	457,549	693,296
Stock slaughtered	404,314	276,607	265,797	186,165	151,978
Animal products	1,266,275	948,872	795,850	524,974	501,540
Total value	$19,375,816	$17,708,076	$4,710,552	$5,642,981	$7,785,704

*Compiled from Dominion Bureau of Statistics, *Eighth Census of Canada, 1941*, vol. VIII, and preceding censuses of Canada and of the Prairie Provinces.

TABLE IV

PRECIPITATION RECORDS, CROP YIELDS, AND PRODUCTION VALUE, 1910-1945*

		MEDICINE HAT				BROOKS	
Year	Price per bushel	Precipitation April-July (ins.)	Annual precipitation (ins.)	Yield per acre (bu.)	Production value per acre	Annual precipitation (ins.)	Yield per acre (bu.)
1910	$0.79	2.6	7.5	7.0	$ 5.53		
1911	0.64	8.3	16.4	18.2	11.64		
1912	0.62	4.7	10.3	15.5	9.61		
1913	0.67	7.1	13.6	11.1	7.43		
1914	1.22	2.8	12.1	3.2	3.90		
1915	0.91	10.9	16.1	37.4	34.03		
1916	1.31	10.7	17.9	23.3	30.52		
1917	1.94	3.3	11.1	20.0	38.80		
1918	2.02	3.5	10.1	2.9	5.85		
1919	2.37	3.7	7.6	2.3	5.45		
1920	1.62	5.4	10.7	7.7	12.47		
1921	0.81	6.7	11.7	7.1	5.75		
1922	0.85	6.5	11.3	9.2	7.82		
1923	0.67		13.6	20.8	13.93	11.3	
1924	1.22		9.8	6.0	7.32		
1925	1.23		14.6	10.0	12.30	14.1	20.0
1926	1.09		11.9	5.0	5.45	10.2	15.0
1927	1.00		25.2	25.0	25.00	21.7	25.0
1928	0.80		7.6	25.0	20.00	11.5	20.0
1929	1.05		9.3	10.0	10.50	9.1	5.0
1930	0.49		12.7	10.0	4.90	13.0	20.0
1931	0.38		9.9	5.0	1.90	8.7	20.0
1932	0.30		16.5	15.0	4.50	14.2	20.0
1933	0.41		14.1	5.0	2.05	12.7	20.0
1934	0.53		13.0	10.0	4.10	9.6	10.0
1935	0.61	7.4	13.6	14.0	8.54	14.3	18.0
1936	0.92	3.1	9.2	7.0	6.44	12.2	20.0
1937	1.02	4.1	9.8	0.0	—	10.1	21.0
1938	0.58	6.2	17.6	11.0	6.38	12.1†	25.0
1939	0.52	7.1	13.7	10.0	5.20	10.3	22.0
1940	0.49	8.21	22.5	14.0	6.86	18.0	28.0
1941	0.50	6.9	12.7	12.0	6.00	12.1	21.0
1942	0.66	9.6	17.4	20.0	13.20	14.9	30.0
1943	0.98	2.4	7.0	5.0	4.90	7.0	20.0
1944	1.04	7.2	13.7	10.0	10.40	14.6	20.0
1945	1.04	4.5	12.9	5.0	5.20	11.1†	18.0

*The figures for the years 1910-34 are from *A Report on the Rehabilitation of the Dry Areas of Alberta and Crop Insurance, 1935-1936*, p. 33; the figures for the years 1935-45 were supplied by the Alberta Department of Agriculture in a letter.
    †Incomplete.

TABLE IV *Continued*

Production value per acre	HANNA				THREE HILLS		
	Precipitation April-July (ins.)	Annual precipitation (ins.)	Yield per acre (bu.)	Production value per acre	Annual precipitation (ins.)	Yield per acre (bu.)	Production value per acre
	7.10	13.6	17.9	$11.99			
	2.8	12.1	8.8	10.73			
	10.9	16.1	40.3	36.67			
	10.7	17.9	29.1	38.12			
	3.3	11.1	18.0	34.92			
	3.5	10.1	5.3	10.70			
	3.7	7.6	5.5	13.03			
	5.4	10.7	15.7	25.43			
	6.7	11.7	7.9	6.39			
	6.5	11.3	6.7	5.69			
	9.7	13.6	20.8	13.93	7.5		
	1.6	9.8	6.0	7.32	13.1		
$24.60	7.6	14.1	20.0	24.60	13.1	25.0	$30.75
15.75	3.6	11.9	15.0	16.35	17.5	20.0	21.80
25.00			25.0	25.00	16.8	25.0	25.00
16.00		11.6	20.0	16.00	14.5	25.0	20.00
5.25		8.9	5.0	5.25	8.5	5.0	5.25
9.80		13.4	10.0	4.90	8.1	5.0	2.45
7.60			5.0	1.90	14.0	10.0	3.80
6.00		11.9	15.0	4.50	21.2	25.0	7.50
8.20		8.5	5.0	4.05	10.9	10.0	4.10
5.30			5.0	2.65	9.2	10.0	5.30
10.98	7.5		11.0	6.71	16.0	25.0	15.25
18.40			2.0	1.84	10.3	12.0	11.04
21.42	5.3	13.7	1.0	1.02	13.9	4.0	4.08
14.50	7.6	16.2	15.0	8.70	16.7	23.0	13.34
11.44	11.4	16.7	15.0	7.80	15.9	28.0	14.56
13.72	10.4	25.1	18.0	8.82	17.4	27.0	13.23
10.50	5.7	11.6†	6.0	3.00	18.6	15.0	7.50
19.80	11.9	20.6	25.0	16.50	15.9†	29.0	19.14
19.60	4.1	9.5	6.0	5.88	16.5	20.0	19.60
20.00	7.2	13.6†	4.0	4.16	11.6†	21.0	21.84
18.72	5.4	13.3	4.0	4.16	17.5	14.0	14.56

TABLE V

SIZE OF FARMS, CENSUS DIVISION NO. 5, ALBERTA, 1921-1941*

A. Number and Percentage of Farms, by Size

Size of farm	1921 Number	%	1926 Number	%	1931 Number	%	1936 Number	%	1941 Number	%
Farms of										
1-50 acres	6	0.1	8	0.1			23	0.5	13	0.3
51-100 acres	10	0.1	723	12.6	Not		12	0.3	10	0.3
101-200 acres	1,386	17.2	2,177	38.1	given		463	10.7	386	10.0
201-299 acres	76	0.9	⎰				41	0.9	30	0.8
300-479 acres	6,624	81.8	856	15.0			1,266	29.3	896	23.3
480-639 acres	⎰		1,955	34.2			697	16.1	554	14.4
640 acres and over							1,815	42.0	1,958	50.9
Total	8,102	100.0	5,719	100.0			4,317	100.0	3,847	100.0

B. Area and Percentage of Land in Farms

Size of farm	1921 Acres	%	1926 Acres	%	1931 Acres	%	1936 Acres	%	1941 Acres	%
Farms of										
1-50 acres	95	0.0	100	0.0	543	0.0	315	0.0	298	0.0
51-100 acres	775	0.0	115,073	3.8	1,455	0.0	972	0.0	848	0.0
101-200 acres	221,439	6.7	692,986	22.8	131,819	3.6	73,825	2.5	61,622	1.8
201-299 acres	18,893	0.6	⎰		13,077	0.4	10,581	0.4	8,682	0.2
300-479 acres	3,049,248	92.7	400,111	13.1	618,341	17.0	412,072	13.7	292,631	8.4
480-639 acres	⎰		597,016	19.6	459,897	12.4	341,077	11.3	270,216	7.7
640 acres and over			1,240,689	40.7	2,390,241	66.1	2,172,026	72.1	2,857,479	81.8
Total	3,290,450	100.0	3,045,975	100.0	3,615,373	100.0	3,010,868	100.0	3,491,776	100.0

*Compiled and calculated from Dominion Bureau of Statistics, *Eighth Census of Canada, 1941*, vol. VIII, and preceding censuses of Canada and the Prairie Provinces.

TABLE VI

TENURE OF FARMS, CENSUS DIVISION No. 5, ALBERTA, 1921-1941*

A. Number and Percentage of Farms, by Form of Tenure

Form of tenure	1921 Number	%	1926 Number	%	1931 Number	%	1936 Number	%	1941 Number	%
Operated by owner	6,361	78.5	3,087	54.0			1,833	42.5	1,210	31.5
Operated by manager	45	0.4	36	0.6	Not given		4	0.1	16	0.4
Operated by tenant	734	9.1	963	16.8			933	21.6	1,083	27.9
Operated by part owner, part tenant	962	11.9	1,633	28.6			1,547	35.8	1,538	40.0
Total number of farms	8,102	100.0	5,719	100.0			4,317	100.0	3,847	100.0

B. Area and Percentage of Land in Farms, by Form of Tenure

Form of tenure	1921 Acres	%	1926 Acres	%	1931 Acres	%	1936 Acres	%	1941 Acres	%
Operated by owner	2,286,081	69.7	1,176,703	38.6	1,285,169	35.6	778,105	25.8	553,546	15.8
Operated by manager	29,921	0.9	40,889	1.3	12,132	0.3	5,280	0.2	118,563	3.4
Operated by tenant	348,510	10.6	469,931	15.4	484,064	13.4	497,401	16.5	687,675	19.7
Operated by part owner, part tenant	625,938	19.0	1,358,452	44.6	1,834,008	50.7	1,730,082	57.5	2,131,992	61.1
Area owned	2,637,598	80.2	1,842,149	60.5	2,137,529	59.1	1,482,758	49.2	Not given	
Area rented	652,854	19.8	1,203,826	39.5	1,477,844	40.9	1,528,110	50.8		
Total area in farms	3,290,450	100.0	3,045,975	100.0	3,615,373	100.0	3,010,868	100.0	3,491,776	100.0

*Compiled and calculated from Dominion Bureau of Statistics, *Eighth Census of Canada, 1941*, vol. VIII, and preceding censuses of Canada and the Prairie Provinces.

TABLE VII

	1931	1936	1941
Total no. of farms		4,317	3,847
Farm values			
Land	$28,067,700	$17,409,000	$12,500,800
Buildings	$8,167,300	$5,019,100	$3,813,700
Residence	Not given	$2,669,100	Not given
Implements and machinery†	$7,772,800	$4,625,118	$5,097,700
Livestock	$4,560,507	$3,723,722	$4,340,275
Total value	$48,568,307	$30,336,881	$25,752,475
Total amount of mortgage debts	$6,378,000	$4,137,000	$2,330,800
No. of farms reporting mortgages	2,194	1,541	1,118
Status of "fully owned" farms			
No. of "fully owned" farms		1,833	1,210
Acres in farms	611,563	778,105	553,546
Acres improved	811,261	515,607	343,152
Value of farm property	$9,603,300	$8,680,400	$5,602,900
Amount of mortgage debts	$6,378,000	$2,279,600	$1,105,600
No. of farms reporting mortgages	1,354	811	480
Debts covered by liens			
Total amount of debts covered by liens	Not given	$557,300	$364,730
No. of farms reporting liens	Not given	1,461	734

*Compiled from Dominion Bureau of Statistics, *Eighth Census of Canada, 1941,* vol. VIII, and preceding censuses of Canada and the Prairie Provinces.
†Including automobiles.

TABLE VIII

DESCRIPTION OF OCCUPIED DWELLINGS
ACADIA ELECTORAL DISTRICT, ALBERTA, 1941*
BASED ON A 10 PER CENT SAMPLE†

	Farm	Non-farm
Population	16,826	9,482
Occupied dwellings	4,442	2,683
Estimated number of single dwellings	4,424	2,348
Percentage of owner-occupied dwellings	73.7	50.2
Average no. of rooms per dwelling	4.6	4.5
Average no. of persons per dwelling	3.8	3.4
Average annual earnings, wage-earner family heads		$1,302
Average monthly rent, tenant-occupied dwellings		$11
Average value owner-occupied dwellings	$927	$1,190
Percentage of dwellings with		
External repairs needed	55.0	32.0
Frame exterior	95.8	90.4
Furnace heating	15.1	31.8
Running water	2.1	14.6
Flush toilet	1.6	9.7
Electric lights	5.2	64.6
Gas or electric cooking		6.3
Refrigeration, ice or mechanical	6.6	20.0
Radio	86.4	89.0
Automobile	61.7	40.7
Telephone	29.7	14.4
Electric vacuum cleaner	2.0	21.5
All four preceding conveniences	1.0	5.7

*Acadia Federal Constituency is larger than Census Division No. 5, and includes relatively good lands to the west and northwest. The condition of the dwellings for the drought area alone would be considerably worse than this table indicates.

†Dominion Bureau of Statistics, *Housing Census of Canada, 1941*, Preliminary Housing Bulletin no. D-6.

TABLE IX

VALUE OF FARM BUILDINGS
CENSUS DIVISION NO. 5, ALBERTA, 1921-41*

Year	Value of buildings
1921	$11,086,058
1926	7,914,149
1931	8,167,300
1936	5,019,100
1941	3,813,700

*Compiled from Dominion Bureau of Statistics, *Eighth Census of Canada, 1941*, vol. VIII, and preceding censuses of Canada and of the Prairie Provinces. In evaluating the decrease in the value of buildings, account must be taken of abandonment of land and of increased size of holdings.

TABLE X

POPULATION BY CONJUGAL CONDITION AND SEX
CENSUS DIVISION NO. 5, ALBERTA, AND CANADA, TOTAL AND RURAL, 1941*

Status	Sex	Census Division No. 5, Alberta	Canada (Total population)	Canada (Rural population)
Total Popuation	M	10,684	5,900,536	2,821,766
	F	8,242	5,606,119	2,432,473
Population 15 and over	M	8,081	4,281,237	1,970,166
	F	5,807	4,026,867	1,609,866
Single	M	6,383	3,322,827	1,697,360
	F	4,114	2,907,741	1,297,472
Married	M	3,934	2,363,528	1,027,982
	F	3,716	2,292,478	1,000,107
Widowed	M	301	170,743	80,795
	F	355	354,378	123,215
Divorced	M	17	6,569	2,381
	F	12	7,463	1,482
Separated	M	48	36,201	12,956
	F	45	43,936	10,179
Not stated	M	1	668	292
	F		123	18

*Compiled from Dominion Bureau of Statistics, *Eighth Census of Canada, 1941*, vol. II.

TABLE XI

POPULATION BY PRINCIPAL RACIAL ORIGINS
CENSUS DIVISION NO. 5, ALBERTA, 1921-1941*

	1921	1931	1936	1941
British races				
English	11,023	6,844	5,839	4,658
Irish	4,792	3,759	2,769	2,537
Scottish	6,361	4,638	3,552	3,177
Others	386	322	260	311
European races				
French	960	562	478	406
Austrian	619	195	142	231
Belgian	101	93	75	79
Czech and Slovak	Not given	119	164	180
Finnish	55	42	48	38
German	2,732	3,753	3,364	2,319
Hungarian	Not given	114	282	326
Italian	141	93	135	138
Jewish	291	68	56	45
Netherland	550	584	359	426
Polish	216	695	453	530
Roumanian	Not given	400	145	122
Russian	1,539	1,017	670	1,083
Scandinavian	2,998	2,562	1,936	1,700
Ukrainian	172	521	460	474
Others	401	71	51	45
Asiatic races				
Chinese	}156	113	72	55
Japanese		7	7	6
Others	31	61	35	27
Indian	5	1		
Negro	27			
Unspecified	163	17	7	13
Total	33,719	26,651	21,359	18,926

*Compiled from Dominion Bureau of Statistics, *Eighth Census of Canada, 1941*, vol. II, and preceding censuses of Canada and the Prairie Provinces.

TABLE XII

ARRIVAL OF FOUR LARGEST GERMAN-SPEAKING IMMIGRANT GROUPS IN ALBERTA*

A. Number Arriving in Given Period

Time of Arrival	Russian-born	German-born	United States-born	Polish-born
Before 1901	1,100	630	530	300
1901-10	2,500	1,250	3,100	800
1911-15	1,550	1,200	1,450	490
1916-20	650	100	1,450	10
1921-25	1,700	850	500	300
1926-31	2,700	3,500	600	2,100
Total in Alberta, 1931	10,129	7,789	7,586	4,111

B. Percentage of Total Immigration into Alberta

Time of Arrival	Russian-born	German-born	United States-born	Polish-born
Before 1901	3.6	2.7	2.6	1.5
1901-10	2.6	1.7	3.3	0.9
1911-15	2.7	2.2	2.6	0.9
1916-20	1.2	0.5	4.3	0.0
1921-25	5.6	2.9	1.6	1.0
1926-31	2.4	4.3	2.8	5.5
Percent of total foreign-born population, Alberta, 1931	3.4	2.7	2.6	1.3

*Adapted from E. B. Gerwin, "A Survey of the German-speaking Population of Alberta." Miss Gerwin based her estimates on personal and written accounts and census figures.

TABLE XIII

IMMIGRANT POPULATION BY PERIOD OF IMMIGRATION AND SEX CENSUS DIVISION NO. 5, ALBERTA, 1941*

Sex	Total immigrant population	1940-41†	1936-39	1931-35	1921-30	1911-20	Before 1911	No stated
M	4,013	4	31	82	1,068	1,182	1,626	20
F	2,713	4	48	107	768	985	797	4

*Dominion Bureau of Statistics, *Eighth Census of Canada, 1941*, vol. II.
†Five months of 1941 only.

TABLE XIV

POPULATION OF FIVE VILLAGES OF CENSUS DIVISION No. 5
WITHIN THE SEVERE DROUGHT AREA, 1916-41*

Name of village	1916	1921	1926	1931	1936	1941
Cereal	89	180	150	185	131	142
Chinook	189	241	198	176	134	142
Oyen	286	390	346	401	298	326
Richdale		109	58	44†		
Youngstown	305	410	457	372	187	188
Total	869	1,330	1,209	1,178	750	798

*Compiled from Dominion Bureau of Statistics, *Eighth Census of Canada, 1941*, vol. II, and preceding censuses of Canada and the Prairie Provinces.
†Disorganized 1931.

TABLE XV

POPULATION OF FIVE VILLAGES OF CENSUS DIVISION No. 5
NOT WITHIN THE SEVERE DROUGHT AREA, 1916-41*

Name of village	1916	1921	1926	1931	1936	1941
Craigmyle		231	232	236	214	186
Delia	179	312	329	286	279	315
Morrin		164	162	149	146	216
Munson	149	207	223	164	146	139
Rumsey		116	89	83	81	90
Total	328	1,030	1,035	918	866	946

*Compiled from Dominion Bureau of Statistics, *Eighth Census of Canada, 1941*, vol. II, and preceding censuses of Canada and the Prairie Provinces.

BIBLIOGRAPHY

Bibliography

ALBERTA, DEPARTMENT OF EDUCATION. *Thirtieth Annual Report, 1935.* Edmonton, 1936.

ANGELL, R. C. *The Family Encounters the Depression.* New York, 1936.

ANNETT, R. R. *Especially Babe.* New York, 1942.

ARENSBERG, C. M. and KIMBALL, S. T. *Family and Community in Ireland.* Cambridge, Mass., 1940.

BELL, E. H. *Culture of a Contemporary Rural Community—Sublette, Kansas.* U.S. Department of Agriculture, Bureau of Agricultural Economics, Rural Life Studies, 2. Washington, 1942.

BOJER, J. *The Emigrants.* Translated by A. G. JAYNE. New York, 1925.

BOWSER, W. E. and McCALLA, A. G. *Cropping for Profit and Permanency.* University of Alberta, Bulletin no. 44. Edmonton, 1944.

BOYD, H. *New Breaking: An Outline of Co-operation among the Farmers of Western Canada.* Toronto, 1938.

BRITNELL, G. E. *The Wheat Economy.* Toronto, 1939.

BRUNNER, E. DE S. *Immigrant Farmers and Their Children.* New York, 1929.

BRUNNER, E. DE S. and LORGE, I. *Rural Trends in Depression Years.* New York, 1937.

BURNET, J. R. "Town-Country Relations and the Problem of Rural Leadership," *Canadian Journal of Economics and Political Science,* XIII, no. 3, 1947, 395-409.

CANADA, DEPARTMENT OF AGRICULTURE. *P.F.R.A.: A Record of Achievement.* Ottawa, 1943.

CANADA, DEPARTMENT OF AGRICULTURE and UNIVERSITY OF ALBERTA, DEPARTMENT OF POLITICAL ECONOMY. *Classification of Land, Sounding Creek Special Area, Alberta.* Preliminary report, 1938.

COTTRELL, W. F. *The Railroader.* Stanford, Calif., 1940.

CUNNINGHAM, J. B. and CASE, H. C. M. *Father-Son Farm Business Agreements.* University of Illinois College of Agriculture, Extension Service in Agriculture and Home Economics, Circular 587. Urbana, 1944.

DAVISSON, W. P. *Pooling Wheat in Canada.* Ottawa, 1927.

DAWSON, C. A. *Group Settlement: Ethnic Communities in Western Canada.* Vol. VII of *Canadian Frontiers of Settlement,* edited by W. A. MACKINTOSH and W. L. G. JOERG, 9 vols. Toronto, 1934-40.

DAWSON, C. A. and YOUNGE, E. R. *Pioneering in the Prairie Provinces: The Social Side of the Settlement Process.* Vol. VIII of *Canadian Frontiers of Settlement,* edited by W. A. MACKINTOSH and W. L. G. JOERG, 9 vols. Toronto, 1934-40.

DOMINION BUREAU OF STATISTICS. *Sixth Census of Canada, 1921,* vols. II and VIII. Ottawa, 1924-9.

———— *Seventh Census of Canada, 1931,* vols. II and VIII. Ottawa, 1932-5.

———— *Eighth Census of Canada, 1941,* vols. II and VIII. Ottawa, 1944-7.

———— *Census of the Prairie Provinces, 1916.* Ottawa, 1918.

———— *Census of the Prairie Provinces, 1926,* vol. I. Ottawa, 1931.

———— *Census of the Prairie Provinces, 1936,* vol. I. Ottawa, 1938.

———— *Housing Census of Canada, 1941.* Preliminary Housing Bulletin no. D-6 (processed). Ottawa, n.d.

EASTERBROOK, W. T. *Farm Credit in Canada.* Political Economy Series, no. 2. Toronto, 1938.

ECKERT, P. S. *Father-Son Farming Arrangements.* Ohio State University, Agricultural Extension Service, Bulletin 219. Columbus, Ohio, 1945.

EDWARDS, A. D. *Influence of Drought and Depression on a Rural Community: A Case Study in Haskell County, Kansas.* U.S. Department of Agriculture, Farm Security Administration and Bureau of Agricultural Economics, Social Research Report no. VIII (processed). Washington, 1939.

FAY, C. R. *Agricultural Co-operation in the Canadian West.* London, 1925.

GALPIN, C. J. *Rural Life.* New York, 1923.

———— "The Social Agencies in a Rural Community," *First Wisconsin Country Life Conference,* Bulletin of the University of Wisconsin, serial no. 472, General Series no. 308. Madison, 1911, pp. 12-18.

GARD, R. E. *Johnny Chinook.* Toronto, 1945.

GARDNER, R. W. "Wheat Production Costs," *Canadian Chartered Accountant,* XXXIV, 1939, pp. 165-9.

GERWIN, E. B. "A Survey of the German-speaking Population of Alberta." Unpublished Master's thesis, University of Alberta, 1938.

GIFFEN, P. J. "Adult Education in Relation to Rural Social Structure, a Comparative Study of Three Manitoba Communities." Unpublished Master's thesis, University of Toronto, 1947.

GILLETTE, J. M. *North Dakota Weather and the Rural Economy.* University of North Dakota, Department of Sociology and Anthropology, Bulletin 11, reprinted from *North Dakota History,* XII, nos. 1-2, 1945. Bismarck, N.D., 1945.

GREAT PLAINS COMMITTEE. *The Future of the Great Plains.* Washington, 1936.

Hanna Herald, Dec., 1912—Sept., 1946.

HARRISON, M. *Go West—Go Wise!* London, 1930.

HICKS, J. D. *The Populist Revolt.* Minneapolis, 1931.

HOPKINS, E. S., ARMSTRONG, J. M., and MITCHELL, H. D. *Cost of Producing Farm Crops in the Prairie Provinces.* Canada, Department of Agriculture, Bulletin no. 159, new series. Ottawa, 1932.

HOPKINS, E. S., PALMER, A. E., and CHEPIL, W. S. *Soil Drifting Control in the Prairie Provinces.* Canada, Department of Agriculture, Publication no. 568, Farmers' Bulletin 32. Ottawa, 1938.

HUGHES, E. C. "A Proposal for Study of the Dynamics of Rural Culture and Institutions." Unpublished paper presented at the Seminar on Rural Life, University of Chicago, Nov. 6, 1945.

JENKINS, D. R. *Growth and Decline of Agricultural Villages.* Columbia University, Teachers' College, Contributions to Education, 819. New York, 1940.

KRAENZEL, C. F., THOMSON, W., and CRAIG, G. H. *The Northern Plains in a World of Change.* N.p., 1942.

McCOURT, E. A. *Music at the Close.* Toronto, 1947.

MacGIBBON, D. A. *The Canadian Grain Trade.* Toronto, 1932.

MacINNES, C. M. *In the Shadow of the Rockies.* London, Eng., 1930.

MACKINTOSH, W. A. *Agricultural Co-operation in Western Canada.* Publications of the Faculty of Arts in Queen's University. Kingston, 1924.

——— *Economic Problems of the Prairie Provinces.* Vol. IV of *Canadian Frontiers of Settlement,* edited by W. A. MACKINTOSH and W. L. G. JOERG, 9 vols. Toronto, 1934-40.

——— *Prairie Settlement: The Geographical Setting.* Vol. I of *Canadian Frontiers of Settlement,* edited by W. A. MACKINTOSH and W. L. G. JOERG, 9 vols. Toronto, 1934-40.

McMILLAN, R. T. and DUNCAN, O. D. *Social Factors of Farm Ownership in Oklahoma.* Oklahoma Agricultural Experiment Station, Bulletin no. B-289. Stillwater, 1945.

MITCHELL, E. B. *In Western Canada before the War.* London, 1915.

MITCHELL, W. O. *Who Has Seen the Wind.* Toronto, 1947.

MOE, E. O. and TAYLOR, C. C. *Culture of a Contemporary Rural Community—Irwin, Iowa.* U.S. Department of Agriculture, Bureau of Agricultural Economics, Rural Life Studies, 5. Washington, 1942.

MOORHOUSE, H. *Deep Furrows.* Toronto, 1918.

MORTON, A. S. and MARTIN, C. *History of Prairie Settlement and "Dominion Lands" Policy.* Vol. II of *Canadian Frontiers of Settlement,* edited by W. A. MACKINTOSH and W. L. G. JOERG, 9 vols. Toronto, 1934-40.

PARSONS, K. H. and WAPLES, E. O. *Keeping the Farm in the Family.* University of Wisconsin, Agricultural Experiment Station, Research Bulletin 157. Madison, 1943.

PULLEN-BURRY, B. *From Halifax to Vancouver.* Toronto, 1912.

A Report on the Rehabilitation of the Dry Areas of Alberta and Crop Insurance, 1935-36. Edmonton, 1936.

RÖLVAAG, O. E. *Giants in the Earth: A Saga of the Prairie.* Translated by L. COLCORD and the author. New York, 1927.

Royal Commission on Dominion-Provincial Relations, 1937. *The Case for Alberta.* Edmonton, 1938.

SALTER, L. A., Jr. *Land Tenure in Process.* University of Wisconsin, Agricultural Experiment Station, Research Bulletin 146. Madison, 1943.

SOROKIN, P. and ZIMMERMAN, C. C. *Principles of Rural-Urban Sociology.* New York, 1929.

Special Areas Act, Statutes of Alberta, 1938, c. 92; 1939, c. 34; 1940, c. 28.

STEWART, A. and PORTER, W. D. *Land Use Classification in the Special Areas of Alberta and in Rosenheim and Acadia Valley.* Canada, Department of Agriculture, publication no. 731, Technical Bulletin no. 39. Ottawa, 1942.

STRANGE, K. *With the West in Her Eyes.* Toronto, 1945.

STUART, MAJOR D. *Our Creeping Desert, Its Causes and Its Cure.* Calgary, n.d.

SUTHERLAND, J. K. Unpublished radio broadcasts, given over the network of the Canadian Broadcasting Corporation from Calgary, Alberta, in 1939 and 1940.

VEBLEN, T. B. "The Country Town," *Absentee Ownership and Business Enterprise in Recent Times: The Case of America.* New York, 1923, pp. 142-65.

—— "Farm Labor for the Period of the War," *Essays in Our Changing Order.* New York, 1934, pp. 279-318.

—— *Imperial Germany and the Industrial Revolution.* New York, 1915, Note IV, pp. 332-40.

WEBB, W. P. *The Great Plains.* Boston, 1931.

WHETTEN, N. L. "The Social and Economic Structure of the Trade Centers in the Canadian Prairie Provinces, with Special Reference to Its Changes, 1910-1930." Unpublished Ph.D. thesis, Harvard University, 1932.

WILSON, W. H. *The Evolution of the Country Community: A Study in Religious Sociology.* Boston, 1912.

WOOD, L. A. *A History of Farmers' Movements in Canada.* Toronto, 1924.

WYATT, F. A. and NEWTON, J. D. *Soil Survey of Sounding Creek Sheet.* University of Alberta, College of Agriculture, Bulletin no. 16. Edmonton, 1927.

——*Soil Survey of Sullivan Lake Sheet.* University of Alberta, College of Agriculture, Bulletin no. 31. Edmonton, 1938.

INDEX

Index